ANGELS GATE

Based on a true story of:
THE GREATEST HEIST–NEVER TOLD!

ANDREW J. RAFKIN

&

LOUIS PAGANO

outskirtspress

DENVER, COLORADO

Outskirts Press, Inc.
http://www.outskirtspress.com

ISBN: 978-1-4327-8002-9

Outskirts Press and the "OP" logo are trademarks belonging to Outskirts Press, Inc.

This book is dedicated to the memory of
August Felando

August Felando, a dear friend of Louis Pagano, spent his last months with Louis, fishing golfing, going to games, and just spending quality time together, during which he told Louis the story of the greatest heist never told. Later, Louis Pagano joined an old friend and award-winning author, Andrew J. Rafkin, to write this amazing story titled — ANGELS GATE.

PROLOGUE

During the post-WWII lull in the late 1940s, Southern California sea routes reopened on a peaceful Pacific, and illicit drug trafficking again grew exponentially by sea, land, and air, smuggling anything from bonded booze to Mexican black tar heroin.

One night, Captain Vito Taracina, at the helm of his 50-foot fishing boat the *Santa Maria*, headed to his port of call, San Pedro. A white blanket of mist wrapped around the windows of the bridge making visibility poor and dangerous.

He had one of his crew standing stalwart at the prow, on watch for other craft, and the historic Angels Gate Lighthouse out there ahead in the gloom.

The lookout finally heard the old, deep-throated, two-tone foghorn affectionately known to the locals for decades as "Moaning Maggie," and signaled the captain on the bridge. A few minutes later, Captain Taracina spotted the familiar flashing light looming on top of the lighthouse built in 1913 that stood at the end of the break-water, still welcoming ships into the harbor of the City of Angels, Los Angeles.

Maggie didn't care if their cargo was seafood or dope, for a lighthouse has one function: bringing in vessels, safe from the sea.

Tonight, Capt. Taracina wasn't bringing in fish; he was bringing in a load of opium, cursing the treacherous fog that forced him to travel at half-speed. He looked at his watch, eyes squinting to see the hands on the darkened bridge. He still thought he had time enough to make his meeting with his contact.

The captain took the *Santa Maria* down the harbor's main channel to Berth 73 and tied her up at the dock, amongst the fishing boat fleet, some craft named for saints and others sometimes serving sinners' appetites.

He left his crew to guard the cargo and piled into his battered 1942 Ford truck. He drove into seedy downtown San Pedro, parking in front of the neon-splashed Shanghai Red's, which was a popular bar and hangout for seamen, fishermen, longshoremen, and Navy sailors who rode the ferry from Terminal Island to get to the action.

They never tired of visiting the many vice dens, tattooists, chop suey parlors, card rooms, and other landmark joints on notorious Beacon Street, a latter day likeness of San Francisco's Barbary Coast, reputed to be "The Toughest 10 Blocks in the World." If they exaggerated, it was anything but little, for at times 5,000 seamen from many nations crowded those ten blocks on the dank waterfront, where underground tunnels linked many structures for myriad unsavory purposes.

Capt. Taracina worked his way through the crowd, took a scarred table, waved over a busty waitress, and ordered a beer. She delivered a large schooner, froth pouring over the edge as she set it on the table. Taracina took a pull to quench his thirst then sat back, waiting for his contact.

The place was presided over by Shanghai Red, a Scandinavian fellow, rumored to be the strongest man in town. The place was full with noisy locals and sailors, plus a few hookers, who looked to Red as their protector. Often, he was.

There wasn't a night that one fight, or maybe more, didn't break out and cops with well-worn nightsticks dragged combatants away to jail, only a few blocks down the street.

Taracina recalled the time he tried to pick up a longshoreman's daughter and damn near had his throat cut. He spent the night in jail on the seventh floor of City Hall, 638 S. Beacon, with a few more drunks and rabble-rousers. The top floor was known as "Seventh Heaven," a hell of a place to spend a Saturday night, bruised and spitting blood, without even a good buzz on yet.

Vito was getting impatient, glancing at the clock on the wall, as his contact appeared and slid into the chair across from him.

"How was your trip?" he asked, as he signaled the waitress to bring him the same as Vito was drinking.

"Fog slowed us down a little. You ready to pick up the load?"

"Sure, after we finish our beer, I'll follow you to your boat." The waitress delivered his beer and he took a long drink, then wiped the foam off his mustache with his forearm. "How's business?"

"Great—and growing," Taracina replied. "Now that I can finally get more products to port, the future looks promising."

Through the '50s and '60s, San Pedro slowly shed the rough reputation it had as a sinister waterfront, where men were still drugged and shanghaied to fill a ship's short crew roster.

The seaside town was becoming a bedroom community of the City of Los Angeles with its enclaves of Italians, Croatians, Hispanics, and other nationalities, who'd emigrated decades earlier to catch fish in the fertile waters off the coasts of California and Mexico.

As the attractiveness of fishing declined, their children and grandchildren pursued professional careers. Some chose to remain in the family commercial fishing business while a few entrepreneurs took the crooked path, becoming smugglers who supplied the ever-growing demand for illicit drugs.

By 1983, L.A. grew to over 3.8 million people living within the city limits and 12.9 million within the sprawling, outer metropolitan area of inland valleys and rolling hills.

At the same time, maritime technology developed cargo container shipping using giant cranes to unload or load the ships outbound for Pacific Rim destinations. The Port of L.A. exploded with growth. In 1983, 734,000 efficient containers were handled; by 1984, it rose to 908,000 and in 2009, the tally was over 7.8 million.

L.A. became one of the world's centers of business, international trade, manufacturing, and technology, making it one of the most substantial economic engines within the United States of America, and of course, the home base of Hollywood, "Entertainment Capital of the World."

Two gateways supported the increasing flow of people, goods, and services: Los Angeles Airport, the aerial highway into the City of Angels, and Angels Gate Lighthouse, the entrance to the largest port on the West Coast.

As the city grew in population and commerce, so did the demand for drugs, like marijuana and cocaine; the smugglers relied on the same gateways to bring in their illicit, though extremely profitable, cargo.

Angels Gate, based on a true story of the largest monetary heist in history, is a tale never before told officially, engineered by some local surfers and a drug smuggler, who are integral parts of this story.

1

Randy picked the third wave in the set, spun his board around and paddled, catching a perfect head-high wave which he shredded, got tubed, kicked out, and paddled back through the surf to join his friends, Scott McCarran, Terry Clark, and Jeff Holland, all silhouetted by the setting sun.

Not only best of friends in youth, they also worked together at Western Airlines in the baggage and freight department. Their shift started at 6:00 A.M., and by 4:00 P.M. they were in the water at their favorite surfing spot, off El Porto, whose village business district was rated with the three B's. . . bars, bikers, booze, and now drugs.

El Porto stretched between 38th to 43rd streets in north Manhattan Beach. Early on, a scattered patch of seaside cottages served as residences for employees in the oil business. It was unincorporated L.A. County land until 1981, when all of its 34 acres became part of the city of Manhattan Beach, but it never lost its colloquial name and bohemian reputation.

They could call it part of Manhattan Beach, but they could never close the door on El Porto's wide-open personality, the enclave whose name in Spanish meant "The Door."

Randy, Jeff, and Terry shared one of those seaside cottages, and Scott, their foreman, lived with his wife and two children in the "tree section" of Manhattan Beach, a hilly area of the city that extended to Pacific Coast Highway. He was twenty-eight, six-foot one, had long blond hair, a full mustache, a great tan, and was in excellent physical shape.

His three single friends went to high school together. Randy was the best looking of the group. He stood six-foot four, had green eyes, and a full head of curly long black hair. He was a little on the thin side, but definitely the alpha male of the group. Jeff, the best surfer of the four, had long blond hair, was five-foot ten, had a stocky build, and liked his beer.

In different environments, Terry looked more like a hippie than a surfer, with straggly blond hair and a full beard, closely cropped. But all in all, they were good-looking, tanned surfer dudes, who'd just gotten back from a surfing trip to Costa Rica.

Scott wished he could have joined them, but having a wife and two little kids brought added responsibilities. While he waited for the next set to roll through, he thought, "Maybe next time I could talk Karen into taking a family vacation there, and surf with my buds who already say they want to go back."

The four of them sat on their boards, waiting for the next set of waves. The sun was morphing into a giant orange ball of flame, as it touched the horizon, casting glimmering streaks of fire across the water and the cloudless sky. An offshore wind held up the face of the waves, and as they broke, blew misty veils of water in the air, setting off little rainbows that fell back to the sea.

"What a bitchin' sunset. Reminds me of the ones we watched in Costa Rica," said Terry. "Man, it's too bad you weren't there."

"Yeah, wish I could have made it. Maybe next time," said Scott.

"You have to come, if you're going to invest in our new—" Randy sang out, "Hotel Costa Rica."

"How the fuck do you think you guys could afford to buy a hotel? You can barely afford your car payments and rent," laughed Scott, as they paddled to position themselves for the next wave.

"Maybe we can start selling drugs," said Jeff.

"Yeah, and end up in—in the—Hotel Leavenworth," chuckled Scott.

Randy locked eyes with Scott. "I think it's worth the risk. Our jobs are okay, but we're not going to get rich shuffling baggage around. Together we could come up with enough money to buy a large quantity of pot, sell it, and repeat the process."

"We're not pot dealers."

"Yeah, but look at Ernie, he makes a helluva lot of dough selling pot. He's been supplying us for years, and he's never been caught. He once told me that he has customers throughout the beach area and San Fernando Valley.

"All we need to do is find a big dealer to supply us, and do what Ernie does. We're a lot smarter than he is, and there are four of us. Just think. We could buy this piece of land right on the point near Tamarindo. It's for sale, and we talked to a real-estate agent down there. He says, with a small down payment, we could buy the land now and make monthly payments. We would only sell drugs until we save enough money to pay off the loan and build the hotel."

Jeff butted in. "The area's starting to grow; Americans are retiring there, and people are flocking in to surf and fish. The realtor told us that a couple of international hotel chains are looking to build resorts nearby."

"We could all retire down there; not when we're sixty-five, but now," said Randy.

"Sounds great! But most pipe dreams do," said Scott.

"It may be a pipe dream to you, but we plan to go for it. I hope you'll consider joining us. Shit, I used to buy pot from you when we were teenagers."

"Yeah, but I only sold enough so I could smoke for free. That's a big difference compared to what you're proposing."

"Well, think about it anyway. We need your smarts to pull this off."

* * *

The four of them cut up a few more waves then paddled in before it got dark. They walked up to their beach house and had a beer. Then Scott drove home, listening to the end of "Good Vibrations" by the Beach Boys. The next song was "Hotel California" by the Eagles. Scott laughed, thinking about Hotel Costa Rica and Leavenworth.

He reached over to turn the station, then stopped and said, "Fuck it," and sang along with Don Henley, lead singer of the Eagles.

When he walked into his 900 square-foot house, he found Karen, in the tiny kitchen, cooking dinner. Scott met Karen while surfing at Manhattan Beach Pier, when he was twenty-two. She was nineteen, had long blond hair, was five-foot five, had a perfect body, a great tan, and could surf almost as well as he could.

They dated for six months, he asked her to marry him, and four months later, they got married. A year after that, they had a baby girl, Kati, and twelve months later had a son, Josh. Scott gave Karen a kiss and a pat on her still-youthful ass, said hello to his children, took a shower, and joined his family for dinner.

Later, he read the paper, watched a little TV, and decided to hit the sack. He woke up around midnight, with Karen at his side, and "Hotel California" playing in his head.

The next morning, he drove to work, parked in the employee lot, and headed for the lunchroom to join his friends for a cup of coffee. Randy was sitting at one of the tables. Scott poured himself a cup of java and joined his friend.

The three roommates carpooled together. "Where's Jeff and Terry?" asked Scott.

"They're both in the head. You see the surf this morning?"

"No, I wasn't paying attention. How is it?"

"Bigger and better than yesterday; we're going out after work, you coming?"

"Probably not, I have a lot of shit to do around the house."

"You give any further thought to our Costa Rica plan?" asked Randy.

"Yeah, I'm interested, but only if we can do something better than just becoming street peddlers. If not, it's just too risky for me. If you had a family, you'd understand."

Jeff and Terry walked in and joined them. Scott looked at his watch; their shift started in ten minutes so he left his friends and headed to the office to pick up his paperwork for the day.He was the foreman and reviewed the manifests for the incoming and outgoing traffic prior to their shift. The day started just like every other boring day. They just finished unloading the baggage from a flight arriving from Mexico City, and were driving in a bag tug pulling three tandem flatbed bag carts to the distribution area. As the luggage was being loaded onto the conveyers, Scott walked into the baggage handling area watching the incoming and outgoing luggage moving up and down the multitude of conveyors.

He thought, "The guys are right, this job sucks, and we'll never get rich. But selling pot? I have to be out of my mind to even think of it."

He spotted the luggage coming in from Mexico City on Flight 1720 going one way, and baggage from another incoming flight from New York going the other. He stood there suddenly stunned, realizing that they processed the international and domestic luggage in the same terminal. He knew that domestic luggage was never inspected, but U.S. Customs officials inspected international baggage when it reached the Bradley International Terminal.

He'd been working there for eight years and it had never dawned on him just how easy it would be, to switch any international luggage to a domestic conveyor and domestic to international, for anyone with an enterprising reason to do so.

You know, with a little work, and the right contacts, we could smuggle in quantities of pot, and make some real money, with a lot less risk than selling on the street, dealing with God knows who. Here we have a reliable crew on a regular schedule.

He looked at his watch. Another flight was due to arrive in five minutes. He walked toward the arrival gate, whistling that enchanting greatest hit by the Eagles.

2

Scott couldn't wait to tell his friends, but quickly realized it wouldn't be a good idea to discuss the topic of smuggling drugs, anywhere remotely near the airport. He needed more time to figure out the logistics to engineer a reliable, doable, luggage switch. It was Friday; they had Saturday off, so he decided to have a meeting at the guys' house around noon.

He pulled Randy aside. "I've been thinking about your proposal. I'm interested. And I have some additional ideas."

"All right! Let's get Terry and Jeff and talk it over."

"This isn't a good place to discuss things of this nature. How about we meet at your house for lunch tomorrow? I'll bring some sandwiches from Annex Deli; you supply the beer."

"Sounds like some serious shit; now you're talking."

"Oh yeah. It definitely is."

After work, Scott drove straight home. He told his wife he needed some time alone to work out some logistical changes in the way they handled luggage, and would work on it out on the patio. He chuckled to himself, "At least I'm not lying to her."

He picked up a pad and pencil, grabbed a beer out of the fridge, and headed out to the backyard. It took an hour to complete his plan. There were two major factors. First, the luggage from both planes to be switched onto different conveyors had to arrive within fifteen to twenty minutes of each other. The second was the critical deal breaker: he was the only one who had access to the manifests. If anything went wrong, he'd be the first person the police would suspect.

He weighed the risks and rewards, and decided with care, that it was workable. While he was giving the plan a final look-over, Karen stuck her head out the door. "Honey, dinner is almost ready, and the kids want to spend time with you."

He tore off the sheets of paper, folded them, slid his plan into his pocket, stood up and headed for the door. "Perfect timing, I just finished."

Scott took a quick shower, threw on some shorts and a T-shirt, and sat with his kids watching cartoons on TV until it was time to have dinner.

He helped Karen clean up the table and the kitchen, and then they joined their children. They put the kids to bed at eight, watched *Magnum P.I.* and *Cheers*, then went to bed.

He woke up, had breakfast, and completed more chores around the house from the "honey-do list." At 11:30, he cleaned up and left for the big meeting.

He stopped at the Annex Deli on Highland Avenue and picked up four large torpedo specials, got back in his Cherokee, headed for El Porto, turned left on 39th and parked. The guys' beach house sat right on the Strand. The cottage was built in the forties, and looked as if it hadn't been painted since.

It had a Cape Cod style design, and what little paint remained, was bluish gray, with white trim. There was a large deck facing the beach, and a fireplace that actually worked, in the living room.

Scott didn't knock; he just opened the door, finding his three friends sitting at a table that was probably bought at a garage sale. In fact, everything in the house had been purchased at a swap meet, garage sale, or was donated by friends.

The furniture in the two bedrooms, the loft, and the rest of the house came from different generations, giving it a sort of bohemian surfer theme; it was a comfortable place to hang out.

By the looks on their faces, they were anxiously waiting to hear his plan. Scott handed out the sandwiches, while Randy opened the fridge and pulled our four bottles of Coors. He passed them out and sat down at the table. "Well, we're all ears."

As they attacked their sandwiches, Scott started to go over his plan. "After you 'ambitious dickheads' sprang it on me about becoming drug dealers, I decided not to get involved. I have a family, and the risks are too high for the return. I agree that our jobs aren't going to make us rich. But, they're secure, and I can't afford to get busted." He noticed the disappointment on his friends' faces. "I liked your idea about Costa Rica, and I'm sure if we budget our money, we might be able to buy the land.

"Now—to build a hotel on it, and move there? I didn't think we could raise that kind of money by selling pot on the street, and I still don't think it's a good idea. What's changed?" Scott said, tantalizingly. "Plenty!"

"As of ten o'clock yesterday morning, I started to devise a plan that I feel can make us more than enough money to buy the land, build a hotel, and have enough left over to retire there."

That got all three of them to straighten up and pay attention.

"We handle a lot of baggage every day coming in or out of LAX, from domestic and international flights. During our shift, we're usually by ourselves in the baggage handling area. The domestic baggage never gets inspected, but the other luggage does, when it reaches the international terminal. The customs guys and their dogs check everything, and when the passengers pick up their luggage and go through the process, it's very possible that the luggage could be carefully scrutinized."

"So, that's nothing new. What's the big deal?" said Randy.

"The big deal is . . . we have someone check in at the International Airport in Mexico City, board a flight to LAX, check in two suitcases stuffed with quality pot, then another person boards a plane out of Houston, and checks in identical suitcases, loaded with clothes.

"We make sure the arrival times of the two jets at LAX are within an hour. If not, we sit the first bags aside, until the others arrive.

"When we unload the planes, we pull both sets of luggage, switch the bag tags and send them off on conveyors, where our man from Houston picks up the now-domestic suitcases via Mexico, and the international traveler picks up the suitcases full of clothing via

Houston and safely goes through customs.

"We have someone pick up our man from Houston and the suit-cases are delivered to Ernie or someone functioning like him, and we get our cut. What do you think?"

"That's fuckin' fantastic!" yelled Randy. "Shit, we could do this almost every day."

"Yeah we could, if we had the contacts in Mexico or Colombia, and had the money to buy the pot. I figure we could smuggle up to 40 pounds of quality pot per suitcase. Let's say we pay one hundred dollars a pound. That's $4,000 per suitcase or $8,000 per shipment, and we did one or two shipments per week. It would take twenty-four to thirty thousand dollars to front the operation and get started.

"We can't afford to do this, but maybe Ernie can. Or maybe he knows someone who could. We have the way; we just need to find somebody that's trustworthy and has the means. Our cut wouldn't be as large, but our risk would be a lot less. Guys, I think we could make a ton of easy money, and just maybe—have our dreams come true.

"But we have to be careful. We just have to make sure our dreams don't become a nightmare."

"Sounds like we need to have a little talk with Ernie," said Terry. "Scott, you've known him longer than the rest of us. Give him a call. Let's get this plan in motion."

Scott picked up the phone and dialed. "Ernie, it's Scott McCarran. How's it going?"

"It's going good. What can I do for you, bro?"

"Well, it's not what you can do for me, but what I can do for you."

Scott didn't want to reveal his plan over the phone, but divulged just enough to spike Ernie's interest, and then set up a meeting with him at the beach house at five. He hung up the phone, pulled out and unfolded the three sheets of ruled paper, and spread them out on the table.

"When I got home yesterday, I worked out the logistics to pull this off. I think we should go over them to see if I missed anything, or if you guys can add something to the plan."

In the next hour, they made a few slight changes, unanimously agreeing that the plan seemed solid. Scott had some work to do at home and said he'd be back at quarter to five, while the three bachelors grabbed their Strand cruiser bicycles and rode down the beachfront walkway to check out the chicks.

* * *

It was five-fifteen when Ernie pulled up in front of their place. He took the steps to the porch two at a time, and knocked. Randy opened the front door. "Hey, dude, good to see you."

Ernie walked into the living room. He had scraggly, long hair, a full mustache, wore a T-shirt with Willie Nelson on the front, worn-out jeans with a big Harley Davidson buckle on his belt, and black army-style boots. He was from the San Fernando Valley.

They all shook hands and gathered around the table. Ernie pulled out a joint and lit up, took a hit and passed it to Randy, while Scott began to go over their plan.

"Dude, do you really think you could pull this off? Ten minutes off a flight's schedule could get you ten years."

"Yeah, we can definitely do this," said Randy.

Ernie turned to Scott. "What do you think?"

"I spent some intense time working on the logistics. We *can* do this."

"Fuck, this could be a winner," said Ernie. "But it would take a lot of money."

"I know. That's why I called you," said Scott.

"I don't have that kind of dough, but I think I know someone that would be interested in working with us. He definitely has the contacts and the money to pull this off."

"Can he be trusted?" Scott asked.

"I've been doing business with this guy for years. I'll give him a call and arrange a meeting; hopefully he's around."

Ernie wasn't the type to stay in one place too long, and pushed his chair back and stood. "I've got a lot of shit to take care of to-night. I'll call my friend in the morning, and set something up." He looked at Scott. "Is it okay to call you at home?"

"Yeah, no problem. I planned to refinish the patio set tomorrow, so I'll be home all day."

They shook hands, as if they had actually made the deal, and walked to the door. Ernie pulled a couple of joints out of his shirt pocket. "This is some new shit from Thailand; tell me what you think. Talk to you tomorrow."

They all got a beer, lit a joint, and celebrated the future of their venture.

3

Scott was finishing lunch when the phone rang. "Hello."

"It's Ernie, how's the refinishing going?"

"Good, I'm going to start varnishing the pieces after lunch. What's up?"

"He's interested and wants to meet tonight."

"That's great. Where?"

"The Proud Bird, at six. Okay with you?"

"No problem, I'll let the guys know."

"See you then." Ernie hung up, and Scott called his friends.

Randy answered the phone. Scott said, "I've got some good news. Ernie's contact is interested and wants to meet tonight at the Proud Bird restaurant—right there at LAX, the scene of the crime of our dreams."

"All right. When do you want us there?"

"We're going to meet at six; I'll pick you guys up; talk to you later." Scott hung up, then headed for the garage to finish varnishing the furniture, thinking of putting a shine on all their futures.

* * *

Scott picked up his partners, and ten minutes later, pulled into the Proud Bird's parking lot at the same time that Ernie slid his El Camino into a nearby spot. They greeted each other and headed for the restaurant, just in time to see a brand new 1983 black Turbo Carrera pull up to the valet stand.

"Nice wheels," admired Randy.

"Yeah, and they belong to our new partner," said Ernie.

They stood there checking out the low, curvy Porsche, a little intimidated, when Ernie's friend stepped out. He was cool and looking the part being around 5-foot eight, with jet-black hair, a mustache, well built, wearing a black leather jacket, jeans, and deck shoes.

Ernie walked up to him and shook hands. "August, good to see you. These are my friends, Scott McCarran, Randy Bowman, Terry Clark, and Jeff Holland."

August shook their hands, saying, "Nice to meet you," as each was introduced.

The Proud Bird opened in the early sixties and offered guests an excellent dining experience with a "one-of-a-kind" view, right next to one of Los Angeles International Airport's busy runways. The restaurant had a great bar and front row seats where the guests watched the jetliners land, not more than one hundred yards away.

Along with a great view and food, it was themed after the era surrounding World War II, loaded with sleek masculine aviation memorabilia. As they entered, August remarked, "I love this place."

"Yeah, so do I," said Scott. "You know, this is one of the best aviation museums with old fighters and bombers in the area. When you step through the front door, you feel like you've stepped back in time."

"I love to fly older planes. One of my friends owns a restored P-51 Mustang and it's a blast to fly."

"Sounds fun. Maybe you could give me a ride in one."

"Unfortunately, there's only room for one person, but we could take up an SB2C Helldiver, if you're interested."

August chuckled, "Helldiver, sounds like my kind of plane."

The bar was already filling up. August took one look and said, "It's too noisy in the bar, why don't we get a table? We can have our drinks there."

They followed August, who was greeted by the maitre d', "Good evening, Mr. Taracina, your table is ready, please follow me."

Terry gave Randy a look, as if to say, I'm impressed.

They sat at what looked like the best table in the restaurant. August ordered a few appetizers and asked them what they wanted to drink. Scott ordered a rum and Coke, August, a dirty martini, and the rest of them had Coronas.

The waiter brought the drinks and appetizers.

"Why don't we order dinner before we get down to business?" asked August.

Four ordered prime rib, Randy ordered pork chops, and August ordered fresh char-boiled Pacific swordfish, and took the liberty to order two bottles of wine. He raised his martini glass. "Here's to a successful venture, salute." They all clicked glasses and beer bottles, waiting for Mr. Taracina to continue.

"So, Ernie tells me you have discovered a way to smuggle in drugs through the baggage and freight handling area at the airport. Who would like to explain this intriguing operation?"

"It was my idea, so I'll go over the details," said Scott. "The four of us work for Western Airlines in the baggage and freight department. We always work the same shift and I'm the foreman.

"All of the international and domestic luggage is processed in the same baggage distribution area and loaded on the conveyors to their respective carousels. The domestic baggage never is inspected. The other baggage goes to the international terminal, where customs officials use dogs to sniff out pot and other drugs.

"After the passengers pick up their luggage, they still have to go through U.S. Customs, which checks their passports—and might elect to inspect their luggage before they're cleared into the country.

"If we had someone fly into LAX from—let's say, Mexico City, who checked in a suitcase loaded with pot, while another person checking in with the same identical type and color suitcase departed from San Francisco, we're set for the switch.

"When the luggage arrives, one of us would pull these two identical bags off the conveyor. We change the flight tags, send the one full of pot to the domestic flight carousel, and send the other suitcase filled with clothes to the international terminal, to be picked up by the passenger from Mexico, who would routinely go through customs. Meanwhile the domestic passenger would leave the airport, get picked up, and deliver the goods to you."

August cracked a big smile. "That's a great plan. We could ship two large suitcases, holding no more than thirty-five to forty pounds of pot each. Seventy to eighty pounds isn't a very big shipment, but it looks like we'd have a free pass, with little risk, to bring in the goods. I think we should give it a try. But let's start slowly." He paused, in thought. "Yeah, we'll make a couple of test runs. I'm going to have some of my associates from Guadalajara set up sample shipments of thirty pounds of medium-grade pot, properly bagged and sealed, put into a suitcase, and deliver them to Mexico City. Then I'll have someone carry them on a flight to LAX.

"At the same time, I'll get someone to fly into L.A. from San Francisco or Phoenix checking in suitcases packed with clothes. You guys tell us what flights they should be on and they'll be there. You do your magic, and we'll see what happens. So whaddya think?"

Scott looked at his friends, who all nodded. "We think it's a great plan, but it's not that simple. What we're going to do is give you, or you could buy, two suitcases that are exactly the same, so we can recognize them in the baggage handling area."

"To make sure my guy doesn't end up with the forty pound bag blues, I'll provide some nifty green-striped leather Ralph Lauren suitcases. I use them when I travel, can't miss them on the carousel. You just make sure they get switched."

"Sounds good to me. Now the only thing left is to agree on what our cut will be."

The waiter began to serve dinner, so they changed the subject until he left, giving August some time to think.

"Let's get through the trial shipment first, to see if it works. I have a few items to look into before I can determine how much it will cost to bring in the marijuana. I do think it will be a profitable venture, if we only bring in the crème de la crème, quality grass.

"Ernie will be my go-between, and I'll take care of him from my side. So if that's agreeable for now, let's finish dinner. I'm tired, and tomorrow is going to be a busy day."

They ate and talked about flying, surfing, and fishing, all having a pleasant evening with business concluded. August ordered a glass of fine expensive port for everyone, and made a toast. "Here's to a long and profitable partnership."

They parted ways at the valet station and headed for their cars, while Mr.Taracina tipped the valet ten bucks, slid into his new Carrera and sped away.

The meeting left August in a good mood and he decided to take the coastal route back to San Pedro. He turned left on Highland and drove through the cities of Manhattan Beach, passing Chico's, then Hermosa Beach, going by the Comedy Club, and the Windjammers in Redondo Beach.

August was a pot smuggler working out of the Port of Los Angeles. He was born and raised in the port town of San Pedro and grew up in a commercial fishing family, developing a solid knowledge of the boating and maritime industry.

He started his operation in the sixties and employed some of his friends from high school and a local car club he belonged to, in various capacities, such as running shipyards, employing boat operators, drivers, pilots, and others. He established himself with various people by loaning them money, or helping them out during rough times, and then leveraged them in with reassurances.

One of his old buddies from the Sea Scouts, Daniel O'Brien, was also a smuggler and a sailor, and his dad, Daniel, Sr., was an official for some of the unions at the port, like shipfitters, dockworkers, and crewmen and captains of tug companies.

August built up an offshore company, and with the influence of Daniel's father, was allowed to acquire some of the leases on facilities in the ports of Los Angeles and Long Beach.

He was able to get the Port Laundry Operation contract; collected their soiled garments off freighters and tankers in port, and returned them cleaned, with his boats.

Laundry was dropped off the side of the ship onto barges, and August's company would tug them to port. There were times when the loads of laundry bags weren't laundry—and not clean in some eyes—and, of course, those bags were never returned.

Now established, he was able to lease a couple of small boatyards and gained control of some of the other small businesses in the harbor.

He took over part of the old Bethlehem Steel yard, located on the main channel of Los Angeles Harbor. Southwest Marine leased the south side of this huge facility. The north side housed August's marine survey and salvage operation where he docked his two 100-foot salvage and research vessels, the *Valero* and the *Peacock*.

August now had a well-oiled operation with control of enough waterfront facilities to conduct his smuggling operation successfully. But he still had to be vigilant, gaining the reputation of being careful and never reckless.

Daniel O'Brien's friend, Todd Sims' younger sister, Sharon, was dating a young DEA agent, Ricky Philips, who became totally enthralled with her, and rightfully so, because she was drop-dead gorgeous.

As they became more involved, dating frequently, they used Sharon's car to go out on the town. Daniel asked Todd to let him know when the DEA agent left his car in their family's home driveway. While the DEA agent's car was there unattended, August's men were able to break into it, using a Slim Jim, get to his radio unit, and use a decoder to read all the frequencies that the DEA agents used and frequently changed.

August's organization installed their own monitoring equipment on top of the Palos Verdes Peninsula and now had the ability to monitor all DEA radio transmissions from Santa Monica, San Fernando Valley, Los Angeles, Riverside, and Orange counties.

This mountaintop communication center, with a stunning coastline view, was one of his most valuable assets, and contributed to his success in controlling the harbor smuggling operation.

By 1980, he had control of boatyards and sufficient dock space on Terminal Island, where his fleet of vessels could unload the bundles of marijuana smuggled out of Mexico or Colombia. He also had a fleet of speedboats that were used to offload marijuana from ships offshore, with the capability to deliver to various ports along the California coast, enhancing the distribution of pot throughout the country.

August was now passing the Velvet Turtle Restaurant in the Hollywood Riviera business district. "Negotiated a lot of deals there," he thought, smiling, as he blew through the town and entered Palos Verdes Estates, a bastion of old money and mansions fit for their owners.

August had another meeting to attend in his hometown and was already fifteen minutes late. He passed the quaint Malaga Cove business district, with its Neptune fountain and the PVE Police Department. The road was empty. *Okay, let's see what you've got.* He downshifted into third gear, accelerating as he entered the first curve. The new Turbo Carrera hugged the road like a Formula-One car racing at Monte Carlo.

August pushed the car to the max, as he drove down Palos Verdes Drive West. He flew by Lunada Bay, entering Rancho Palos Verdes. Another one of his haunts, the Admiral Risty Restaurant, was a blur, as he passed it at well over one hundred miles per hour.

He only slowed down when he reached the notorious landslide area at Portuguese Bend, where the road is full of potholes and cracks caused by the land mass moving continually, fractions of an inch per year, seaward.

The green light at 25th and Western turned orange, as he flew through the intersection entering San Pedro. The Carrera lost its grip, as August turned left onto Gaffey Street, but quickly recovered. He reached 9th Street, turning right, then left into Peppy's Restaurant parking lot, now only one minute late.

He went upstairs where Johnny Prophet was performing. August spotted his contact, who was hard to miss, with his thick black hair, square jaw and pronounced cheek bones, handlebar mustache, and deep obsidian eyes. Put a sombrero on him and he'd look like he rode with Zapata during the Mexican Revolution.

Joe Cruz smiled, showing his white teeth, and waved him over. Joe was a member of a small syndicate that smuggled various drugs from Mexico. They owned a small fleet of fishing boats, and various planes, and occasionally would sell a load of marijuana to August, who would send his fleet of speedboats offshore to pick up bales of pot, and deliver them to various local ports. Early the following morning, August arranged to pick up ten thousand pounds from one of their fishing boats.

They shook hands; August ordered a drink and sat back enjoying the entertainment. Years earlier, Johnny Prophet was the opening act for Dean Martin. His fans thought his voice was better than Frank Sinatra's. Not having Sinatra's connections made it difficult to compete in the entertainment world; his career peaked in the late seventies. Many people still loved his voice, and came to Peppy's to listen to him, including August and many of his friends.

He finished his set and Joe Cruz spoke, "I talked to my captain; they'll be on time."

"Perfect, I'll have my boats waiting at our agreed coordinates."

"Payment arrangements the same as last time?"

"No, it's been a little hot around here, not with the law, but with the local gangbangers, having turf wars, so I think we should meet in Long Beach." August slid a piece of paper across the table. "Have Carlito meet me here at ten in the morning. I'll give him the front cash."

"No problem."

Johnny Prophet walked back on the stage, the band started playing "My Way," and Johnny stepped up to the microphone as everyone clapped. The meeting was over, and even if it wasn't, you couldn't hear each other, so they waited for the set to finish. Joe picked up the tab, put down a generous tip, and they left the restaurant.

August turned right on 9th Street, which changed to Miraleste Drive as he entered Rancho Palos Verdes. He turned left on Palos Verdes Drive East and flew through the curves, snaking through the hills to turn right on Crest Drive, right on Starline and right on Newridge. He pushed the garage-door opener and pulled into his driveway, next to his girlfriend Sandi's red Mercedes 380SL roadster. He walked out front and looked around the perimeter.

Everything looked quiet, so he walked back in, shut the garage, and went into the house.

He entered the kitchen and drank a glass of water. As he set the glass on the counter, a soft hand slid around his neck. "Hi."

"Hi." He turned to face Sandi. She was only wearing her panties and the lights from the living room silhouetted her perfect naked body. He wrapped his arms around her waist and pulled her close, kissing her passionately, as he ran his fingers through her long blond hair. "Mmm, you smell good."

"Thank you, but I have to tell you, you don't, and you look stressed out. How about we take a shower together and I'll wash your back? Then we'll go sit in the Jacuzzi."

August followed her, like a dog in heat, into their bedroom taking off his clothes as fast as he could without tearing them. He heard the shower, and when he entered the bathroom, Sandi was waiting, posing nude. She backed into the large steaming shower, holding her arms out, inviting August to join her. She looked down and smiled at his erection.

She grabbed a washcloth and soaped it up, scrubbed his whole body, then shampooed his hair. Then she poured a handful of conditioner into her hands, scrubbed some into his hair, poured more into her hands and rubbed her breasts, closing her eyes and smiling. She hugged August and slowly slid her hand down to "Augi Junior," giving it a little rub.

A second later, they were all over each other, and as he entered her, she locked her legs around him as tight as she could. She moved her hips with the beat of a jungle drum, their animal instincts taking over, as they climaxed together.

Naked and dripping wet, they went out the French doors to the patio, walked around the pool, and slid into the Jacuzzi. August had just rented the house, which sat on the side of the hill, with an unobstructed view from Catalina Island, down the coast to Oceanside, and most important, all of Los Angeles and Long Beach Harbors.

From this vantage point, using a pair of powerful binoculars, he could overlook his drug smuggling operation.

They enjoyed the view and fucked their brains out, once again, in the Jacuzzi. Sandi wrapped her arms around August's neck, and said, "If I stay in here any longer, I'll shrivel up into a prune."

"Well, I certainly don't want that to happen to either of us. Let's go to bed."

They climbed out, dove into the pool to cool off, toweled, went in, slipped into the satin sheets naked, kissed, and fell asleep in each other's arms.

August woke up at three-thirty, wondering if his boats had been stopped or boarded by the Coast Guard, who were always on the lookout for drug smugglers. *What the fuck am I doing? Why am I nervous? I know it's because that fucking cop Belson is out there on the hunt. That has to be it.*

Sandi woke up. "What's wrong? Can't sleep?"

"Yeah, just a lot of things on my mind."

"Well, let's see if I can help you relax."

She slid under the sheet and began to kiss and lick his inner thighs, slowly working toward "Augi Junior," who was now at attention. She gave it a kiss. "Feel better?"

At the same time, he heard the foghorn bellow from Angels Gate Lighthouse and smiled, knowing that the fog would give his boats excellent cover and safe passage into Los Angeles Harbor.

"Oh yeah, much better." He put his hands behind his head and lay there, smiling as he got one of the best blowjobs ever.

4

By 7:00 A.M., August was receiving calls from his men, discreetly verifying that his boats successfully picked up their bales of pot, unloaded them, and distribution had commenced.

August paid one hundred dollars a pound for the high-grade marijuana and now owed one million dollars to Joe Cruz and his group. The agreed payment arrangements called for him to give Carlito $200,000 today and the balance in a month, giving August time to collect from his distributors.

The address he gave Joe the previous night was for an apartment located in North Long Beach. He felt his new Porsche might definitely look conspicuous in that neighborhood. One of his employees, Dennis Freeman, worked at his boatyard in Huntington Beach and lived at that apartment. He planned to drive to his boatyard and take Dennis's Toyota pickup.

He took the stack of hundred-dollar bills out of his safe, put it in a money-counting machine, sorted it into twenty ten-thousand dollar bundles, and put them into a brown paper bag. He left the bag on the kitchen table, went to the front door and stepped out on the front porch to see if any uninvited people, cops, or henchmen were hanging around.

Everything looked peaceful. He went back in, locked the door, picked up his Beretta 9-millimeter automatic, tucked it inside his belt by the small of his back, grabbed the bag of cash, and headed for the garage. He pulled out of the driveway and headed for his boatyard, located across the street from the Golden Sails Marina.

He drove over the Vincent Thomas bridge, stopped at the toll-booth and gave the attendant a quarter, passed through Terminal Island, and entered Long Beach. He took Ocean Boulevard, turned right on Second Street, drove through Belmont Shore, over the bridge at Alamitos Bay, then through the moneyed, canal-laced neighborhood of Naples.

August turned left on Pacific Coast Highway, then right into the Golden Sails Marina. He already had Dennis's apartment and car keys, so he switched cars, turned right on P.C.H. to Walnut Street, turned left and pulled up to the apartment building, fifteen minutes before his meeting with Carlito. Dennis lived in the front unit. August grabbed the bag, climbed the stairs up to the apartment, and let himself in.

He sat next to a window with a clear view of the street. He saw Carlito, one of Joe Cruz's right-hand men, pull up to the curb on the opposite side, get out with a briefcase in hand, shut the door and begin to walk across the street. A gray Buick Riviera came to a screeching halt behind his car. Two guys jumped out with guns drawn, Carlito instantly saw them and ran, while pulling out his gun.

August watched, in horror, as Carlito was gunned down, falling next to the curb. He was trying to get up, but one of the guys walked over, and methodically executed him, putting a bullet in the back of his head. He grabbed the briefcase and jumped into the Riviera, which burned rubber as they sped off.

Curious neighbors were coming out into the street, and August knew the police would arrive any minute. *How the fuck could anyone know about this location or the deal? There's no way. This means they were onto Carlito, and followed him here, but they didn't know exactly where he was going, or what was in the briefcase.* He looked at the bag of cash. *I better get this to Joe Cruz before he thinks I had something to do with this.*

He grabbed the bag and got up to leave. He reached for the door-knob and stopped. *No one knows I'm here, and the police could drive up any second, and I would be standing there, left "holding the bag."* He chuckled at his own joke. *Time to sit tight and give Joe a call.*

He walked into the kitchen, pulled out his wallet and found the number, grabbed the receiver and dialed.

"Hello."

"Joe, it's August. There's no fucking good way to say this. Carlito was gunned down, just now, right in front of the apartment where we were going to meet." He could hear the sirens outside. "I'm still in the apartment and the police just pulled up."

"Wait! Wait, they're with you now?"

"No, they're outside, and I'm upstairs in the apartment with the money."

"Okay, that's good."

"This is really a bummer, amigo. Fuck, it happened so fast. I was looking out the window when he pulled up. A gray Buick Riviera pulled up behind him, two guys jumped out with guns. Carlito ran for cover, while pulling out his gun. They shot him in the back, and he fell, but was still alive. He tried to get up, but one of those motherfuckers walked over and put a bullet in his head, grabbed Carlito's briefcase and took off.

"Believe me, if I could have stopped it, I would have."

"Wait till they open that fuckin' briefcase, and see that it only had a sample of a couple pounds of pot I wanted you to try. Those motherfuckers! August, you need to find out who did this. I'll pay whatever it takes. You need to do this for me, my friend."

"I think I might know who's behind this."

"When you confirm it, don't do anything, just call me, okay?"

"I still have your money and will deliver it to you personally."

"I've got a place in Riverside; I'll meet you there. Let's say around six tomorrow night. Okay with you?"

"That'll be fine."

"Got a pencil?"

"Yeah, go ahead."

"It's 32 San Jacinto Road."

"Got it."

"I need to inform his old lady before the story of his murder hits the front page, and square up the money I owe him, so she can make arrangements to have his body transported back to Calexico, where his family lives."

"Carlito never told me he was married."

"Yeah, and he had two little kids. His wife is going to be devastated. This is fucked up. Those guys could have left him alive and just taken the briefcase. Why the fuck did they kill him? Don't forget; just identify these assholes for me. We'll take care of them."

"I'll do what I can."

"Be careful, and I wouldn't leave that apartment until the heat dies down."

"I fully intend to stay here for now. See you tomorrow."

August hung up, and then called his boatyard.

"Boatyard, this is Brad, can I help you?"

"It's August, get Dennis for me."

A minute went by. "August, what's up?"

"My contact was murdered in the street right in front of your apartment. There are cops all over the place. I'm not going to be able to leave your apartment until things cool off."

"Jeesssus . . . What do you want me to do?"

"First, don't tell anyone about this. Next, no one knows he was coming to this apartment so I think everything will be fine. Why don't you check into the Golden Sails Hotel? I'm going to hang out here tonight, and leave early in the morning. I'll leave your truck parked by my Porsche, with your keys inside the gas cap lid. Have a great dinner and charge it to your room. I'll take care of the bill."

"You're the boss. Oh, there's beer in the fridge and some leftover pizza from last night, and a bottle of bourbon and vodka in the cupboard above the phone. Be careful."

"Always." August hung up the receiver, and opened the cupboard. To his surprise, there was a full bottle of VO and a six-pack of soda on the shelf. *Ah, all I need is a glass and ice.* He opened the freezer and filled his glass with ice, poured in three fingers of VO and the rest with soda, chugged down half of it, and filled it back up with VO. He grabbed the bottle, walked over to the window, and sat down to watch the commotion outside. He took another swallow, and shook his head in worry and awe. "Fuck me."

The police, the coroner, and even a couple of news vans stayed on the scene until six. Some of the neighbors got bored, others had just come home from work and were curious. By seven, the street was clear. August went to the kitchen, opened the fridge, got out the pizza and opened the lid, put all four slices on a platter, and put them in the microwave. He got a beer, took the steaming pizza into the living room and turned on the TV to catch the seven o'clock news.

"This is Phil Cross at NBC Evening News. The space shuttle Challenger has completed a successful voyage, including the first space walk in nine years." Phil continued the report then talked about the pending 1983 State of the Union speech delivered by President Reagan, then turned over the mike to Cynthia Leonard to cover local events.

She reported a truck pile-up on the Grapevine due to the Tule fog. "Over twenty-two trucks and fifteen cars were involved, and the north side of Highway 99 has been closed since nine this morning and is not expected to reopen until 11:00 P.M.

"There was a gangland murder in Long Beach this morning; a man was gunned down in the middle of the street. One eyewitness saw a man with a briefcase get out of his car. A gray Buick Riviera pulled up behind the subject's car. Two men jumped out with guns drawn. The man started to run and pulled out his gun, but never had a chance to fire, because he was shot in the back and fell to the ground. The witness said that he thought the man was trying to get up, and one of the assailants walked up to him, shot him in the back of the head, took the briefcase, and fled.

"The authorities do not have any suspects at this time and think the murder was gang, and possibly, drug-related. They're not sure if the killers were following him or chasing him. The murdered victim, a Mexican national, lived in Calexico, California.

"Well that's it for this evening. This is Cynthia Leonard and Phil Cross with the NBC

Evening News. Good night and stay tuned for another thrilling adventure of the A-Team."

So the police think Carlito was being followed or chased. Let's hope it stays that way. August got another beer, picked up another piece of pizza and settled back to watch B.A. Baracus, Hannibal, Murdock, and Faceman take on the bad guys.

* * *

August was up at four and drove to the boatyard where his catch boats are maintained. He switched cars, took care of Dennis's hotel bill, and then drove back to his house. He cruised past his home and neighborhood; all looked normal, so he pulled into the driveway and drove into the garage. Sandi's Mercedes was gone.

He unlocked the back door and slipped in, drawing his Berretta. He went through all the rooms. Satisfied that he was alone, he set down the bag of cash, picked up the phone, and called his best friend and business associate.

"This is Mickey."

"Can you come over right now?"

"Sure, what's wrong?"

"I'll tell you when you get here."

"Be right there."

Mickey G grew up with August, went to the same schools, was in the same car clubs, and was a crime partner and road dog. He had long sun-bleached brown hair, stood five-nine, 185 pounds, and was sort of a hippie lowrider.

August watched Mickey pull up and walk toward the door; he opened it.

"Man, you look like shit," said Mickey.

"Good morning to you too, asshole."

"What's wrong?"

"I went over to Dennis's apartment to meet Carlito to give him his dough. I was looking out the window when he pulled up. As he got out of his car—"

"Ah fuck. I saw it on the news last night. I had no idea it was about you and Carlito."

"You know, we've had our run-ins; we've been shot at; we've seen people dead. But I watched Carlito try to get up and that cold-blooded motherfucker shot him in the back of his head. It was like slow motion; first I could see him grimace with pain, then half of his face exploded into pieces."

"Did you recognize any of them?"

"No. But they looked like a couple of serious motherfuckers.

"You should have called me."

"Nothing you could do. The police were all over the place so I decided to spend the night at Dennis's apartment. After a few VOs, beer, and pizza, I thought I could get some sleep, but every time I shut my eyes, I saw Carlito's face blow up. I'm going to personally deliver the money to Joe Cruz; he's driving into town today. I need to get some rest. I also need to find out who the fuck was responsible for killing Carlito."

"You think it could be Eddie Burger?"

"I don't know for sure. But why so heavy? A 187 (California penal code section for murder) for nothing. It was like an execution. Something's up, Mickey. Whoever did this is trying to make a state-ment, and whoever it is, will eventually show themselves; we need to be ready for them. I think we should contact Diz and the Nieto brothers, and tell them we need to have a meeting about Carlito's demise. It's definitely time to beef up our security, if people are go-ing to start getting whacked."

"Do you think we should set up a meeting to discuss how we can tighten everything up?" asked Mickey.

"Yeah, set up a meeting with our crews, as soon as possible. Make sure you pick a spot where we don't catch any surveillance by Belson, or get jammed by that scumbag Eddie Burger."

5

August managed to get a few hours of sleep. He felt like shit, and was starving. He took off his clothes, got the shower steaming hot, and stood under the spray until he couldn't stand it. He turned off the hot water, leaving it ice cold, and repeated the process.

He pulled on some designer jeans and a polo shirt, slipped on a pair of Top Sider deck shoes, slid his Berretta inside his belt, and put on his black leather jacket. He grabbed the bag of cash and left the bedroom. Sandi was sitting at the dining room table reading the paper. She looked up concerned. "How ya doin'?"

She's looking at me as if she knows what happened yesterday. Nah, no fuckin' way. "I feel a lot better after taking a nap."

"Were you up all night?"

"Pretty much. I've got another appointment. I'll be home tonight."

She stood up and gave him a kiss. "Be careful."

It was only three-thirty. He decided to drive straight to Riverside, have an early dinner at the Mission Inn, pay Joe Cruz, and then go directly home and get some rest. He planned to organize the smuggling operation via Western Airlines the following day and put the plan into action.

August put the bag of cash in the trunk. When he pulled into Mission Inn's driveway, he ignored the valet, who would have had access to the trunk and the cash. He parked and locked the doors.

He was early and got a nice table. He ordered scotch on the rocks, half dozen oysters on the half shell, and locally raised rack of lamb for dinner. While sipping his scotch and slurping down the oysters, he sat back trying to block yesterday's events out of his mind.

He finished his dinner, paid the bill and left a nice tip. He went to the head, took a leak, and walked to the parking lot, scanning the area, making sure no dickheads got the drop on him. *Come on, August, get hold of yourself.*

At ten minutes to six, August pulled up to 32 San Jacinto Road, pulled into the circular driveway, and parked next to a black Lincoln Continental. He got out and looked around, making sure he wasn't followed or the house wasn't under surveillance. Satisfied, he opened the trunk, grabbed the bag of cash, walked up to a pedestrian gate, and pressed the doorbell button.

The door strike buzzed, August opened the gate, walked past a huge fountain, and headed toward the entry.

August was about to knock when the door was opened by a guy as big as the doorway. They shook hands, well actually, Mr. Mountain who stood six-foot three, weighed around two-ninety, and was built like a wrestler, grabbed August's hand that disappeared into his giant paw. "Frank Mendez. Nice to meet you, Mr. Taracina."

He turned, and motioned for August to come in. He squeezed between Frank and the doorjamb, while the big guy shut the door behind them. "Mr. Cruz is out on the patio."

August followed him. He could see the bulge from a big handgun tucked under his belt in the small of Frank's back, through an untucked loose-fitting shirt.

Nothing was spared in decorating the interior of this Mexican drug smuggler's house. It was a little garish for August's taste, but colorful.

Joe Cruz, sitting by the pool, spotted him, quickly stood up, walked over, and gave him a hug. "August, so good to see you—; too bad it's under these circumstances. How about a drink?"

Not one to mix drinks, August asked, "Got any scotch?"

Joe handed the bag to Frank. "Take care of this and bring us a couple of Glenlivets on the rocks." He gestured with his hand, "Sit down and make yourself comfortable."

August pulled out a pack of Marlboros and offered Joe a cigarette. "Gracias." He pulled out a solid gold Dunhill, lit August's and then his own.

Joe blew out a plume of smoke. "What a fucked-up day. First, I had to tell Carlito's wife that he had been murdered. Then I sent one of my guys down to give her a little money, so she could arrange to have his body sent down to Calexico. Now I'm trying to fill Carlito's position."

"Anything I can do?"

"Thanks, just find the motherfuckers who shot him."

"That's one thing I wanted to talk to you about," said August. "Over the years, our businesses have grown and the amount of cash we handle is becoming dangerous. There are more shootings now than ever.

"I only deal in marijuana and I've had a few problems, but people in the cocaine business are killing each other every day. I think many of the newcomers are drawing so much heat that they're being taken out by the old pros. And it's getting out of hand."

"You think it's bad out here? There's literally a war going on in Southern Florida with the Colombians killing each other," said Joe. "But out here we're lucky. We've kept the Colombians at bay because they think us Mexicans are like Aztecs, and that we eat human hearts."

They both laughed. "Well, you want to keep it that way," said August. "I think we should use offshore numbered accounts; I'll wire you the payments. I know I have to get the cash out of the country, but at least I'll have complete control."

"You've always been a cautious man, and I respect that. I think it's a good idea. We already have a lot of numbered accounts. If you need any help setting this up, let me know. Now, back to Carlito's killers, have you learned anything?"

"Not yet, but I've instructed the Nieto brothers to look into it."

"Oh that's good; let me know what Chuck finds out."

Joe motioned to Mr. Mountain. "Frank, bring me that bag of pot."

Big Frank handed Joe a brown shopping bag. "I have a new load at the border; I want to see if you like it. It's all buds and flowers. I brought it up from Oaxaca. It's extra high quality, and the price is the same as the grade we sell." He handed August the bag. "This is five pounds of the same stuff that Carlito had in the briefcase that he was going to deliver to you. Let me know if you're interested."

August saw the opportunity to call it a night, and stood up. "I'll let you know."

"You don't have to leave. How about another drink?"

"I'd love to stay, but I didn't get any sleep last night and tomorrow's going to be a busy day."

Joe Cruz stood. "Well, maybe next time." He walked August to the door. "Take care of yourself, and let me know if you learn anything."

August put the sample in the trunk and jumped into the Carrera. His Berretta was poking his back so he pulled it out and slid it under the seat. He drove down the hill and turned left onto the 91 Freeway. Less than a minute went by before a police car pulled up behind him, with the lights and siren on. *You gotta be fucking kidding me.*

He pulled over, pulled out his wallet, and rolled down his window.

The cop walked over, flashlight in his hand. He shined it through the window, blinding August.

"See your license, please?"

August pulled out his driver's license and handed it to him. "What did I do? I wasn't speeding or anything."

"That's not why I pulled you over. You don't have any license plates."

August's eyes began to adjust; he could see the cop had his hand on his service revolver.

"I just bought the car two weeks ago, and haven't received them yet."

The cop flashed his light at the right side of the front window.

"So, Mr. Lira, where's your temporary registration?"

In the early seventies, you didn't need a passport to go to South America; you only needed a copy of your voter registration, birth certificate, and Social Security card and other types of ID.

August felt he needed an alias when traveling, or if ever stopped by the law. He did his research, picking Tony Lira, who had died shortly after birth.

August rebuilt the name of Tony Lira by getting a driver's license. As the ID got older, it became validated and eventually he paid taxes and opened accounts under that name. He also got a passport under that name, taking on another identity. Later, he was able to obtain various passports under different aliases, so he could travel anonymously throughout the world.

August's (a.k.a. Tony Lira's) eyes followed the beam of the cop's flashlight. He could see the tape residue on the right corner of the windshield, but no registration. *Oh man, am I fucked.* "I don't know. It must have fallen off." *Come on, think of something.* "I've only lowered the top once. That was yesterday, maybe it tore off."

The cop handed him his license. "You're going to have to follow me to the station so I can run a check on this vehicle because my radio's down. We're only a few minutes away, shouldn't take too long."

"No problem, officer, I'll be right on your tail." *Yeah, no problem, officer, unless you make me open the trunk, or look under my seat.*

August followed the cruiser to the Riverside Police Station and pulled into a visitor spot. He got out, quickly went to the passenger side and opened the door to look for the registration. The cop was watching him. He looked up. "I thought I'd take a look, but it's not here." He shut the door and hit the remote locking it up, as he walked up to the cop.

"Okay, Mr. Lira, come with me and take a seat at the counter, while I run your VIN number. Nice car, Tony; what do you do for a living?"

"Work in the film biz."

"You don't live out here in the flats. Your license says you live in Marina Del Rey. Is that correct?"

"Yes, sir."

"So, where do you work?"

"Twentieth Century Fox."

"What do you do there?"

"Foreign film distribution."

"Sounds like the pay would be pretty good."

"Yeah, it pays the bills."

"I guess so; you drive a brand new Porsche Turbo Carrera."

A burly old overweight cop, and his partner who looked like he just came out of the academy, walked into the station. "Hey, Parker, who owns that Porsche out there?" asked the senior officer.

"Mr. Tony Lira here owns it."

"Hey, did you check the car for money and drugs, Parker?"

"No, why?"

"Haven't you seen the Glenn Fry video called 'Smugglers Blues'? That guy drives a Turbo Carrera, has guns, drugs, and money in his car."

"I haven't seen it, Babbitt. This guy's clean, has a good job, and a clean record."

"Well, Mr. Lira, you can go. Make sure you get another temporary registration as soon as possible."

"Will do, Officer Parker." August walked out of the station while thinking, "What the fuck! I can't wait to get home."

6

August entered San Pedro, still way too hyped up to go home, and decided to pay Mickey a visit. He pulled into his driveway, opened the trunk, and took the sample of marijuana with him. He knocked on the door; Mickey opened it. "August, how'd it go?"

"Fucking unbelievable. I drove up to Joe Cruz's pad in Riverside, and gave him the money." He held up the bag full of pot. "He gave me a sample of the same stuff Carlito had in his briefcase. I put it in my trunk and took off. I jumped onto the 91 Freeway, and thirty seconds later a fuckin' cop was on my ass with his siren and lights on."

"Jesus Christ! What the hell did you do?"

"I didn't do a fucking thing. I don't have any license plates yet, and I don't know how, but the temporary registration taped to my front window was missing. I think the cop thought I stole the Porsche. Anyway, I had to follow him to the station and wait until they ran the VIN number. They found some parking tickets on my record. Some of the fees were late, but fortunately, none had gone to warrant, or I would have been fucked. From now on, any tickets I get are going to be paid the same day."

"Want a drink?"

"How about a Stoli Greyhound?"

Mickey pulled the bottle of vodka out of the freezer and made up a couple of drinks.

"So how's the deal going with the airline guys?"

"I think it's a winner. The only problem is the quantity. A passenger can only check in two large bags without looking conspicuous.

Let's say we pack each with thirty-five pounds, that's only seventy pounds per flight. The guys said they could do this three times a week; that's only 210 pounds a week. I mean shit, we just unloaded ten thousand pounds last week.

"The best part of this deal is that there's little risk. I thought, what if we bring in the crème de la crème, handpicked and clipped, stuff that can't be pressed into blocks. All lime green, purple-tipped Oaxacan colas, vacuum-sealed, and considered the triple-A+ grade of marijuana on the market. We could get a thousand dollars a pound out of New York. That's $210,000 a week."

"So what's your plan?" asked Mickey.

"I'm going to put Antonio in charge. We'll do a couple of trial runs from Mexico City. I'll have him load each suitcase with twenty-five pounds of medium-grade pot, packaged exactly like we intend to send the rest. We go through the whole process, even the delivery to us. If all goes as planned, we get moving."

"What about the airline guys; you trust them?"

"Yeah, they're decent guys who love to surf and they're just trying to make some extra money so they can fulfill their dreams."

"What kind of dreams?"

"They want to have a little hotel in Costa Rica, retire there, and surf every day."

"Not a bad goal, if they can pull it off."

"I hope they do because that would mean we made a lot of money from this little operation. But the only fly in the ointment is Ernie, that greedy fuck."

"You're fuckin' kidding me," said Mickey. "You better keep an eye on him because he could fuck up his own wet dream."

* * *

The following morning, August was on the phone, giving instructions to Antonio. "Make sure you pack and hermetically seal them so the dogs can't get a scent, and use those Ralph Lauren suitcases with the model number I gave you."

"No problem. I'm going to personally see this through, every step of the way, until my guy boards the plane. I have a partner and his girlfriend prepared to take a flight next week. I'll be waiting for your phone call to tell me exactly what flight my guy should take."

"How long before you're ready to go?" asked August.

"We'll be ready by tomorrow morning—that okay?"

"Yeah, that's fine. I'll call you with the flight number tonight."

Scott's pager went off; he told Randy to cover for him while he left work and drove to a pay phone at the Chevron Gas Station on Century Boulevard. He put in a dime and dialed the number.

"August, speaking."

"It's Scott. How are things going?"

"We'll be ready tomorrow morning. All I need is the flight number departing out of Mexico City and the corresponding flight from San Francisco."

"I already have them. Flight 1793 leaves Mexico City at 8:20 A.M., arriving 10:25 A.M., Flight 766 leaves San Francisco at 8:20 A.M. and arrives at 10 A.M. If those times are good, just give me a call. We'll be ready."

August called Antonio with the departure time, then made arrangements with two chicks from Laguna, who were mules working for the Brotherhood, to fly out of San Francisco with the suitcases only filled with clothes.

The Brotherhood of Eternal Love was a group of guys originating in Long Beach and Orange County who settled in picturesque Laguna Beach. They became a cooperative group of dealers and smugglers. They personally liked to trip out on LSD and smoke pot. August came to trust the group and worked with them during the sixties and seventies.

* * *

Antonio picked up his man at 6:00 A.M. He took the off-ramp for Benito Juarez International Airport and followed the departure signs. He drove into the designated parking lot for Western Airlines at 7:00 A.M. and followed his man, keeping an eye on him from a distance. His mule checked in his luggage with no problems and headed for the loading gate.

Antonio took a seat a few rows from him. The attendant at the counter announced that Flight 1793 was boarding. He watched him hand the attendant his ticket and enter the gate, then waited until the DC-10 lifted off the tarmac. Antonio went directly to a phone booth, called August's pager, and left the number.

A few minutes later, the phone rang.

"Hey compadre, my man is in the air."

"Gracias, amigo." August smiled, as he hung up.

While Antonio's guy was in the air, August's two mules, a couple of good-looking chicks that turned a few heads as they entered Gate C-11, boarded a Western 737 out of San Francisco International, bound for LAX.

The flights landed at Los Angeles International Airport as planned, first the domestic flight, and ten minutes later, the flight from Mexico City. As the passengers deplaned, their luggage was unloaded and taken to baggage handling, where the guys were anxiously waiting.

Randy spotted the green-striped leather Ralph Lauren suitcases coming in from San Francisco, and nonchalantly set them aside. When the baggage came in from Flight 1793, he pulled off the two exact suitcases loaded with marijuana, switched the baggage tags, and placed them on the proper conveyors.

As the switched luggage arrived at the international terminal, customs officials walked their trained dogs through the entire load of assorted baggage and canvas duffel bags, not finding any trace of marijuana or other drugs.

The travelers waited at their respective carousels, picked up their luggage and left the airport. Ernie picked up the two female mules and their luggage; Antonio's man hailed a cab to visit his brother in East L.A. He would stay overnight, and return to Mexico City the following day.

The plan was for Ernie to pay the women and drop them off at the Hacienda Hotel in El Segundo, then deliver the pot to one of August's warehouses on Channel Street in San Pedro.

Mickey opened the overhead door at the warehouse, and Ernie drove in, the door closing behind him. They pulled the two suitcases out of his car. August opened them up.

"Looks like everything went as planned."

"This is so fuckin' easy, we could do this every day," said Ernie, chuckling with greed.

Mickey looked at August, rolling his eyes.

August frowned. "It's not all *that* fucking easy, Ernie; there's a lot of working parts to pull this off. All you did is put the guys from Western together with me. You have your job, and you'll get your cut."

"How much do I make on this load?"

"I don't fucking know! This is just a trial shipment, and I intend to do one more. You have any problems with that?"

"Yeah I do. I don't do fucking free felonies."

"Well no one's asking you to. But don't get fucking greedy, because I don't know what we're going to make yet, and whatever it is, it will be fair. No one is doing this for free. If you don't like your cut, you can do this with somebody else."

"Look, all I want is a payday, August."

"That's what we all are looking for, so lighten up. Did you drop off the girls at the Hacienda Hotel?"

"I not only dropped them off, but made sure they checked in with no problems."

"Good," said August, who started pulling on the chain that opened the overhead door. "Don't worry, man; I'll have some cash for you guys."

"How about if I take it in material?"

"Okay, maybe you can take the whole thing. How long do you think it would take you to flip it?" August asked.

"I don't know; maybe a week."

"Nah, on second thought, I'll handle it so we can get working on the next shipment. I'll call you when I have some cash for you guys, probably day after tomorrow. Is that okay?"

Ernie nodded, got into his customized El Camino and drove off.

August looked at Mickey. "You think I was being too tough on him?"

"Hell no, he needs to know who's calling the shots; he's so fuckin' greedy and delusional that he thinks he is doing this whole deal himself."

7

After two trial shipments with no glitches, August started bringing in the best quality pot on the market. One shipment a week, using one mule to bring up 70 pounds of triple-A grade, purple bud sinsemilla, hand-packed in Mexico. At one hundred dollars a pound, August paid $7,000 a load.

He also had to pay $3,000 in total to the cops in Mexico at the airport to turn their backs, and the Mexican mules to carry the pot on the plane. Another $2,500 went for the two girls to fly down to LAX and pick up the switched suitcases, and $500 for hotel and miscellaneous expenses, for a total of $13,000 per load.

August paid $5,000 to get the load back to New York by car, for a total cost of $18,000 for 70 pounds of top-grade marijuana.

The triple-A grade pot was sold to Sweet Willie, a long-time friend and business partner of August's, for $1,000 a pound, total $70,000, less the $18,000 in expenses, for a gross profit of $52,000.

He paid the guys $6,000 each, Ernie's cut was $4,000, leaving August with a $24,000 net profit; not the biggest deal, but it was a clean deal.

Unfortunately, the operation was short-lived, and in May, Western Airlines started to change their terminal policies. The airline was not aware of their smuggling operation, but realized that they were vulnerable and needed to make some changes. U.S. Customs was pressuring them to change their baggage handling operation, sending all international luggage directly to the Bradley International Terminal.

Scott's boss, Wayne Harper, walked up to him and said, "We're having a meeting at five in my office. I know it's after your shift. Can you make it?"

Scott's heart pounded and his stomach turned. *Aw fuck, we're busted.* "Sure, no problem."

"Good, see you then."

Yeah, see you with some DEA agents, who are going to take me away in handcuffs.

Scott was feeling faint and a bit sweaty when he walked into his manager's office. To his surprise, all the rest of the baggage and freight supervisors were there. They were told that the new Bradley International Terminal would be handling all international flights and luggage in preparation for the '84 Olympics, as of September 1.

The meeting ended and Scott walked out of the office feeling as if a jury had just acquitted him of a major crime.

* * *

August was sitting out on his patio, enjoying a Cuban cigar and a scotch and soda, when the phone rang.

"August, it's Scott. I got some bad news today. I think we need to meet."

"How serious is it?"

"Not serious, but we have a serious change coming up."

"All right, how about tonight, at the beach house—let's say— eight o'clock?"

"That's fine, we'll see you then."

There was a knock at the door; Randy let August in and they joined the other three at the dining room table.

"So what's up?" asked August.

"I had a meeting with my supervisor today. They said Western's going to change the baggage handling process. As of September 1, all international baggage will be unloaded and taken directly to the international terminal for processing."

"That fuckin' sucks. This has been such a sweet operation, no glitches, and profitable," said August.

"I think we can continue doing this till the beginning of August," said Scott.

"I don't think so," said August. "The closer it gets to September 1, the more customs will be nosing around. We need to shut this operation down by the middle of July at the latest."

"Maybe we can smuggle in some other commodities with higher profits? We're only going to have a few more shots at this before we have to shut it down," said Randy.

Now they think they're big-time smugglers."Hey, I understand where you're coming from, but I'm not interested in dealing in cocaine or heroin," August said, emphatically. "You guys have made a lot of money in the last few months. Take my advice. Don't get greedy because that's when you'll make a mistake and get us busted."

"You're right," said Scott.

August could see the disappointment on their faces. "Hey, we still have a few weeks; make the best of it. This has been a good deal for all of us; there's no reason to take any bigger risks. Maybe we could double up on the last few loads?"

"Yeah, that's a great idea," said Randy.

"You think we can make that work?" asked Scott.

"Yeah, I'll contact my guys in Mexico, and get things worked out with them. You think you'll have any problems on your side?"

"I don't think so. In fact, I've been studying the daily manifests and there are plenty of flights that would work out," said Scott.

"Okay then, I'll set up my side and have Mickey take over and work with Ernie and you guys. I need to tend to some other business. You okay with that?"

"Sure, no problem."

"Good, you know we've worked well together; when this thing ends maybe we can come up with something else to do in the future."

8

August continued doing what he knew best, smuggling mari-juana. Even though his operation was well oiled, he always feared Murphy's Law: "Whatever could go wrong, will go wrong." One thorn in his side was State Narcotics Agent Mike Belson, who worked out of downtown Los Angeles, but was assigned to the Harbor Division State Narcotics Task Force.

Belson was in his middle thirties, had the reputation of a hot shot, hot dog type, confident to the point of arrogance and prone to admire himself and his style, beyond reason. Belson worked the lower level, investigating drug dealers and drug users. He raided homes and tried to turn the people that he caught. Mainly, the people he busted were using, and he'd try to flip them, to gain information about people holding larger quantities of drugs.

After he busted one of these guys, the first thing he would ask them was, "Tell me about August Taracina. Anybody that tells me where August Taracina is or lives, or where he hangs out, will get a free pass. He is number one on my hit list; I want to know where the fuck he is."

Belson worked closely with Detective Tyrell, out of the State Narcotics Division located in Torrance. During those years, Tyrell, Belson, and other state agents were constantly breathing down August's neck. They never got close to August, but August felt the constant pressure. He had to live and run his operation out of the Harbor Area, remaining vigilant of Belson's whereabouts, because he did know some of August's associates.

If a good-looking chick got busted, Belson would hit on her. He would make her a deal. If she knew anything or could find out anything about Taracina, he would make sure that she wouldn't be hit with a heavy charge like possession to sell, and have it downgraded to some misdemeanor, or maybe get the charges dropped, if she was "nice" to him.

August and his associates found out that Belson had been hitting on an ex-girlfriend of a lifelong friend, Dennis Tarino. Carolyn was a hot chick who had previously gone with Dennis for a couple of years; they had remained friends.

Dennis suggested that August talk to Carolyn, so he arranged to meet with her. She told August about Belson putting a full court press on her, and that if she gave in to him, he'd be wrapped around her like a wetsuit. She didn't like him. He was a decent-looking guy, but she knew what he was after.

She was willing to help, so she arranged with August to pay her monthly, as long as she dated and seduced Belson. This would give August the opportunity to record their conversations, and keep a close eye on him. The pillow talk might also be useful to bring pressure, and even incrimination, on Belson, if it came to that.

August had his electronic whiz kid bug her house, and install the recording equipment next-door. August could now monitor what was going on, while Carolyn was seducing Belson on a daily basis, and later, fucked and talked out, the asshole would go home to his wife and kids in their suburban nest.

She eventually persuaded Belson that she was his cohort and would be his crime partner. It didn't take long for August to become privy to Belson's plan. He was going to try to ensnare August by entrapping him, not to bust him, but to rip him off. He knew that August dealt in millions of dollars and planned to clean him out of cash, so that he and Carolyn could leave the country and live in paradise, wherever that was.

Knowing Belson's plan enabled August to avoid being caught.

Belson told Carolyn to pass some information on to her ex. He wanted to meet with August to give him the state radio frequencies of their private radios and walkie-talkies. He planned to use this ploy, like a carrot on a stick, hoping August would bite, taking him in as a business partner, setting the stage to rip him off eventually.

August pretended that he was interested, and set up a meeting in the parking lot of Twenty-Second Street Landing, a posh marina and upscale waterfront restaurant. He told Belson to be there at eight and to come alone.

Knowing that Belson was a snake, August had the Nieto brothers with him for protection, just to make sure that Belson wouldn't try anything.

Belson pulled into the parking lot at eight sharp. He got out of his older Mercedes Benz and walked over to August, who was leaning on a railing next to the forest of yacht masts. This was their first face-to-face conversation. The tension between them was like a violin string, too tight and ready to snap. Belson shook hands, and said, "Well, I finally get to meet the phantom, August Taracina. You're a hard guy to track down."

"I make it my job to be. I don't have a lot of time, so what do you want?"

Belson looked past August, spotting two figures lurking in the shadows. Chuck Nieto and his brother "Flea" were not only keeping an eye on Belson, but also watching the parking lot and the street, making sure Belson hadn't set a trap.

"All right, I'll get right to business. I want to give you the state's radio frequencies." He pulled a couple of folded sheets of paper out of his shirt pocket and handed them to August, who unfolded the sheets of paper and looked at them.

"Why would you want to give me these?"

"I want a truce and I want to get a piece of your action in the harbor. For a measly ten thousand dollars a month, you'll be able to do anything you want in this port."

August looked at him for a moment, then handed Belson back the list of frequencies. "I already own this port. Why would I want to pay you ten thousand a month?"

"You may think you own the harbor, but eventually your luck

will run out without my help."

August looked into his eyes, and held his stare. "You make your own luck."

"Yeah, but with me on your side, you wouldn't have to worry about the heat."

"Yeah, but I'm not interested in having any partners," said August. "I'll watch my back, and you watch yours."

"That wouldn't be a threat, would it, August?"

"Of course not; just a little friendly advice."

They got into their respective cars, and left. August knew he would always be a little leery, knowing that Belson would constantly be out there. Belson would never know about August's ace in the hole, that he had microphones recording twenty-four-seven in Carolyn's apartment. If anything came down, he would use the recordings against him, and that was a comfort.

However, Belson never did come close to ensnaring him. Still, August always maintained the philosophy, "Keep your friends close, and keep your enemies even closer." He knew that this amoral asshole with a badge, who didn't even respect himself, or his job, would always be lurking in the shadows.

9

By the last week of July, the airline smuggling enterprise had ended. On September 1, the group met at the Shangri-La Hotel in Santa Monica to settle up. They finished dinner, and the waiter brought the bill. August picked it up, and then pulled out a fat manila envelope for Scott and the guys. He also handed one to Ernie. "Well, this is the last of it. Too bad this operation had to stop, but it was good for as long as it lasted."

Scott put the envelope in his backpack. "It's been great. When we first met, I told you we wanted to own a hotel in Costa Rica and retire there. Well, thanks to you, we now own twenty hectares right on the water, and the waves are perfect. We still have some money left, not near enough to build a hotel, but we'll eventually be able to do it."

"Like I told you before, maybe you'll come up with a new idea. Maybe we could smuggle some hash through some European airline. It doesn't really have to be drugs; maybe there's something else of value, for example, chemicals like ergotamine tartrate or other precursors or compounds like methaqualude. Anyway, let's keep in touch."

August pulled out a wad of cash and peeled off some hundred-dollar bills to pay for the meal. "That should be enough." They got up, shook hands, and left.

* * *

A few of weeks went by. August got a call from Scott, who told him he had come up with another idea, and asked if he could meet with them at the beach house. They agreed to meet at six the following night.

They sat around the familiar dining room table once again. "Well, Scott, what've you come up with?" asked August.

"We receive periodic shipments consigned to Brinks, Loomis, and Wells Fargo."

August's ears perked up. "What kind of shipments?"

Randy interrupted, "Sacks of gold coins, gold bullion, gold ingots, and these big plastic bags, probably filled with cash."

"How's it stored in the plane?"

"It's stored in a bonded cage in the cargo area."

"Where do the armored trucks receive the shipment?" asked August.

"Directly off the plane; they drive their armored trucks right up to the bag belt, personally transfer it onto their truck, lock the doors, and drive off."

"How do you plan to steal the shipment?"

"We were hoping you might have an idea," said Scott.

"Guys, guys, I'm a marijuana smuggler, not a professional thief. I wouldn't have the foggiest idea how to pull something like that off. But it has possibilities. I think you should try to figure out a way to make this happen. If you do, and need someone to help, give me a call."

They drank a couple of beers and talked about Costa Rica; then August left. As he drove back home, he thought, "Nice guys, but to fucking rob a load of gold or cash from Brinks? They're fuckin' nuts; there's no way. They try something like that and they'll get shot or killed, and—for sure—if they get caught, they're going to prison. I hope they come up with something else doable. Then, on second thought, what if they find a way to pull it off? Now you sound crazy. Stick to what you know best, August."

And that's what August did. During the baggage swap deal, he was in a full-blown smuggling operation, far from knocking off armored cars like old-time gangsters.

He had cut a deal with Ken and Slim in Florida to pick up loads of marijuana off the coast of California and distribute the pot through his network.

Slim was from old Floridian money. He was a flashy, six-foot three, Florida blue blood, spotted driving around in his Rolls Royce and associated with people like Carlos Lehder, who went rebel, becoming a big-time cocaine smuggler.

His partner, Ken, was a Georgian from Atlanta, and a sociopath. He was the nuts and bolts technician of the group. He stood five-nine, thinly built, and looked more like a stockbroker than a big time smuggler. They were hooked up with the Florida Jewish mob.

They used seaplanes to smuggle drugs out of Colombia. A new Federal Task Force had been going head-on with the smugglers in the Caribbean, and they were losing load after load, having an increasingly hard time bringing their drugs into the U.S.

They decided to curtail their operation in the Caribbean, attempting to open up Pacific routes on the West Coast. They planned to use ships to transport the drugs, and purchased used 150-foot "United Fruit" vessels that had previously brought bananas and other produce from Central and South America to U.S. ports on the West Coast.

The vessels were in good condition and reasonably priced; the shipping companies were being forced to use larger ships, and the containerization of goods was becoming increasingly popular. Some of these older ships still sailed up and down the West Coast, making their new venture less conspicuous.

Their plan was to load 35,000 pounds of marijuana on one of their ships anchored off the Pacific coast of Colombia, and bring it up to the U.S. It was a new route from Colombia's Pacific side to California; they were confident the smuggling could be done, using August's California off-loading operations, already proven and well known to insiders of the trade.

They planned to send their first ship to Buenaventura Bay. The area was still primitive and barren. There wasn't a landing strip, port, or docks to tie up to, just a naturally protected bay and the location of a small Jahida Indian fishing village.

They planned to transport the pot in droning DC-4 cargo planes loaded with ten thousand pound payloads of marijuana coming out of the interior of Colombia. Having no airport at Buenaventura, they would simply fly over the picturesque bay, and kick out the thirty-five kilo gustalies (bundles) of marijuana packaged to be waterproof and to withstand the impact of slamming into the sea.

The Indians would row their pangas out, retrieve the bundles, bring them back to the beach, stack them, and cover them with camouflaged material. When the transport of 35,000 pounds was complete, they would send the ship to Buenaventura Bay, drop anchor, then an armada of pangas would bring the bundles back out to the fruit carrier vessels, and reload.

The ship had high gunwales, making it impossible for the Indians to unload their pangas by hand. The banana boat had two booms forward and aft for loading and unloading. Cargo nets were lowered to the panga guys, who could now throw the bundles into them. The load was then lifted onto the ship, lowered by groaning hydraulic winches into the hold, and stacked.

Now loaded, the captain set a course for the California coast, making sure they remained in the designated international shipping lanes.

August had to figure out how to unload the bales of pot to his speedboats while the ship was running off the coast, stateside, then get the load safely ashore and distribute it.

He bought two aeronautical airline life rafts, deflated and in their original containers, which could hold over one hundred passengers each. He had them flown down to Colombia and stowed on the ship.

On course, fifty miles off the coast of Southern California, the captain kept his ship under way, in the dead of night, while August's high-speed pickup boats and one commercial fishing vessel moved into position, maintaining the same speed.

The captain slowed the ship down to eight knots. Then the crew tied off a raft, still deflated and folded in a large bundle, on each side of the ship, with ropes long enough for the rafts to reach the ocean surface. As the raft went over the side, the CO-2 canisters inflated it.

When the raft reached the water, it was open and ready to go. Then the cranes lifted the bundles of marijuana out of the hold and set them on the deck. The crew would rush to throw the bales over the side into the tethered rafts as fast as they could. As soon as all the bundles were off-loaded, the crew would release the rafts; the moping old ship would pick up to normal speed and move on.

The crew on the commercial fishing boat took on one of the life raft's cargo, while the crews on six twenty-eight foot customized Skipjacks transferred the bundles onto their boats. After they secured and hid the bundles, the guys on the speedboats punched holes in the expensive, one time-use airline rescue rafts, making sure they would sink to the bottom, leaving no evidence for the Coast Guard.

Each customized Skipjack cost August over $75,000. They were equipped with twin 350 horsepower engines, blue-printed and balanced, with double starters, double fuel filters, extra oil reserves, and stainless steel props with kelp cutting blades, that could travel at over 60 miles an hour, loaded with 3,000 pounds of marijuana.

He had eight of them, six for the catch and two backups. As the old freighter maintained its course toward some bogus ports of call, the six speedboats headed for the Port of Los Angeles, while the commercial fishing boat steamed to Channel Islands Harbor in Ventura to off-load about half the total shipment.

August would have his speedboats pulled out of the water and trucked to a warehouse where they unloaded the pot. They refueled the speedboats, and towed them up the 405 freeway to Ventura Harbor, where they would be put back into the water, rendezvous offshore with the fishing boat, pick up the second half of the load and return to Ventura Harbor. Then the speedboats were pulled onto their trailers and towed back to another warehouse in the L.A. area.

Although tripling the work, by using two drop-off points, August always felt that if one shipment was stopped and confiscated, he could cover his cost after selling the other load.

10

August changed cars now and then, and parked his new Porsche inside one of his warehouses. He moved two of his favorite cars to his hillside home in Palos Verdes. His pride and joy was a 1965 Porsche Carrera II that he bought from the actor James Coburn, the original owner. They were extremely rare, with less than fifty in the United States. It was the car that Shelby Cobra tried but failed to beat in the 1965 Le Mans. It was a 165 mile an hour, twin-chained, twin-plugged mean machine. The other was a small Dino Ferrari, parked next to his girlfriend's Mercedes Benz 250 sports car.

Every morning, August would go for a walk, then come home and decide which car he was going to take to work. Around nine, he would back it out of the garage, and park it on the slanted driveway to wash it with loving care.

There was another beautiful home next to his. Every morning a woman watched her twin girls on the swings. They faced his driveway; August would always wish them a good morning, and the woman would do the same, nothing formal, just polite and congenial.

One morning, he backed his Ferrari out and started washing it. He looked over and said, "Good morning." To his surprise, she was nervously nonchalant, betraying herself, trying too hard to act normal, while she kept swinging her children.

August kept washing his car, the change in their morning ritual sent up a red flag. Something was up. He glanced at the windows of her house facing his home, sensing that someone was peering down at him. He knew, at that moment, the authorities had set up surveillance and were watching him, and had told this woman that he was a bad character and suspected of selling drugs.

Not wanting to alert anyone watching, he continued to wash his car, dry it off, then drove it back into the garage and shut the door. He entered the house; Sandi was in the kitchen. "Hey babe, sorry to say this, but we have to move out."

"When?"

"Right now!"

She knew the drill, followed him to their bedroom and started packing, while August went directly to his closet, opened the safe and cleaned it out. There was jewelry, handguns, lots of cash, and some incriminating documents in it. He knew the authorities were coming and would have a search warrant. He went out the side door, down the hill, toward the canyon, and buried the goods.

He went back into the house and called Mickey, who answered on the first ring. "Mickey, I need you to get a couple of the guys, go rent a Ryder truck and get to my house, ASAP. I'm moving."

"You're moving?" asked Mickey.

"As quick as I can."

Mickey didn't have to ask why. "I'll be there as fast as I can."

August started rolling up the Persian rugs, taking down the paintings, and packing up everything. An hour and a half later, the Ryder truck backed up into the driveway.

Mickey and two of August's employees climbed out, and started loading the truck. "You want us to put this stuff in one of your warehouses?" asked Mickey.

"Shit, that hadn't even crossed my mind. In fact, I'm not even sure where I'm moving to."

"My rental house in the back is vacant; it's small but whatever doesn't fit can be stored."

"Good idea, thanks."

As sure as the sun rises, state narcotics agents abruptly jumped the walls and came running in, guns drawn, yelling, "Police, stop! Freeze!"

Everyone stopped what they were doing. "What's going on?"

asked August.

"Who are you?" asked the officer.

August held out his hand. "Tony Lira, this is my house."

The officer ignored the gesture to shake hands and held out a document. "I'm Agent Jacobson; I have a warrant to search this house. You moving out?"

Just for a couple of days while the floors get refinished, and my Oriental rugs get cleaned," said August.

The agents started to search the house, not really knowing who August, a.k.a. Tony Lira, was, at that moment in time.

Later, August found out what happened to cause this assault on his home. An associate of August's from the Brotherhood in Laguna Beach, Jimmy Critinton, had gotten pulled over by Los Angeles County sheriff's deputies, on Western Avenue as he entered San Pedro.

Jimmy had three bales of marijuana hidden in the back of his truck. He pulled to the curb, leaving the engine running. He waited for the sheriff's deputies to get out of their vehicle and then floored it. The deputies jumped back into their unit and gave chase, but not quickly enough.

Jimmy was hauling ass down Western, past First Street, and veered off onto bucolic Weymouth Avenue. He knew he had evaded them but not for long. He turned left onto Sixth Street, almost out of control, as he raced through the residential area, and slammed on the brakes, while pulling over to the curb, next to Gaffey Canyon. He and his girlfriend got out and made a break for it, running down into the brush-choked ravine and up the other side. They split up, running between houses, jumping fences, trying to elude arrest.

The deputies, who gave chase, eventually located the truck, and found Jimmy's girlfriend hiding behind a store on Bandini Street. They took her purse and found a phone book with names and numbers listed in it.

Later, they traced all the numbers listed in the phone book. One was to August's residence in Ranch Palos Verdes. His elegant home was in proximity to the truck, making the inhabitant a person of interest; they were curious to find out who lived there.

Thus, the case was handed over to the State Bureau of Narcotics Enforcement, who paid a visit to August's only neighbor, getting approval to set up a surveillance team in the house next-door. Of course, they never told the neighbor that they really had no idea who their suspect was in the first place, allowing her to use some fearfully creative imagination. They didn't have to make up a story to get her cooperation.

While the agents searched the house, August and his friends sat down and waited, under the watchful eyes of two Lomita sheriffs. They found the safe and Jacobson asked August to open it. He knew the code, but acted as if he didn't, pulled out his wallet, and said, "I don't use the safe, but I've got the code some place. Ah, here it is."

He turned the dial, right, left, right, and opened it. Jacobson looked, only to find a stack of rubber bands inside. He faced August, looking disappointed. "Okay, Mr. Lira, go sit with your friends."

Almost two hours went by before the ranking state narcotics agent, Lieutenant Jacobson, walked up to them. August stood. "We're finished; sorry for the inconvenience." The agent started to walk out, stopped, and turned. "So, Mr. Lira, where are you staying while your carpets are being cleaned?"

"We're staying at the Torrance Marriott."

"What about all your furniture?"

"Leaving it in the truck; we'll be moving back into the house in a couple of days."

Jacobson waved at his men, who followed him out of the door.

August looked at Mickey. "Let's get the fuck out of here." Everyone jumped up and went to work. While the guys loaded up the truck, August went back down the canyon, dug out his stuff, and put it in the Porsche.

"Mickey, take the Ferrari, and have the guys unload everything in the Channel Street warehouse, leave the Ferrari there. Sandi, follow them, pick up Mickey and go to his house."

"Where you going?" she asked.

"To check into the Marriott, just in case Agent Jacobson checks up on me." August opened the car door. "Oh Mickey, have my nephew come back here and play gardener, and keep an eye on the house. I want to know if anyone comes snooping around." He jumped into the Porsche, backed out of the driveway, and took off.

While Lieutenant Jacobson drove back to the office in Torrance, something about Tony Lira bugged the hell out of him. The guy looked familiar, but he'd never heard that name before. He was so positive they'd find something, and it pissed him off that he'd gotten skunked.

When he got back to the station, he went to his office and checked his messages; there wasn't anything important. He leaned back, the hectic morning still preying on his mind. One of his friends, Agent Garcia, walked in. "How's it going?"

"Shitty." He went over the morning's raid. "Not even a joint or a seed on the floor. You're out in the field, have any ideas?"

"Yeah, why don't we go over our current investigations, pictures, crimes; maybe we'll find something."

"Good idea, but first, I need some lunch. Let's go, I'll buy."

After lunch, they went to work. Twenty minutes later, they realized what they had—and who they almost had. Two unmarked units and two squad cars headed back to August's house.

August's nephew was watering the front lawn when the four cars came roaring up the street, screeching to a halt in front of the house. While the lawmen surrounded the property, Jacobson and Garcia walked up to the gardener. "Have you seen the owner?"

He answered in Italian, raising his hands and shrugging his shoulders as if he didn't understand.

They found a side door open and went in. The house and the garage were empty; August Taracina was long gone.

August drove to Torrance and checked into the Marriott, paying cash for two days, then drove back to Mickey's house.

"Well, let's see where I'm going to live now."

The three of them entered Mickey's rental behind his home. "Shit, I could put this house in my living room," laughed August.

They drove back to the warehouse, meeting a few employees

who drove in a couple of August's vans. They picked up what would fit in the house and helped load it in the vans.

A few hours later, August stood in his furnished little house.

Mickey left and August poured Sandi and himself a drink. "Things are getting a little hot around here. I think you should go to Hawaii and visit your family."

"What do you mean? Aren't you coming with me?"

"No, I have things to take care of here. I think it's better that you go to Hawaii by yourself."

"Are you breaking up with me?"

Never thought about that, maybe a good idea. "No, but Sandi, I just don't want to be responsible for you right now."

She frowned, and gave him a kiss. "Okay, I'll start packing. Well fuck it August. I'm already packed."

11

On a foggy morning at LAX you could barely see your hand stretched out in front of you. Randy was cautiously driving the bag tug and carts out to a plane that was already a half-hour late, due to weather conditions.

Two more planes landed and were waiting to dock. He thought, "Looks like they're going to start backing up; we'll be getting overtime today."

As he passed one of the waiting planes, he noticed the running lights turn off, and at the same time, a light in his brain turned on. "The pilots sometimes shut down if their wait is too long. Shit! If they shut down in the fog—we might—fuckin'-a—they won't know if the cargo doors are open or shut. We could do it! And no one would ever know."

Randy pulled up to the plane parked at the gate. The rest of his crew was waiting. He jumped off the bag tug and ran over to Scott.

Smiling from ear to ear, he said, "Scott, it's time to get an architect and design our Hotel Costa Rica."

"What the hell are you talking about?"

Randy got close to his friend's face and whispered, "I know how we're going to rip off the plane."

"Not here. Let's talk when we get to your place."

After their shift, they met at the beach house, popped open some beers, and sat down to listen to Randy's plan.

"Okay, we're all ears," said Scott.

Randy stood and began to pace back and forth. "When I was

driving the bag tug to the plane, that we were going to unload, I passed one of the planes waiting in line because of the fog delay. I noticed the running lights were turned off. It dawned on me that the pilots shut down the engines if the wait is too long.

"I stopped the tug and realized that no one could see me in the fog. What if we drove up to that plane and opened the cargo door, pulled out a Brinks or Wells Fargo shipment, shut the door, and took off. No one would know, not even the pilot.

"All we'd have to do is figure out what to do with whatever stuff we took. We could do it! No one would ever know, and after things cool down we could all be retired and surfing in Costa Rica."

He turned to Scott. "You said we should wait till we got home to talk about my idea, so while we were at work, I had time to polish up my plan. A 737 is 94-feet long, and the fuselage is 12-feet, 4-inches wide at the cargo doors, which are located at the bottom of the right side of the fuselage, one in front of the wing, the other behind it. We know that the bonded cargo is stowed in the rear compartment.

"When the planes are backed up, the right side is facing the airstrip, the body of the plane blocks any staff from seeing the cargo doors.

"After verifying that the captain's shut down, we back up the bag cart under the tail section, hugging the right side of the fuselage until it's under the cargo door. We pull out the spring-loaded handle from its flush position, turn it counter clockwise, push in the cargo door, turn the handle to the normal position and let it spring back to its normal position, then push the door in and up.

"Then we unload the stuff, pull the door release cable, pull the door down, pull the handle out, rotate to secure the door and store the handle. Then we leave, driving under the tail section, undetected. We open these fuckin' doors every day. I could do it with my eyes closed. Whaddya think?"

Scott thought a moment. "There's one problem. Even when the captain shuts down the main engines, the auxiliary power unit, that powers all the electronics and supplies pneumatic pressure to re-start the main engines, would still be on." He paused. "The cargo warning lights in the cockpit would still be working and would show that the cargo door was open."

"Damn, I thought we had it made," said Randy, with a disappointed look.

"I think it has possibilities. I'll do some more research, see if we can pull it off," said Scott.

The following day, Scott drove a jitney over to the maintenance hangars and snatched a service manual. When he got home, he read it from front to back, and then called the guys.

"Maybe there is a way," said Scott. "I'll see you in fifteen minutes."

Scott jumped into his Jeep Cherokee, drove to the beach house, parked, and went in. The guys were anxiously waiting on the front deck.

"So what's up?" said Terry.

"I went through the 737 service manual and I think we can actually pull this off. There's a micro-switch in the doorjamb that operates the indicator light on a 737. If we time it right, we could open the door and push in the micro-switch so fast that the indicator light would only flicker. Even if the pilot saw it flicker, he'd ignore it, the light flickers under normal operation."

"How do you know that?" Randy asked.

"Because an insert in the manual pointed that fact out. Timing is everything. I think we should buy some walkie-talkies, have three of us drive a jitney under the plane, open the cargo door, one of us holds the micro-switch down, and two of us jump in and start moving the goods. When we're ready, the one pushing the switch will call the driver of the bag tug. The driver backs up under the cargo door; we unload the goods, shut the doors and boogie. The indicator light would flicker, stay off, and no one would be the wiser."

"What do we do with the goods?" asked Terry. "What are the goods going to be?"

"Shit, I haven't thought that far ahead," said Scott. "Have any ideas?"

"Maybe we could hide them somewhere and move them out

later?" Jeff suggested.

Scott shook his head. "Way too risky. Don't forget how Caveman and Horny Thorny ended up getting busted by the feds and going to prison. They were stealing shipments from PSA freight, where they worked, by putting a transfer ticket on a container full of computers, diverting it to another airline's freight department, where they had an associate move the stuff out of LAX."

"Yeah, and how about Janice, ah . . . can't remember her last name, but some guys called her 'Bone Marrow.'" The guys laughed. "She worked in baggage, and used her free passes to fly to Florida and back to LAX with bags of pot in her suitcase with no ID on it. She got busted by dogs and is now doing time," said Randy.

"She wasn't the sharpest tool in the shed," chuckled Scott. "So that's why we don't want to end up like her. The longer the goods sit in LAX, the risk of getting busted grows. That's why we need to get the shit out of the airport immediately, while it's still foggy and no one knows it's missing. When they discover that the shipment disappeared, there's going to be cops and FBI agents all over the place."

They went over different scenarios, but found faults in every one of them. Terry went to the fridge for another beer. "We could cut a hole in the perimeter fence and have someone pick it up in a van or something. They do it in the movies, so why can't we?"

Randy chuckled, "Yeah, you see a lot of shit like that in the movies, but in reality? No fuckin' way."

"Wait a minute. Maybe Terry's got something there," said Scott. "First, we would have to do this in the most remote spot in the airport."

"How about the boneyard, in the southwest corner, off of Imperial Highway?" asked Jeff.

"Perfect. All there is out there is a bunch of old equipment and containers scattered all over the place; no one goes out there except the local rabbits and skunks. We'll cut the hole a day or so before we do this and use some baling wire to hold it together. That whole area is overgrown with weeds and tall grass, so we pull out a bunch and use it to camouflage the hole in the fence.

"There are a couple of problems. We need all four of us to pull off the first phase; it would take too long to drive to the Imperial side and back. We'd be missed in the baggage area, then when the goods are discovered missing, we could be implicated," Scott explained. "We'll have the bag tug and a jitney under the belly. I think three of us should go back to the baggage handling area, one of us drive the bag tug and cart to the Imperial side. Or maybe one of us could call in sick and take off that day to drive the van. Or maybe we could use Ernie?"

"You think we could trust him?" asked Randy.

"I don't know. It's just the first name that came to mind. We have time to think that through. When do you think we should pull off the heist?" asked Scott.

They agreed that the best time to pull off the caper would be in the winter; it gets dark earlier and stays dark longer, increasing their odds of success. They decided that they would make their move during January or February, based on two important factors.

First, they needed a heavy layer of fog to delay air traffic. Next, the shipping manifest would indicate a Brinks, Loomis, or Wells Fargo shipment due to arrive at the right time.

They decided to do a couple of trial runs to be certain that it was doable and to gain experience.

* * *

The first foggy morning, they drove a jitney under one of the 737s waiting to dock with the main engines off. They estimated how long it would take to pull off the robbery and just sat there. In fact, they stayed twice as long as needed, and then went back to work.

A couple of weeks went by. It was foggy and planes were beginning to stack up. This was going to be their dress rehearsal.

They drove out, spotting a 737 with the running lights and main engines off. They drove under the belly. Terry pulled out the spring-loaded handle, turned it counter clockwise and Randy and Terry pushed the door in and up while Scott held the micro-switch down.

They counted to ten, pulled the cargo door release cable and closed the cargo door, pulled out the handle and secured the door, letting the handle slip back to its flush position in the door. They gave each other high-fives as they drove off into the fog.

They kept their ears open for the next few days; nothing was mentioned about any cargo door malfunctions. It was Friday night and they celebrated, looking forward to the real thing.

By November 1, they were ready to go. They decided to contact August closer to the actual heist, if they elected to have him get involved at all. There was one hang-up: should they use Ernie to pick up the loot?

12

There was another smuggling group working out of the port of Long Beach that used the same connections out of South America, a competitor of sorts to August's operation. The head guy's name was Bruiser, slipshod and rough around the edges, as criminals go.

He enlisted many hippies, and marina boat live-aboards, and would use anything afloat to go out to the cargo ships and unload the pot. They were bold, careless, and unsophisticated. They were successful, but sloppy, and drew an enormous amount of unnecessary heat into the harbor.

Occasionally, August's communication guys would monitor the feds following or chasing Bruiser and his men, and would let him know, saving Bruiser's ass, for whatever reason.

Eventually, they developed an acceptable relationship, and because of Bruiser's inefficiencies, they needed August's help to do some unloads.

José Gonzalo Rodriguez Gacha, known as "The Mexican," was the partner and best friend of Pablo Escobar, the head of the Medellin Drug Cartel. The other major leaders of the cartel were Carlos Lehder Rivas and the Ochoa brothers. Each of these people had built up his own business, before teaming up.

Cocaine was becoming the major commodity smuggled out of Colombia. During the early eighties, the Colombian-based cartel was doing fifteen to eighteen billion dollars worth of business every year. *Forbes* magazine noted that Pablo Escobar was one of the top ten richest men in the world; José Gonzalo Rodriguez Gacha was in the same category.

While most of the cartel concentrated on the cocaine business, including Gacha, he continued to be the major grower and supplier of marijuana from Colombia. He had a fifty-six thousand pound shipment coming up the West Coast consigned to Bruiser, who finally admitted that he couldn't handle that large of a shipment. So, Gonzalo sent one of his men, José Luis, to visit Bruiser and August to set up the catch.

On Monday, December 5, the three of them met for a waterfront lunch at the Ports O'Call Restaurant in San Pedro. Bruiser was being sort of an asshole. José Luis was annoyed, and looked at August while rolling his eyes. "I think you two should split the load in half," said José Luis.

Bruiser was about to complain when José Luis interrupted. "Gonzalo would want it that way." So it was agreed that each organization would off-load twenty-eight thousand pounds.

"I made the original deal with Gonzalo and I think August should only get paid for the catch. I'll make the sales," blurted Bruiser.

August chuckled, "No fucking way. You handle your half and I'll take care of mine. I'm not going to take all the risks to pick up the load and just deliver it to your fucking warehouse."

"That's bullshit," said Bruiser.

August began to stand up. "Fine, then find somebody else."

"Look, Bruiser, you're splitting the load," said José Luis.

August sat back down, and paused. "Not only that, but I'm unloading first."

"Fuck that, we'll unload at the same time," said Bruiser.

"No, I'll unload first, and make sure we're not hot," said August.

Bruiser's face was turning red and he was about to object. "I think that sounds fair," said José Luis, while he glared at him.

Reluctantly, Bruiser said, "Okay, fine, but you better not cherry pick the load."

"Fuck you, I'm not like you. That's something you would do."

Bruiser laughed.

"You and Snydo come over to see me and we'll get all the coordinates down," said August.

"Fine, where do you want us to meet you?"

"At Chip's house. Snydo knows where it is."

Bruiser nodded, got up and walked out, without saying another word.

"We're going to have to keep an eye on this guy. He's getting a little out of line," said August.

"Yeah, I'll discuss it with Gonzalo; let me know if you have any problems with him."

* * *

As the freighter was steaming up the coast, August began to gear up for the catch taking place Friday morning at 1:00 A.M. He planned to send five of his boats to pick up three thousand pounds each, to go through Los Angeles Harbor, and a seventy-five foot yacht to pick up the balance of thirteen thousand pounds to be offloaded in Marina Del Rey.

At 1:40 A.M., the five Skipjacks were pulled out of the water onto trailers and hauled to one of August's warehouses on Channel Street in San Pedro. The boats were unloaded and washed, then hauled to Marina Del Rey and launched off the boat ramp. The crews headed out to the yacht, drifting off D marker buoy, to pick up the thirteen thousand pounds. Then the boats were pulled out of the water and trailered to an El Segundo warehouse, where the process was repeated.

August met his crews at the warehouse and invited them to spend the night at the Airport Hotel just outside of El Segundo.

They finished breaking down the equipment and drove their rigs to the hotel parking lot, and August's driver, Dan, pulled the Mercedes 500 SEL into a spot. August got some rooms for his men and they all went to his suite for drinks.

August raised his glass. "Here's to all of you for doing a fine—" His pager went off. The number was from his communication center.

He grabbed the phone and made the call.

"Jerry, what's up?"

"You have a radio with you?"

"Yeah, of course."

"You better turn to channel 970; the DEA agents are talking about you."

August immediately tuned in to the federal communication channel. They all listened to the agents talking about August Taracina from radio to radio; they mentioned that August was at the hotel, and that they're camped outside waiting for him to make a move. One of the agents said that they identified his car, giving the correct license number to his supervisor, asking if they should go after him.

"You think this guy is registered under his own name? Just stake out his car and when he leaves, follow him."

August knew that the agents had no idea that his crew was in the hotel and their trucks and equipment were parked in the lot. He turned down the radio. "Listen, guys, they think I'm here, but I'm certain they don't know that you're here. I want you to leave separately; do not go back to any of my locations. Just drive around until you're out of town, certain that you're not being followed, then get to a phone and page me with a 711. As soon as I receive your pages, I'll leave and take the agents with me. I'll page all of you in a couple of days with a number to reach me and we'll settle up for this catch."

It took thirty minutes before he began to receive the 711 pages. After the seventh page, Dan and August left the hotel.

Dan had been August's driver since he got out of the Marine Corps. He was twenty-three, buffed out, and loyal. As they walked to the Mercedes, August whispered, "See anyone watching us?"

"There's no one in the parking lot except us."

They got into the car. "Where to?" asked Dan.

"Head south on P.C.H."

Dan turned right on Pacific Coast Highway. When he crossed Manhattan Beach Boulevard, August asked, "Anyone tailing us?"

"There's only one car behind us. I think it's a Plymouth or a Dodge station wagon, maybe a '74 or '75. Where we headed?"

"Long Beach."

It was twelve-thirty at night as they drove through Manhattan Beach. The traffic was extremely light. "That wagon still behind us?" asked August.

"Yeah, they're maintaining the same distance from us; it's a dark blue Dodge wagon."

"Don't make any drastic changes, but start to slow down a little, and take your time at the lights."

Dan started to slow down, and eventually the station wagon began to catch up to them. As they entered Redondo Beach, Dan timed it so that at the next red light, the tail would have to pull up alongside them, but the Dodge turned into their lane and stopped behind them.

"Can you make out the guys inside?" asked August.

"Yeah, there are three guys with hats on. Not the baseball type, but like fishing hats, and there's fishing rods sticking out the back window."

"Yeah, I wonder what they're really trying to hook. Just maintain the legal speed limit; let's see if they continue to follow us."

They passed Palos Verdes Boulevard, then South High School, as they entered Torrance. The tail maintained its distance. August looked to his left and spotted the Hot 'N Tot restaurant neon sign. He knew it stayed open twenty-four hours, and blurted out, "Pull in there now!"

Dan slammed on the brakes, and then accelerated, making a hard left into the driveway, slowed and pulled into a parking space. August heard tires screeching as the Dodge station wagon tried to stop, but passed the first driveway and turned into the next, drove around the restaurant, and parked a couple of spaces away from them.

This was the first time they really got a look at the guys, who did have fishing hats on with lures and flies hanging from them, all used for freshwater fishing, while the rods hanging out the back window were definitely saltwater tackle.

August shook his head. "Fuckin' unbelievable. Let's get a cup of coffee."

They got out of the car and August walked up to the driver. "Hey, how's the fishing?"

That caught the agent off guard. "Ah, um, we haven't gone yet, but we're ready to go."

"Well, good luck," said August as he caught up with Dan, both laughing quietly as they entered the restaurant. They went to the bathroom, then took a seat at the counter and ordered a cup of coffee.

"I'm surprised that only one car is tailing us," said Dan.

"Yeah, so am I, after listening to the DEA agents on the radio, I thought we'd see a lot more. They still haven't stopped us, or ID'd us, so when we leave, make a left on P.C.H., go to the next light which is Oak, turn left, punch it, and get the hell away from them as fast as you can. When you reach Lomita Boulevard, hang a right. As soon as you make the turn, be prepared to make another right into a complex. That is, if I tell you to. There are six small buildings on the lot. Go to the rear and pull behind them; we'll hide until the guys go by, and then get out of there."

They finished their coffee, paid the bill, and left. The fishermen were still sitting in the Dodge. Dan started the engine and backed up, pulled out on P.C.H., then floored it. He hit Oak, pedal-to-the-metal, fishtailing as he turned. They were going one hundred miles an hour down Oak, taking only seconds to reach Lomita Boulevard.

August was looking out of the rear window; the Dodge hadn't turned on Oak yet. Dan hit the brakes and turned right.

"Turn into the driveway!" yelled August.

Dan, an expert driver, turned and drove to the rear, pulled behind one of the buildings, and turned off the lights. Three minutes later, the Dodge drove by, headed east.

"It won't be long before they're on the radio reporting in," said August. "They have our license plate number so we'll have to avoid them and the cops as well. Go through Palos Verdes, over the hill and get back to Redondo."

That's what they did, eventually going north on Palos Verdes Boulevard, then Prospect, passing Texas Loosey's, a place similar to Hooters. They crossed Sepulveda, turned left on Knob Hill, crossed P.C.H., turned left on Catalina and pulled into a complex on the

Esplanade, where August rented a beachfront penthouse apartment that he used as a safe house. They parked in August's underground parking garage.

They took the elevator up to the top floor and went in. August poured each of them a drink, sat down in the living room, and turned on the TV. Dan watched attentively, while August lay back thinking, knowing that after this incident the law was definitely onto them. The gig was up, and from that point on, the pressure would only accelerate.

It became obvious that he would have to curtail his operation for now and see what the future might hold.

13

A couple of weeks went by since the incident at the Hot 'N Tot. August, Diz, and the Nietos' nephew, Little Chucky, were sitting at a table at the Jet Strip Club on Aviation Boulevard, close to LAX. August was going over some business with the club's owner, Big Mac "Horse" McKenna, who was a good friend of his.

Mac was a big, black, forty-year-old Mr. Universe-looking guy, who August met inside Terminal Island Prison in the seventies, while waiting to be transferred to the Pleasanton Federal Prison where he would do his time for a bust. He was using airplanes to smuggle pot at the time.

In the early seventies, Mac and August's friends, Roy, Burl, and Gary rode choppers together. Mac was a CHP motorcycle officer earlier in his career. When he was finally released from prison, Mac and a good friend, a previous lieutenant in the CHP, started the Jet Strip located by LAX.

In the early eighties, Mac moved to Rolling Hills Estates on Colt Road, a horse community on Palos Verdes Peninsula. August lived close by; they became good friends and partied at each other's homes.

They had various business dealings, but mostly Mac helped August launder money. Everyone knew that Mac's money came from prostitution and strip clubs that he owned throughout Southern California, and that he handled a lot of cash.

At times, Mac would ask August to ride around with him while he picked up money from other strip club owners. He extorted them for a percentage of their income to be paid on a monthly or bi-monthly basis.

Anyone who wanted to open a strip club in Southern California had to have the okay from Big Mac and even though most of them didn't like to pay their vig to Mac, they did it, because Big Mac McKenna, was a bad motherfucker.

Later, in 1990, Mac was killed, machine gunned in his limo in front of his heavily secured home in Orange County's remote Carbon Canyon. It was believed that the other strip club owners were tired of paying the vig and put a contract out on him. Later, the authorities arrested Mac's partners, Mike Woods and English Dave, for the murder.

One of Mac's girls walked up to the table and told him that he had a phone call. He excused himself. Diz turned to August. "Mac's got a good thing going on. It's too bad we can't get a piece of that."

"Mac's got this down; let's stick to what we do best. Fuck! I don't think I could handle fifty naked bitches every day anyway."

"Yeah, you're right." They both laughed.

Diz was six-foot tall, good-looking, and strong as an ox. He was half-Italian and half-Mexican, born and raised in Compton. He grew up on the streets in a tough neighborhood, and was in and out of juvie; he later did some time in state prison.

Diz was tough and smart, knew how to come out on top, and where to put his alliances. He was a no-nonsense, solid motherfuck-er that you didn't want to cross or screw with. August developed a strong alliance with him and the Nieto brothers; eventually Diz became a partner in some of his operations.

August's pager went off. He looked at the number and knew the call came from Chip Jones. They went to high school together. He became the student body president, was popular with the girls, and a good friend of August's, who eventually went to work for him. August walked over to the phone booth and made the call. Chip answered.

"It's August. What's up?"

"Bruiser, Snydo, and one of Bruiser's men are here."

Snydo was a skinny, blond-haired surfer dude whose family had operations in the harbor.

August had a bad feeling that Bruiser was behind pressuring Snydo to take him to Chip's house to convince Chip to contact him. "This guy a hired gun?"

"Could be."

"Are Bruiser and this guy armed?"

"Yeah . . . They asked me to call you. He wants you to come by and have a meeting."

"He asked you, or threatened you?"

"Bruiser said he was unhappy about the way the deal went down. Apparently, some of the off-load from Gonzalo's shipment was wet and he didn't get the money he expected, and got charged back from Gonzalo."

"Does he really want a meeting or is he gunning for me?"

"I don't know, but he thinks he has some additional money coming to him."

August heard Bruiser say, "Give me the fuckin' phone. I think you cherry picked the load, and I want to negotiate a settlement."

"Look, asshole, I told you I don't do that sort of shit."

"Then come over here and convince me."

"Put Chip back on the phone."

"Yeah, August."

"Tell him I'll be there in half an hour, and be sure to stay out of the way when we get there; it could get ugly."

"Okay, I'll tell him."

August knew it would only take twenty minutes to get to Chip's house, but intended to be there early. Diz jumped into the driver's seat of August's Mercedes; August got in the front passenger seat and Little Chucky Nieto got in the back.

While they drove to Chip's house, August laid out his plan. "Let's not get hot with these guys and start shooting immediately. Let me try to get these motherfuckers out of Chip's house quietly, so the man doesn't show up."

"Those motherfuckers are the ones that caused the scene by

going to Chip's house in the first place, packin' guns. We need to fuck these guys up! You pay me for security, if you don't need me, then fuck it," Diz protested.

"Come on, Diz, you know I need you, but there's a time to use force and a time not to."

"Look, August, these guys are packin' guns, they're not fuckin' around, and there's no chance for us to make any mistakes. We need to make a point."

"Okay, Diz, let's just see how they're going to act, before we do."

Twenty minutes later, Diz drove by the house and parked a block away. August knew that Bruiser and this guy were waiting inside, and if August just walked in, they could get the drop on them.

He had Little Chucky sneak around to the backyard while he and Diz hugged a hedge bordering the property and moved up to the side of the house. Then they quietly approached the front porch and climbed the stairs, while pulling out their guns.

Each side of the front door had louvered glass panels two feet wide, running from the top of the doorframe to the bottom for ventilation and light. Diz wasn't going to wait to see how these guys were going to act. He swung his silenced .380 automatic through the louvered strips of glass, shattering them as he drove his gun to the bottom, then stepped through the opening followed by August, both firing their weapons.

Bruiser and the hired gun were caught off guard; both started shooting wildly as they moved to the kitchen for cover.

August dove behind a large wing chair, while Diz took cover behind a wall. The hired gun hid around the corner, reached out and fired a few shots, keeping August and Diz pinned down. Then Bruiser and this guy made a break for the laundry room and the back door.

Bruiser opened the back door and Little Chucky opened fire, causing splinters of wood to shatter around Bruiser's head, as he ducked back in, pinning them inside the house, caught in a cross fire. While Snydo and Chip remained flattened out on the floor, Diz and

August moved toward the kitchen, guns held with both hands, ready to shoot at any movement.

While Bruiser fired at Little Chucky, the hired gun covered the entrance to the laundry room. Nieto's gun jammed. Sensing the lack of return gunfire from the rear, Bruiser yelled, "Let's get the hell out of here." He turned and dashed toward the back door, firing blindly, while running for his life. The hired gun opened fire on Diz and August while he backpedaled for the door, but took a bullet in the gut and went down. Bruiser ran out the back door, shooting wildly.

August and Diz kept running, jumped over the body, and out the door.

Bruiser already had a shoulder wound. As he ran through the backyard, he got shot in the ass as he jumped the rear wall and escaped.

August walked up to the hired gun as Little Chucky walked in. "What happened out there?" asked August.

"Sorry, man, my gun jammed. By the time I cleared it, he was over the wall."

August looked at the guy on the floor. He had long blond hair and wasn't wearing any shoes. He turned to Snydo and said, "You know who this fucking guy is?"

"Only that Bruiser was boasting that he was a Vietnam Vet, a real badass, trained in Special Forces."

"The guy's in pretty bad shape. Since you brought him here, I think it's your fuckin' job to dump him off at a hospital. I don't even know this prick."

"I'm sorry, August; I really didn't have any choice."

"Yeah, right. Well, you're damn lucky; if any of my guys got hurt, Snydo, you would have ended up in the hospital next to this cocksucker."

"I'm really sorry, man," said Snydo.

"Sorry doesn't cut it. I know that Bruiser and this motherfucker threatened you. They probably filled their noses with coke, got jacked up, and decided to come to town and fuck with me. You tell that piece of shit Bruiser that he better stay the fuck out of my way, or else."

The wounded former GI started to cry out because his wounds were serious and he needed a doctor. "Shut the fuck up," yelled Diz. "You should have thought about that before you came over here acting like some fuckin' Rambo."

August chuckled at Diz's comment. "Chip, I need to get out of here. Clean up this mess as quick as you can, in case the cops come snooping. I'm sorry your house got fucked up. Have it fixed and give me the bill." He turned to Snydo. "Take this guy to the hospital and dump him off in front of the emergency entrance, and get the hell out of there."

August turned and left, followed by Diz. They jumped into the Mercedes; Diz put it in gear and took off. August shook his head. "Fucking unbelievable."

* * *

A week went by. With revenge on his mind, Bruiser tried to get even. He sent a couple of his men to pour sacks of marijuana seeds in August's boats as evidence. They towed them into the harbor and set them adrift. He hoped that the boats would be retrieved by the Harbor Master or Coast Guard, get searched, and that they'd bust August's operation.

One of the problems in off-loading marijuana was that the decks constantly required cleaning. But, if you wanted to incriminate someone, pouring seeds in their boats or warehouses could do the trick. One of August's friends spotted the Skipjacks being towed out; he warned him in time for August's crew to retrieve the boats.

Bruiser thought he was vindicated, but he had gone too far. August had to put him out of commission. Bruiser was force fed a half-ounce of cocaine, causing him to go into violent convulsions. He was picked up by an ambulance and admitted to the hospital. He never really recovered; his operation eventually dried up.

After the elimination of Bruiser, Gonzalo Rodriguez Gacha contacted August. He still wanted to ship loads of marijuana up the

West Coast and asked him if he was interested in providing his catch operation.

Rodriguez rarely came to the United States. They both agreed that they needed another physical meeting to consummate the deal. August arranged to fly down to Colombia. August never flew out of any airport in the United States, but used Mexico City as his hub to travel worldwide. He would either walk or have someone drive him across the border to the Tijuana or Mexicali airports, then take a local flight to Mexico City's Benito Juárez International Airport, where he would book passage to anywhere in the world. Then he would also return to the U.S. the same way.

But this particular time, knowing and feeling the heat, he wanted to see how much interest the U.S. authorities had in him. He used different aliases in his business, but if they were looking at August Taracina, exclusively, he wanted to know. So he decided to travel under his real name, departing from Los Angeles International Airport.

Mickey and August were on their way to LAX. "You really shouldn't be going down there by yourself; how come you don't have Chip go with you?" asked Mickey.

"Chip's still rattled about the shoot-out at his house. I think it would be better to travel by myself, keeping it low key. Gonzalo needs my operation and I have no intention of fucking him—ever. It'll be fine."

Mickey pulled up to the curb in front of the departure gate of Pan American World Airways at the new Tom Bradley International Terminal.

"How long do you think you'll be down there?"

"Probably a few days, hell, I might make a mini-vacation out of it. Maybe I'll go fishing or hunting, who knows?" said August. "Be sure to check up on the white manufacturing operation because they were ready to move and build another location."

He carried his overnight bag to the ticket counter. "Can I help you?" the ticket agent asked.

"I'd like to purchase a first-class roundtrip ticket, with an open date and time for the return trip from Bogotá, Colombia."

"How would you like to pay?"

"American Express." He handed his card and passport to the agent.

She looked at the passport and credit card. "Any luggage to check in, Mr. Taracina?"

"No, just a carry-on."

The agent swiped the credit card, and he signed the slip. She prepared the tickets and handed the passport, credit card, and ticket to August. "Your plane will be boarding at Gate A22; have a nice flight and thank you for using Pan Am."

August walked to the gate, after having his bag x-rayed and his ticket and passport rechecked. He figured that, if there was any steam on him he would draw it when he landed in Bogotá. He had an hour to kill before boarding, bought a newspaper, then walked into the bar and ordered a beer.

As he left the bar, he heard an announcement: "Flight 1923 will begin boarding at Gate A22."

As August reached the gate, the Pan Am agent announced, "Now boarding, all first-class passengers."

August continued walking, only slowing down as he handed his ticket to the agent, then continued down the loading ramp and into the DC-10, where he was greeted and directed to the first-class section of the plane.

He took his seat; a good-lookin' stewardess walked over, introduced herself, and asked if he wanted a cocktail, and/or appetizers. He ordered a scotch and soda, sat back and enjoyed the hors d'oeuvres.

They took off, and a half-hour into the flight, he was served lunch. August ordered steak and lobster. After a couple of scotches, appetizers, lunch, and a few glasses of cabernet, he lay back and dozed off. Two hours later, he woke up just in time to watch a movie while being catered-to by the same good-lookin' stewardess.

It was an uneventful flight; they landed and taxied to the dock. He headed for the baggage claim and walked directly to the Colombian Customs kiosk. He handed the officer his passport. The officer looked at it and handed the passport to another official behind him.

"Mr. Taracina, would you please follow me?"

"Who are you?"

"Agent Garcia, of the Departamento Administrativo de Seguridad."

August knew about the Department of the Administration of Security; many of the agents, if not all, were corrupt as hell, and could be dangerous, or at least have their hand out. He hoped this was just a random check and that he could remain under the radar while in Colombia.

The DAS agent took him into a small room, photographed, fingerprinted, and interrogated him.

"So, Mr. Taracina, what brings you to Bogotá?"

"I came down to attend a friend's wedding."

"You travel with little baggage."

"Unfortunately, I will not be able to stay long enough to tour your beautiful country. I will only be here for two or three days."

"Is that why you purchased an open ticket for your return to the United States?" Agent Garcia asked.

So that's why I was pulled aside. The open ticket must have raised a red flag. "Yes, because if I can squeeze in another day or so, I intend to see more of Colombia."

"Maybe you find a beautiful señorita and stay longer, eh?" he chuckled as he handed back August's passport. "Enjoy your stay in Colombia."

"I will, and thank you."

August left the airport, got a cab and went to the Continental Hotel, where Gonzalo told him to register. He checked in and went to his room to wait to be contacted. It was six-thirty when his phone rang. "Hello."

"Mr. Taracina, this is José Luis, I hope you haven't had dinner?"

"Not yet."

"Good, I will wait for you in the lobby."

August took the elevator. The door opened; José Luis was sitting in an armchair in the lobby. He stood and walked toward August, extended his arms, and gave him a hug. "Good to see you again, my friend."

They left the hotel; a car was waiting for them. They got in as José said, "Carlos, take us to Andres Carne de Res." He turned to August and said, "They serve the best steak in Bogotá. The beef comes from Gonzalo's cattle ranch."

Carlos pulled up to the curb and the valet opened the car door. "Buenos noches." The doorman opened the door and they walked up to the maître d', who instantly recognized José Luis, greeted him, and led the way to what looked like the best table in the place. And it was quite the place.

With leather-backed chairs, crystal chandeliers, richly finished oak walls adorned with original art, the restaurant had a musky smell to it and was very masculine. The women and men sitting at the tables definitely came from Colombia's elite class.

They ordered drinks; José Luis ordered an array of appetizers and wine, and steaks for both of them. They talked about the growing problems with the Colombian government and about law enforcement creating a lot of trouble for the cartel. Things were changing, they lamented.

José Luis asked, "So, you have any more problems with Bruiser?"

"No, he decided to get out of the business."

José Luis chuckled, "I think maybe you decided that for him."

"Maybe."

August and Bruiser started doing business with Gonzalo about the same time, and were introduced to him by a mutual friend of theirs.

Bruiser jumped at the opportunity and cut a deal with Gonzalo before he conducted any business with August. As time went on, Gonzalo realized that August's operation was far more professional than Bruiser's. Hell, he was like a bull in a china shop. He loved his cocaine and pot and was too much of a cowboy. He was a big intimidating dude, but lacked good old common sense and was apt to make mistakes.

August was halfway through his meal, when he said, "This

porterhouse is the best steak I've ever had."

"People say Gonzalo's beef is the best in South America." They finished dinner; both had a glass of forty-year-old port for dessert, and then left the restaurant. José Luis's car miraculously appeared, pulling up to the curb.

José Luis told August to check out of the hotel before nine the next morning and that he'd be there to pick him up; he would be Gonzalo's guest.

* * *

August had met with Gonzalo a couple of times in the United States, but never in Colombia. His dealings were always taken care of stateside. August had some big dealings with him in the past and became like a brother to him, after saving Gonzalo's son.

It was around two years ago when Gonzalo's right-hand man, José Luis, called August to tell him that Gonzalo's son, Fredy, was onboard one of his freighters that was on its way from Cartagena to Boston loaded with forty thousand pounds of marijuana.

At the last minute, they were notified that the guys that were making the catch got busted and they didn't have anybody to unload the ship. The catch was to go down off the coast of Massachusetts, and because of the bust, the Coast Guard was on alert patrolling the area.

The guys on the ship knew that they could throw the pot overboard, but would probably get arrested. Gonzalo didn't want his son involved because he would never be allowed to come back into the United States, after being red-flagged.

So Gonzalo asked José Luis to fly up to L.A. and ask August if he would be able to snatch his son Fredy from the freighter, which was now cruising off the coast of Virginia, next port-of-call Montreal, Canada. They hoped, if the ship continued on course, that they might slip by the Coast Guard, but were certain, if they turned around, they would be boarded.

August flew to Boston, and through one of his contacts, was

able to procure a fishing vessel that he took out to rendezvous with the freighter. Gonzalo wanted his son off the ship before the crew started to throw the pot overboard. August had the coordinates of the rendezvous spot and pushed the old fishing boat to full speed, finally seeing the ship on the horizon.

The ship maintained speed while August turned the fishing boat around and began to move alongside. There was a four to five foot swell running and it was going to be a tricky move to pull this off.

The crew lowered a rope ladder over the side while the swells were causing the fishing boat to rise, fall, and sway from side to side. August worried that the ship might smash into the fishing boat, or even worse, crush Gonzalo's son, while climbing down the ladder. If he was knocked off, or he lost his grip and fell into the water, the ship's propellers would chop him up, or he would hit something, rendering him unconscious, causing him to drown.

As Fredy stepped onto the last rung, August timed it perfectly. He pulled as close to the ship as he could, as a swell took the fishing boat up. All Fredy had to do was to push away from the ship's hull, step onto the rail of the fishing boat and jump on deck, which he did without a hitch.

As August pulled away from the ship, the crew began to throw the bales of pot overboard as fast as they could.

Fredy didn't have his passport with him, which wouldn't be a problem if August could get him ashore, unnoticed.

On the way back to port, they passed two Coast Guard vessels running at full speed toward the freighter. August hoped they had enough time to dump the load. It was going to be close.

He took the fishing boat into the harbor, pulled up to the dock, and Fredy secured the lines. Gonzalo's son looked like shit, unshaven, and wearing dirty clothes. August hailed a cab and told the driver to take them to the closest Holiday Inn or Best Western. They ended up at a Comfort Inn, checked in for the night, and then went to the closest department store, where August bought him some clothes suitable for the plane ride back to Los Angeles.

August had to charter a plane because Fredy had no passport or identification.When August and Fredy landed in Los Angeles, they went to the Beverly Hills Hotel, where they met Gonzalo, who rarely came to the U.S., waiting for his son. They walked into the suite. Gonzalo hugged his son, while thanking August.

"August," he said, "I realize what a risk it was going back East, and not only making arrangements, but physically going out to sea to rescue my son from the authorities. If there's anything I can do for you, just let me know."

"I'm just happy that I was able to help, and it all worked out for the best."

Gonzalo gave him a hug. "Remember, I am indebted to you."

As August started to leave, Fredy gave him a hug. "Thanks, man."

* * *

August was awake at seven, cleaned up, dressed, and packed. He checked out of the Continental , then had breakfast in the hotel's café.

He stepped outside at nine. The same car that he rode in the previous night was parked at the curb; José Luis was sitting in the front passenger seat. He opened the rear door and slid in. There was another guy sitting in the backseat, obviously, a bodyguard.

"Good morning," said José Luis.

"Good morning."

Carlos drove through the city, and fifteen minutes later, they were driving through the countryside and Bogotá's suburbs. The driver turned off the highway and drove through a tract of homes that you might see in an upscale neighborhood in Southern California.

He turned into a driveway, pulled up in front of the double garage door, and honked. The garage door opened and he drove in. When the door shut behind them, it was pitch dark. The lights turned on and August could see holes in the walls with machine gun barrels poking out of them. *I guess if you weren't invited you'd be fucked.*

José Luis opened his window and talked to the guards brandishing the machine guns, and then the fortified double doors in front of them opened. Carlos drove into a beautifully landscaped courtyard and parked.

There were armed guards everywhere. They got out of the car and walked up to the side door that one of the guards opened. Gonzalo was waiting for him in the kitchen.

He walked up to August, grasped his hand with both of his. "Hey, my friend, how was your trip? How was your dinner last night?"

"My flight was good, and dinner was fantastic, especially the beef; it was the best I've ever tasted. I did have a problem when I walked into the terminal. One of your DAS agents pulled me aside, searched, and photographed me."

"I'm sorry to hear that. You know, at one time, we paid them off and they looked the other way. Now, the American and Colombian governments have turned the tables on us."

"José Luis said that law enforcement down here is putting the squeeze on your operation. Is that why you have so many guards around?"

"Things have changed over the last few years. The government of Colombia, DAS, the Cali cartel, the national police, and other groups are forming to kill Pablo and me. We are no longer free to come and go as we please. Even our families are in danger.

"We're worth billions of dollars and have helped thousands of people in Colombia, including the hundreds of millions of dollars that went to bribe officials in our government and law enforcement.

"Until recently, we had very few problems. Now the United States is bringing pressure on our government to extradite us to the U.S. and throw us into their prisons.

"You know, we have made a lot of money from the cocaine business, but we are being cursed by our success. We have talked about this issue before. That's why I tell you, my Italian friend, stick with smuggling marijuana.

"I want to increase the quantity being shipped through the Western corridor; I'd like you to handle my shipments exclusively."

"That's great, Gonzalo, but how large are the shipments we're talking about?"

"How about 100,000 pounds?"

"This isn't Florida; the coast is too long, and we don't have the right kind of cover. I think fifty thousand pounds would be a good compromise; it can be unloaded safely and quickly."

"Fine, why not? Fifty thousand pounds is good."

"Okay, it's settled," said August.

As Gonzalo sat down, he dusted off his ostrich-skin cowboy boots while saying, "You know August, that's what I like about you. You are not greedy, and you are practical."

They talked about using Gonzalo's DC-4s to drop off the bundles on the Pacific side of Colombia, where his freighters would pick up the loads and bring their illicit cargo up the coast. They set up a tentative schedule to off-load the ships, as well as the terms of payment.

Gonzalo stretched. "Enough business for now." He stood up. "Come, I want to show you something, and then we will have lunch."

They walked out the front door, accompanied by four bodyguards. A Range Rover was parked in the driveway, between two trucks with two men in the cab. Gonzalo and August got in the backseat of the Range Rover and two of the bodyguards jumped into the front. The driver started the engine and the caravan started to roll.

Gonzalo turned toward August. "I just finished building a beautiful rodeo and bullfighting stadium. I donated it to the city of Bogotá. I want to give you a first-class tour; you'll love it."

Twenty minutes later, the driver turned into the stadium parking lot. The size and architectural design impressed August. "It's a beautiful stadium."

"Wait till you see the inside. We have our own professional bullfighters, picadors, and a full stable of pedigree horses." The driver pulled into a VIP parking space at the entrance. Gonzalo jumped out of the Range Rover before the driver could turn off the ignition. "Let's go."

August caught up with him as they entered the stadium. Gonzalo gleamed with pride as he gave August a tour, ending up at the stables.

"I have various purebreds: Arabians, Peruvian Pasos, Spanish Andalusians, and many others trained for the bullfights, and other events." He waved to a couple of stableboys, who ran over to him. He spoke to them in Spanish: "Saddle up two Andalusians for me and my friend." The boys ran off. "We bring in the bulls and other horses for the rodeo events."

He showed August some of the different horses while the stableboys put on the saddles and walked the horses to them. Gonzalo grabbed the reins and mounted his stallion. August mounted his horse and followed Gonzalo into the center of the field. They rode around the ring together. Gonzalo, sitting erect, smiled with pride and waved at the empty stands, looking like royalty greeting his subjects.

They galloped around the ring a few times, and then rode the horses to the stables. There were two restaurants in the stadium and Gonzalo had the chef of the finer restaurant, prepare a late lunch for them, including more of his local-grown prime beef.

They went back to his home, took a siesta, then enjoyed cocktails and appetizers by the pool. Dinner was served at nine. After they enjoyed a Cuban cigar and a glass of Pisco Oro, they talked until twelve, and turned in for the night.

After breakfast, Gonzalo had his driver take them to his personal emerald dealer, accompanied by the two trucks and five bodyguards. He introduced August to the jeweler and told him to take care of his friend.

August and the jeweler bickered back and forth; finally August came to an agreement, paying $25,000 U.S. for six five-carat emeralds. The stones were the same cut and weights, had excellent clarity and color, and were worth substantially more on the open market. Gonzalo told August how to smuggle the emeralds back into the U.S.A.

On the way back to his home, they stopped at a drugstore. He sent one of the bodyguards to buy a bottle of Prell shampoo. When they got home, he opened the bottle and dropped the six emeralds into the liquid. To August's amazement, the emeralds disappeared completely.

"Put the shampoo with the rest of your toiletries and no one will ever know." Gonzalo laughed, as he held the bottle to the light.

August spent a couple of days with Gonzalo. They went out to one of his ranches, hunted for doves and ducks, fished for bass, and roamed the countryside on horseback.

They drove back to the house in the suburbs of Bogotá, had a little fiesta, danced, and partied into the night. When August woke up, he found the beautiful señorita that he was with that evening, lying naked next to him.

Smiling, he rolled over and sat up. Before he could stand, she grabbed his wrist and pulled him back down on the bed. Her big brown eyes told him what she wanted, and he was more than happy to oblige.

August's flight left Bogotá at eleven so they had a late breakfast, then Gonzalo had some of his bodyguards prepare to take August to the airport. They hugged and said their goodbyes, then August climbed into the backseat of the second car, which followed another sedan down the road.

He got out of the car in front of the Pan Am departure entrance, went to the counter, and handed the clerk his open first-class ticket. He secured a seat and headed for the departure gate.

The Pan Am ticket agent got on the intercom. "Flight 792 non-stop to Los Angeles will now begin boarding first-class passengers."

August got up, walked up to the agent, handed her his ticket, boarded the DC-10 and took his seat.

Eight hours and twenty minutes later, his plane landed at LAX. He got his carry-on and disembarked, walked through the baggage claim area, directly to the U.S. Customs kiosk. He handed his passport to the agent at the counter, who typed in some data, looked at the monitor, reached under the counter and pushed a button. A moment later, another agent walked up and took his passport. "Mr. Taracina, I'm Agent Philips. Would you please come with me?"

As August followed Philips to a small room with a table in it, he thought, "What the fuck! Twice in one round trip? Oh man, the emeralds."

Philips searched August, and then went through his luggage. He dumped his toiletry bag on the table, exposing the bottle of Prell shampoo. August was glad that he used it while he was in Bogotá so it didn't look new and prayed Philips didn't take a closer look, or knew the little trick, or he'd be going to jail for smuggling precious stones into the U.S.

The agent stared directly into his eyes, trying to intimidate him. "So why did you go to Colombia?"

August wanted to tell him that it was none of his fucking business, but played along. "One of my friends invited me to his wedding and I stayed with some of his friends."

"But you stayed in a hotel for one night."

"Yeah, and my friend's buddies picked me up the next morning. Is there any problem?" Philips handed him his passport. "No. You're not carrying more than ten thousand dollars U.S. undeclared, are you, Mr. Taracina?"

"Of course not, Mr. Philips."

"Take everything out of your pockets and place it on the table."

August did what he asked.

Satisfied, Philips handed back the passport. "Welcome back to the United States, Mr. Taracina."

August was now certain that this agent knew more than he was letting on. *Maybe it wasn't such a good idea leaving the country via LAX.*

August repacked his bag, put everything back in his pockets, and left the airport. He had planned to call his nephew to pick him up, but after the harassment by customs, he decided to take a cab to the Marriott Hotel on Century Boulevard. He entered the lobby and walked to the counter.

"May I help you?" asked the clerk.

"Yes, I'd like a room for the night."

He paid cash, got his key, and headed for the bar. He ordered a beer and sat facing the lobby, to see if anyone had followed him. Satisfied, he stood to go to his room, and then a lone suit walked in with no luggage.

It didn't look right, so he sat back down and had another sip of beer. The guy took a seat in the lobby, facing the elevators.

August emptied the glass, got up, slipped through a side door, and left the hotel. He walked over to the Sheraton, a couple of blocks away, making sure he wasn't being followed, then checked in, went directly to his room, and called his nephew.

"Hey, Stevie."

"I was starting to get worried; your plane landed two hours ago."

"Sorry, but I couldn't get to a phone. I ran into a little problem, so I'm spending the night at the Sheraton. Pick me up at eight sharp, but not at the front entrance. I'll be waiting in the parking lot."

Stevie was right on time. August walked out of the shadows and jumped in. "Get the fuck out of here, and use the side streets."

Something had changed since he'd left for Bogotá. Something was very wrong, and until he knew exactly what was happening, he intended to use extreme caution visiting any place he frequented.

Instead of going back to San Pedro or his house, he told Stevie to take him to the apartment that Stevie had just rented in Seal Beach. He dropped off his bag at the apartment and made a few calls. One was to his boatyard, which was not far away.

Chuck answered the phone. "Marina boatyard."

"It's August, everything cool?"

"Yeah, just keeping busy, why?"

"Just concerned about the heat."

Chuck understood. "The weather's great. You can even see Catalina."

"Good. Talk to you later." Meaning Chuck hadn't seen any agents or police snooping around.

August knew his guys were careful, but he just wasn't satisfied and had Stevie drive him to his boatyard located across the street from the Golden Sails Hotel on Pacific Coast Highway.

As they drove past the shopping center next-door, he looked to his right and spotted two U.S. Customs cars in the parking lot. *Hmmm, now that's definitely not a coincidence.*

"Pull into the parking lot and stay there, while I walk around the shops to see what these customs guys are up to."

His trained eye found them in plain clothes, window-shopping at local establishments.

August walked into a store and watched the two guys through the front window. They walked up to two more plain-clothes agents and began to carry on a conversation.

August spotted one of his employees walking out of a restaurant carrying two bags of food and a six-pack of beer. He got into his Trans Am and drove off.

He watched the plain-clothes agents hustle to their vehicles, and follow the Trans Am out of the parking lot.

August ran back to his nephew's car and jumped in. "Get me to the Golden Sails Hotel; they're on to us. We've got heat."

Stevie drove as fast as he could to the back of the hotel. August jumped out, ran up the stairs to the second floor, and took a seat on the deck, overlooking his boatyard and the surrounding area. He watched the two vehicles pull up; one of the agents rolled down the window and began to photograph his boatyard across the street.

The guys were working on his Skipjacks. He knew, from that moment, that his rigs were dead in the water.

His nephew walked up to August. "What's happening?"

"Get me a piece of paper and a pen."

Stevie took off. A minute later, he handed August a notepad from the hotel and a pen. August wrote his message and gave it to his nephew. "Walk across the street into the boatyard, go into the marine store at the front and walk through the store, put the note on top of the oil drum by the rear door, signal Chuck to come over and get the note that you left on the oil drum. Then turn around, go back into the store, buy something, and leave."

Stevie followed August's instructions. Chuck picked up the note. It said, "You are being watched from across the street and they're photographing you through the parking lot fence of the Golden Sails. All you guys pack up at your normal closing time and leave. But, do not go home. Drive in four different directions. Call me in a few days. I will arrange to send you money and we'll get back together as soon as it cools off. PS: Eat this note."

After that incident, he knew that his existing offshore "catch" operation was over, and he would have to rebuild in a few months. *Motherfuckers! I just cut the best deal I ever had with Gonzalo and now—how am I going to tell him we're fucked?*

Later, he found out how customs learned about his boatyard. There was another yard where he had some very sophisticated trim tabs installed, to give a more stable ride at high speeds. The agents were asking if anyone was spending a lot of money on fast offshore speedboats. They told them about the boats and the boatyard where they were stored. August wasn't sure if the agents knew who owned them, but it became very evident that they wanted to know. He decided to back off the catch deal.

He needed to inform Gonzalo that they had to cool it for three or four months, and that he would have to acquire some new equipment. The acquisition of new boats and equipment was going to be costly.

14

For years, the DEA agents were frustrated because August always seemed to be one step ahead of them. They determined that the only way August's organization could maintain that advantage was by monitoring their conversations, or having an inside man. Eventually they changed their method of communication by using landlines.

It didn't take long for August's men to hear an agent on the radio say, "Go to a landline." Eventually the feds installed decoders at their repeater stations that scrambled their conversations; August lost his edge.

August was sitting in the captain's chair on the bridge of his sport fisher, smoking a cigar and sipping on his second scotch on the rocks, while waiting for Mickey to go to dinner.

He had always been conservative and extremely careful, taking very few risks, if any at all. He had lost his edge with the feds; the heat had come up to his pad, sniffing as if they owned the place, forcing him to move. DEA agents were following him. They knew he was in that hotel. Fortunately, he stumbled upon those customs officials casing his boatyard operation, forcing him to shut it down.

The risks were finally tipping the scale in the law's favor. He took a pull on his fragrant cigar and blew out a plume of smoke, then savored a drink of that precious liquid. *Time to slow things down—maybe shut it down—at least the catch operation. I could still broker shit, and maybe—maybe I should expand my bennies manufacturing operation and increase the distribution. Demand's still okay, Mexican manufacturing has dried up, the demand in the U.S. is okay, and Ken and Slim said there's a good market in Canada. Hmmmm.*

August reminisced. In the late sixties and seventies, he was big in smuggling whites. The Mexicans were buying the "real" whites, made of Benzedrine, in huge quantities from legitimate pharmaceutical companies in the United States, then selling them back to smugglers with a stateside market.

In the early seventies, the Mexican market started to dry up and they began to sell bullshit whites. The so-called bennies made of concentrated caffeine really didn't work, unless you took twenty of them. August and others stopped selling them.

In 1980, he started to deal in whites again, through Ken and Slim out of Florida. Ken and Slim were affiliated with an entertainment industry attorney, Joe Vick, who had a long history and connections with outlaw biker groups who controlled the distribution of speed.

He had a meeting with Ken and Slim about a load of marijuana coming up the coast. Slim asked August if he could take a thousand pounds from the load, deliver it to Joe Vick, and collect the money for them.

August called Vick and made the arrangements. When August met with Joe, they talked about the potential of manufacturing and distributing whites.

Joe said, "Whites are the work force of America. Everybody is using them. If you could manufacture them yourself, good quality at a decent price, you could make a fortune."

August knew a couple of guys with a lot of experience manufacturing whites; he made a pact to finance and sell their production. He co-partnered with the Butler brothers who were the cookers, and planned to build a plant at a different location every year. They set up a deal with a guy that owned a large piece of property, more than one hundred acres, in a remote area.

There was one little caveat; the brothers said they could make the whites, but needed the chemicals; their sources had dried up. They needed a chemical called phenol acetic acid, which is converted to phenol 2 propanol; it was August's responsibility to locate a reliable source.

He found a source, a chemical company in the Midwest, and started to buy in quantities, having it shipped by rail to California, and stored in a warehouse. From 1980 to early '83, they manufactured tons of whites, netting over $1.5 million dollars a year, divided among the three of them.

The property had to have three prerequisites: a level area centered on the acreage, where they could erect the building that would house the lab, so no one would spot their operation. The land needed to have an old pond that was not being used and naturally fed from melted snow with no underground springs or seepage into a shallow water table, and no streams coming out of the pond that could contaminate other streams and lakes.

After finding an appropriate spot on the property, they would construct their manufacturing plant: a two thousand square foot building of two-by-fours and plywood, with a raised floor, and a clean room known as a "scrubber room."

In the clean room, they would install twenty 2200 flasks that had double cooling stacks. The twenty 2200s were capable of producing hundreds of pounds of Benzedrine a day.

. The center, larger tube had a stirring mechanism in it; that's where they poured in the chemicals, producing a phosphate compound, to be consumed orally.

They made the best-known conventional cross-top whites, the drug of U.S. truck and bus drivers, waitresses, business people, doctors, lawyers, and bartenders; everybody used them. They called them "Mother's little helpers," but the group called them "pocket rockets."

August would use basic material, phenalacitic acid, and convert it to phenol 2 propanol, which was the precursor to making Benzedrine.

The crews wore white suits and gas masks and kept everything self-contained, in order to prevent hazardous material from polluting the environment and leaving their geographic signature.

Although it increased the cost of production, August didn't want to kill plants, fish, or adversely affect the environment, in any way, and mixed all toxic chemicals with compounds that would neutralize them before discarding the wastes.

The brothers would cook the chemicals to produce a final product of white powdered cake. Then the white powder compound would be hauled to another building in Southern California. The cake was dumped into a huge rotary press converting the powder into pills. The process produced fifty thousand pills an hour, filling plastic, fifty-five gallon drums. They would be weighed to determine exactly how many pills were in each drum.

All of the drums had false tops filled with paraffin wax; if anyone opened a drum top during shipment, they would see hardened wax, agreeing with the shipping documents that listed the contents of the drums as "casting material."

They would load the drums on trucks and drive them across the country. His distributors would break the load down to kegs of whites to sell on the open market, through street dealers.

Each year, when the production was over, they destroyed the building and disposed of all the material at the closest public dumpsite. He'd pay the landowner one hundred grand for the use of the property and move on.

The yearly process of locating the property, constructing the building and processing the white cake for pressing took around four months. The yearly operation was invisible to the law.

Then August would methodically procure the chemicals for the following year's production. It took several months to buy all the materials and store them long enough to be certain there was no heat (law enforcement interest) on the cache of contraband chemicals.

It was a very professional and thorough operation, run conservatively. Everyone walked away with a substantial profit from the couple of tons of whites produced yearly, reaping $1,800,000 after expenses. The landowner was paid one hundred grand and the Butler brothers and August split the balance three ways, netting them over half a mil each.

These guys were experienced, going back to the late sixties, so they knew and trusted each other. They manufactured whites for only a couple years as the demand for speed grew. August didn't really want to remain in that business, which was evolving into the production of backyard methamphetamine. The scourge of drugs right along with crack and heroin, the users, abusers, and dealers were something he wanted to distance himself from. They closed down the Pocket Rocket Pharmaceutical Company.

August consulted other associates about reviving the catch operation. It appeared that the Coast Guard's 12th fleet surveillance arm had remained on high alert with daily overflights and patrols of their southern sector from Colombia north, causing crews to scuttle their ships loaded with marijuana; a few freighters were captured and their loads confiscated.

At this juncture, August and his associates started looking at Thailand and the Pacific Rim as a new source.

15

Scott and the guys never consulted August about their own evolving scheme that might go down in history as "The Great Plane Robbery," if it could be pulled off. But at the last moment, considering its magnitude, they panicked and decided that they needed him and should give him a call.

On February 3, 1984, August's pager went off. August picked up the phone and dialed the number.

"Hey, August."

"Who's this?"

"Scott McCarran."

"Hey, Scott, how's it hanging?"

"Perpin—dick—ular." They laughed. "You think we could meet someplace today?"

"Sure, I'll be in Redondo later this afternoon. How about 6:30 at Millie's Seafood Grotto?"

"That's great, see you then."

August was ten minutes late and found Scott sitting at the bar of the historic landmark restaurant overlooking "The Cliffs," which begin at Torrance Beach, extending to Palos Verdes Estates. The sun was setting, folding its rays into a thick fog bank rolling in off the horizon. They shook hands, found a window table, and ordered a drink.

"So, how are you and the guys doing? Everything cool at work?"

"Yeah, but I really don't know how to go about this, so I'm going to lay it on the line. We've come up with a way to rob the airline."

"Really, that sounds great."

"We weren't sure if we needed your involvement. Now that we're ready to pull this off, all of us decided that bringing you in was the right thing to do. We need your help; you're savvy and we trust you implicitly."

"So when do you plan to pull this off?" asked August.

"We need two things to happen. The manifest I received today shows a big shipment coming in tomorrow. We also need it to be foggy, and the weather report says to expect heavy fog tonight through the morning."

A bit annoyed at their gall, August asked, "So, you decide to fucking tell me *on the very night* before you plan to do all this? Hell, I could've been out of the country, or something. It sounds like you weren't planning to include me in this anyway. So why do you think you guys need me now?"

"I'm sorry, August, it's just—as this became a reality, we realized this heist is really out of our league, and we really need your help. Okay, we need your experience and insight."

"Why would you need my help? If you get a bunch of cash or gold, you could just divvy it up and be done with it." Clearly, August was irritated at his one-time partners.

"We don't know anyone capable of holding a large amount of cash or gold. We trust you and know you have the means. We should be able to pull the heist off, but we would rather give you a share and have your experience on our side."

Shit, there could be millions in cash in those bags or millions in gold. Sounds like a win-win for me. "Okay, I accept," August conceded. "What's your plan?"

"During a foggy period, the planes will stack up while waiting for a parking gate to clear up. We can make sure there is a good lengthy delay, just by slowing down the unloading of the baggage a little bit all along the line.

"Anyway, the plane and crew have to sit on the tarmac while they're waiting. The pilot does one of two things. If the pilot knows he's going to be delayed for a short time, he'll leave everything running, but if the delay is ten minutes or more, he'll power down the main engines, leaving the APU . . ." August gave him an inquisitive look. Scott continued, "Auxiliary power unit running. This is needed to restart the engines that he shut down for a time, in order to continue taxiing to the gate. The APU also maintains the electric power supplying all the instruments and lights, including the cargo warning lights.

"There are two freight compartments on a 737, one forward and one aft. The cargo doors are on the right side of the plane, and the bonded cargo is stored in the aft compartment.

"The plane will be taxiing in an easterly direction when it stops and shuts down, leaving the right side facing the runway obscuring the cargo doors from the terminal and the personnel.

"When Flight 1757 rolls to a stop and shuts down, two of us will drive out in a jitney (a small unlicensed airport utility vehicle used commercially for towing trailers or taxiing people), and stop just in front of the aft cargo door. This is when it gets a little tricky.

"One of us will pull out the spring-loaded handle on the cargo door from its flush position, turn it counter clockwise, and push in the cargo door, while I reach in and hold down the micro-switch as we push the door in and up.

"Then we'll back up the bag cart under the tail section, hugging the right side of the fuselage, until it's under the cargo door, unload the Brinks cargo, reverse the process and leave driving under the tail section undetected. We open these fuckin' doors every day.

"As we drive away from the plane, we'll become more visible and vulnerable. We thought of hiding the stuff somewhere at the airport, to retrieve it later, but the risk of getting caught goes way up. So we decided that, while it's foggy, one of us will drive the bag tug to the outer fence, on the Imperial Highway side of the airport, where we've previously cut a hole in the fence, pass it through to one of us, who has conveniently called in sick and took the day off. We'll load up the van and the driver will get the hell out of the LAX area entirely, and the rest of us will get back to work.

"No one will miss just one of us, and by the time anyone discovers the stuff missing, the van will be long gone, and on its way to you. What do you think?"

August pondered their plan. "I think this could possibly work. *Don't really want them to know where I live.* I do see one very vulnerable spot. There are four of you, one would have to drive the van, and at least three of you should be seen at the baggage handling area while this is going down. I think you should have Ernie drive the van. The three of you stay at the baggage area and one drives out to Imperial Highway to unload and pass the goods through the fence, then hustle back.

"Also, if we succeed, you can bet there will be a thorough investigation, and the last thing you need is for them to question why one of you guys took off sick on that specific day. That's the last thing you need. And, bet your balls, it's one of the absolute first things that will happen."

"That's why we wanted you involved. I never thought of that. But we did think of having Ernie drive the van, and have three of us stay behind. But, well, we're not altogether sure that we trust Ernie."

"You shouldn't!" August declared emphatically. "I don't."

"I thought you did. He did all the pickup and delivery of the pot we smuggled in," countered Scott.

"Ernie introduced you guys to me. Remember when I said I would take care of him? There was a reason for that. Ernie is a go-between, mid-level dealer, a scammer type of guy, bit of an ego-maniac who thinks more of himself than others do. He also thinks he's smarter than everybody else and is always looking for that angle. He will indeed, piss me off on occasion, and he has. I don't think he would ever fuck me, but you never know. I'd never tell him where the money or bodies are buried. Really, I don't trust him all that much, but he can be useful. I'm going to have someone follow him from the airport to the drop-off point, in any case.

"You know you guys are the ones taking the biggest risk, and if I were you, I would want to know what's in those bags or boxes, before they leave your possession. My recommendation is, that whoever drives the bag tug to the west side of the airport, open and inspect the contents before you deliver the take to Ernie, and before I take it all."

"I have no reason not to trust you, August, but you do have a point."

"I presume you haven't contacted Ernie yet?"

"No, I wanted to talk to you first."

"Good, let me take care of him. That way I can keep the reins on him. If this goes down, when do you want Ernie there, and has the fence been cut yet?"

"Flight 1757 is scheduled to arrive at 8:45 A.M.; we cut a hole in the fence in the dark on the way to work this morning. I'll need to show Ernie the location tonight."

"Fine, I'll have him call you."

They left the restaurant together; the fog had already started to roll in. "Here comes the fog. Things are looking up," said August, as they walked to their cars. Thinking on his feet, *Ernie doesn't know that I moved. Maybe I should have him deliver the goods elsewhere, closer to the airport.* "Hey, Scott." August walked over to his car. "I'm going to have Ernie deliver the stuff to one of my warehouses right over in El Segundo. We can meet up there after you guys get off work. We'll see what we have and decide what to do with it."

"You're the boss; sounds like a great idea to me."

Now I'm the fucking boss? That could be really good, or it could be really fucked. But it does at least put me in control. August opened his glove box, grabbed a pen and a piece of paper, and wrote down the address of the warehouse and handed it to Scott. "Memorize the address then burn the paper."

They shook hands. "Thanks, man."

"I'll see you tomorrow night; hopefully, we'll all be a lot richer."

* * *

Scott drove to the beach house. The guys were anxious to hear about the meeting. "I'm *really* glad we decided to include August. He spotted flaws in our plan right away and had the solutions."

He went over the plan in detail. "Unless there are any objections, I think Randy should drive the tug, and inspect and take inventory of the goods that we hijack." They all agreed. "Ernie's going to deliver the stuff to one of August's warehouses in El Segundo. We're going to meet there after work."

The phone rang; Randy picked it up. "Yeah, he's right here." He handed Scott the phone. "It's Ernie."

"August told me what was going down, and asked me to give you a call. I've already switched my El Camino for one of August's vans. How about meeting in the Hacienda Hotel parking lot?"

"I can be there in ten minutes. What kind of van are you driving?"

"A white 1982 Ford 150 cargo van. I'll be waiting."

Ten minutes later Scott pulled alongside the van; Ernie was leaning against the hood. Scott rolled down his window. "Jump in; it might look conspicuous with two cars driving along the perimeter of the airport."

Scott pulled off Imperial Highway. "I'm not going to stop; I'll just point out where we cut the fence. Right there, see the weeds sticking through the fence?"

"Yeah, when do you want me here?"

He handed Ernie a walkie-talkie. "The plane's landing at 8:45 A.M. Park across the street; Randy will call you. If it's a go, he'll just say 'surf's up.' If something goes wrong, he'll say 'wipe out.'"

"Easy enough, I'll be there."

16

Scott dropped Ernie off and drove home. Earlier he'd called his wife to tell her he'd be late. She said she was making tacos for dinner and would leave a plate out for him. He opened the back door, went into the kitchen, put his dinner in the microwave, and got a beer out of the fridge.

He wolfed down the tacos, beans and rice, finished his second beer, and headed for the bedroom. First he visited his kids' room, silently wishing them good night, then tiptoed into his bedroom.

"How was dinner?" whispered his wife.

"Muy bueno. I'm going to take a shower."

"Okay, honey. Buenos noches," chuckled Karen, as she turned on her side.

Scott was exhausted and fell asleep as soon as his head hit the pillow. Unfortunately, he woke up at two, head spinning in turmoil, worried about how the next twenty-four hours were going to turn out.

He was out of bed at five and out the door at five-thirty. It was so foggy that he could barely see the lines on the road. The drive to work normally took ten minutes, but the traffic was terrible; he walked into the lunchroom at six, where he found his team nervously waiting. He got a cup of coffee and sat down.

"Where the fuck have you been? We thought something happened to you," said Randy.

"Sorry, it's really socked in; traffic sucked. It's a good thing we have plenty of fog."

"Yeah, but I hope the visibility gets a little better; one of the supervisors just told us that they might have to divert some of the planes if the fog gets any worse."

"Nothing we can do about that." Scott stood. "Let's get to work."

Planes were already stacking up and they worked their butts off. It was 8:30 when they finished unloading the bag carts and took a coffee break. They watched the departure and arrival screens; every flight was delayed.

* * *

August was out until three in the morning, on his sportfisher, with this total fox he'd met at a friend's party. He opened his eyes; there lay this gorgeous naked redhead. As if her sixth sense kicked in, she opened her beautiful emerald green eyes, leaned over and kissed him passionately. She slid her leg over his and straddled him. She moved slowly, rubbing her ample breasts across his chest, while she nibbled on his lips.

She slid her hand down to Augi Jr., and guided him into her. Then she pushed herself up and began to move at a slow rhythm, as she fondled herself. The rhythm began to speed up as she moaned in ecstasy.

August pulled her down and rolled her over, as he drove deeper and harder; both moved in concert, at first slowly, both thrusting themselves at each other driving the exhilaration to a bursting crescendo.

He rolled onto his back and she snuggled next to him. As their breathing slowed, he heard the Angels Gate Lighthouse foghorn bellow and thought, *What a great way to start the day. First, I get a beautiful redhead to fuck my brains out, and then the foghorn confirms that our job is a go.*

He looked at his watch. It was seven forty-five. *Better get a move on. Have to pick up Mickey and get to El Segundo.*

He ran his fingers through her long red hair. "I really hate to say this, but I have to go to work. I had a wonderful time; can I see you again?"

"Maybe, as long as you don't mind being with a married woman."

"Not a good idea to get involved, is it?" She had followed him to the marina in her own car. "Look, I have to go. You can stay here as long as you like. Just be careful getting off the boat."

She gave him a kiss. "I'll leave my number, in case you change your mind."

He got out of bed, admiring this gorgeous married woman; he could see the whole package. He smiled, "I might just do that."

* * *

"Los Angeles Tower, this is Western Airlines, Flight 1757, requesting landing instructions."

"Flight 1757, this is Los Angeles Tower, landing is delayed due to poor visibility. Air traffic is heavy and increasing. Maintain your altitude. Change your heading to 030 degrees."

"This is Western Airlines, Flight 1757, maintaining altitude at 12,000 feet, heading 030."

Flight 1757 was instructed to maintain altitude and given course changes, while circling the area for another twenty minutes. The guys watched the screen; another flight was diverted to Ontario Airport. They were getting more depressed by the minute, due to this threat of diversion.

"Western Airlines, Flight 1757, this is Los Angeles Tower, fog has cleared to weather minimums. You have clearance to land. Change heading to 160, altitude 5,000 feet."

Scott hit Randy and pointed to the screen showing Flight 1757 due to arrive at 9:15.

The captain set her down. "Flight 1757, proceed to taxiway Bravo 8, taxi east to terminal, traffic extremely heavy."

The captain taxied the 737 to Western's terminal and pulled behind a line of planes waiting for their gate to free up.

Scott looked at his watch. "Let's do it!" he said, his mouth suddenly dry.

As they walked to their vehicles, they put on gloves. Randy

climbed onto the tug, and Scott, Jeff, and Terry sat in the jitney. Scott began to drive out into the fog; all of a sudden, he heard a siren and saw red flashing lights, eerily amplified by the fog, coming straight at them. He slammed on the brakes as an airport police car came into view, then passed them by and turned, going around the building.

"Fuck me! I almost shit in my pants," Jeff gasped, then chuckled. "I thought, for sure, we were busted."

"Jesus! Calm down, we haven't done anything yet," said Scott, as he put the jitney in gear and drove slowly through the fog. When they reached the first plane, they couldn't even see the numbers on the fuselage. He pulled up as close as he could; Jeff had to stand up to read the numbers. "Not the right one."

They drove farther away from the terminal, and found Flight 1757 with the running lights off.

Scott drove under the tail section of the 737, stopping just past the rear cargo door. He looked at Terry and Jeff. "You guys ready?" They nodded in unison.

They got into position; Terry pulled out the spring-loaded handle and turned it counter clockwise, Jeff helped Terry push it open, while Scott slid his hand between the doorjamb and held down the microswitch. Terry and Jeff froze, waiting for something to go wrong.

Scott could see the fear in their eyes. Teeth clenched, he whispered, "Come on, get your asses in gear!"

The guys shook it off and climbed onboard, going directly to the bonded shipment cage. The cage was full of cargo; Terry and Jeff started to unstack the boxes and bags, looking for the shipment. There wasn't much space to move the stuff out of the way; both of them were almost boxed into the cage, when Jeff spotted six large heavy-duty plastic bags consigned to Brinks.

They pulled the six bags to one side and began to carefully repack the bonded cargo into the cage. While Terry kept loading, Jeff started to drag the Brinks bags to the cargo door.

As soon as Scott saw Jeff with the first bag, he called Randy. A minute later, Randy backed the bag cart under the tail and in front of the cargo door.

By then, Terry and Jeff had all six bags by the door. Terry jumped down to the cart's bed, and Jeff began to hand the bags down to him. Now, stacked and secured, Terry signaled Randy to take off.

Randy put the bag tug in gear, started to move out under the tail section and disappeared into the fog. Jeff jumped out of the cargo hold, pulled the cargo release cable and helped Terry close the cargo door, while Scott—who held the critical button down—yanked his hand out; just before the inside edge of the door would crush it.

He watched Terry pull out the handle, turn it and secure it flush to the cargo door. They jumped onto the jitney; Scott slowly drove back to the baggage processing area.

Randy passed numerous planes stacked up at each terminal and carefully threaded his way through them, then began to cross the runways to the Imperial Side. His stomach wrenched every time he hit a bump or a crack in the tarmac, heart pounding, sweat running down his face, knowing the airport police might be on him at any second.

He was two-thirds of the way across the airport, when a giant 747 appeared out of the fog, blocking the taxiway. Randy had to stop, and while he waited, a passenger bus pulled up alongside him headed for the international gates at the Imperial Highway terminal. Fortunately, the driver's seat was on the other side of the bus and the driver wasn't paying any attention to him, but it definitely freaked him out.

Finally, the 747 began to move. Randy began to breathe, heading for the fence. He pulled out his walkie-talkie and pushed the transmit button, saying the magic words, "Surf's up."

He pulled up to the fence; there wasn't a van in sight. Randy didn't know what the fuck to do. He pulled out his walkie-talkie and was about to push the button when the white van pulled up."What the fuck took you so long?"

"Sorry, dude, traffic sucks in this fog."

Randy unhooked the baling wire holding the fence together and bent it open. Ernie handed him a box cutter, and Randy cut the security-sealed strap on the bag so he could inspect the contents. "What did we get?"

"Well, I don't see any cash. It's full of stock certificates and bonds. Fuck! Shit! Shit!"

"Come on, Randy, we can't sit here too long," said Ernie. "Pass me the bags so I can get them to August."

Ernie opened the rear doors and Randy passed the bags through the fence. Ernie pulled the last bag through the fence, threw it in the back of the van and shut the doors. Randy, still wearing gloves to prevent prints, was weaving the baling wire through the fence as Ernie opened the driver's door. "See you guys later." He started the van and took off, while Randy piled some weeds over the cut fence. He stood back to look at his work. Satisfied, he jumped into the bag tug and drove away.

Confused and disappointed with the contents of the bag, Randy sulked as he drove back to Western's terminal, eventually pulling into the baggage handling area. His friends were nowhere to be seen. *This sucks, the way our luck is going we'll probably get busted.*

Scott pulled up in a jitney. "Where the fuck have you been?"

Happy to see that Scott hadn't been arrested, he said, "It was slow going in the fog, and I had to wait for a 747 to move off the runway."

"Jump on; we have to go to work." Randy got on and Scott drove off into the fog. "You're not going to believe this. When we got back to the baggage handling area, it was close to our lunch break, so we decided to wait for you. My supervisor walked up to us; he said he needed us to unload another plane . . . Flight 1757—can you fuckin' believe that? We waited for you as long as we could; I left Terry and Jeff at the gate, and drove back, hoping to find you."

Scott could see that Randy was bummed out. "What's wrong?"

"This whole thing is really fucked-up," mumbled Randy.

"What are you talking about? We pulled it off. Did something go wrong on your side?"

"Everything went just fine, until I inspected the contents of one of the bags. They're full of stock certificates, bonds, documents. I dug deeper into the bag, found the same shit. Not a fuckin' dollar bill."

"It's got to be worth something." They pulled up to the plane where Terry and Jeff were moving the bag belt conveyor to the closed cargo door. Scott turned to Randy. "Let's talk about this later."

The waiting Brinks truck driver pulled up to the conveyor belt and parked. The guard came out of the passenger side and walked up to Scott. "Thought we were going to have to drive to Ontario to pick up this shipment. I love that overtime, but I've got tickets to the Lakers game tonight."

"Well, I doubt I'll get to watch it; we'll be unloading baggage till eight tonight."They stood there watching Terry as he pushed the cargo release button and the concealed compartment opened. He turned the door handle and Randy opened the cargo door.

They positioned the conveyor and climbed onboard. The Brinks man handed Scott the bill of lading. He gave it to Terry, who went through the motions to retrieve the cargo from the bonded area.

The guys pulled out some of the bonded cargo for effect; Randy appeared at the cargo door, signaling to Scott with his hands that he couldn't find it.

"What's the problem?" asked Scott.

"We can't find the Brinks shipment," said Randy.

The other guard got out of the truck and walked over to his partner. They exchanged a few words, and then he motioned for Scott to come over. "What seems to be the problem?" asked the Brinks driver.

"We can't find the shipment. Maybe it's mixed up with the luggage?"

"We'll wait."

Of course you will. Scott climbed onboard to talk to his team. "I told them their stuff could be mixed in with the rest of the luggage. Just hang in there and do your job." He turned and climbed down and walked over to the guards. "I told my men to keep a watchful eye. Could you move your truck, so we can start unloading the other baggage?"

The driver moved the armored truck and reported the missing cargo to his supervisor.

One of the guards stood by the conveyor, inspecting the luggage as it came down the line and was loaded onto the bag cart. Ten minutes passed; they were almost finished unloading the plane when the airport police pulled up. The officers got out and talked to the guards, then signaled for Scott to come over.

"How much luggage is left?" asked one of the officers.

"I haven't looked, but there might be a cartful left. Excuse me, but we have to keep unloading." Scott decided he'd better call his supervisor, and got on the handheld radio.

"Harper."

"Mr. Harper, it's Scott. The Brinks guys are here to pick up a shipment, and we can't find it. They called the airport police; they just arrived."

"I'll be right there. Don't let them mess around with our cargo."

Harper hung up and Randy walked over to the Brinks guard. "I spoke to my supervisor. He's on his way."

Scott turned and joined Randy stacking the luggage. He looked at Randy, who rolled his eyes.

Another police car drove up, then Wayne Harper and another one of Western's supervisors pulled up in a golf cart and joined their conversation.

They all watched as the last of the luggage left the cargo hold of Flight 1757.

Before they shut the cargo door one of the supervisors climbed onboard and inspected the interior. He climbed out. "It's empty." He turned to Terry. "Close the door."

The supervisor walked over to Scott. "Take the luggage to the handling area but don't unload it. We're going to inspect it first."

"They did as they were told and stood by. After the Brinks guards, the police, and the supervisors did a walk-by, they watched as Scott and his crew unloaded the carts, sending the baggage down the conveyor to the waiting passengers.

Scott's supervisor walked up to him. "I wonder where those

bags are? They're sure making a big fuss over this. Why don't you guys take your lunch break?"

"Thanks. Are we going to have to work overtime?"

"I'm not sure. We're an hour behind. We'll probably catch up. Talk to you later."

His boss walked away. To himself Scott thought, "God, I hope not, I'm so fucking tired, I can barely stand up. My fuckin' nerves are shot and I want to get the hell out of here and go see what the fuck is in those bags."

* * *

While all the commotion was going on at Western's terminal, Ernie drove to August's warehouse. The roll-up door opened and he drove in. Mickey G shut the door behind him, and joined August and Ernie who started to unload the bags. "How did it go?" asked August.

"Smooth, except Randy was really pissed off when he looked inside one of the bags. He said it was full of stock certificates and bonds. I told him we needed to get moving. I loaded the bags in the van and left while Randy was working on the fence, cursing to himself. The last thing I heard was 'not even a fucking dollar bill.'"

"Well, let's take a look," said August.

Ernie grabbed a box knife and cut the straps off the other bags, then opened one to look inside.

"Hey, Ernie, your job's finished. I'll do the inspecting."

"Yeah cool, I'll go back to the office, kickback and watch TV."

"Great. Well, Mickey, let's see what the fuck these guys stole."

August opened a bag and peered in, then grabbed a stack of documents. "I'll be damned; they're all stocks and bonds. Can you fuckin' believe this? These guys pull off the heist of the century and steal six bags of worthless shit. Jeeez, if these bags were full of cash it could be worth millions."

Mickey was examining one of the documents. "Hey, look at this. You've heard of clipping coupons, haven't you?"

"Yeah, so what?"

"This bond has some of the coupons missing. Maybe there's some real value to some of this stuff."

August looked at the bond. It was issued by New York City Water District for twenty thousand dollars, at 8% interest. Each coupon was stamped with a redeemable value of $133.33. "Well, maybe there is something here. Let's look in the other bags."

After inspecting every bag, August knew that the guys wouldn't be able to do anything with the stocks or the bonds, and wondered how he could possibly make something out of this mess. It was going to take some time to find someone to buy the shit, and August would need to have possession of the goods while he tried to peddle them.

He didn't want the guys to know where he was living because people were looking for him, including the authorities, so he began to devise a plan.

At the end of their shift, the guys drove to August's warehouse. Ernie let them into the office. "August's in the warehouse."

Scott scanned the room. The El Camino and the van were there, August and Mickey were standing by the bags having a smoke. "August, how's it going?"

"Not so good. The bags are full of stock certificates and municipal bonds. I know the stock certificates are worth nothing to us, and I'm not sure we can do anything with the bonds."

"You mean we just pulled off a perfect heist, risking our jobs and the possibility of spending twenty years in prison, for nothing?"

August saw the disappointment in all their faces. "I'm not ready to give up. We still might be able to do something with this. First, I'm going to get rid of the stocks and municipal bonds and keep these." He held up a New York City bond. "I'll keep the bearer bonds and see if I can fence them. It's a long shot, but it's better than nothing. It's not going to be a slam-dunk; in fact, I'm not sure where to start. So this is what I'm going to do. With your permission, I'm going to take possession of the bags and go through every certificate and bond.

"I know the stock certificates are worthless to us and eventually need to be destroyed. As for the bonds, I'll take inventory of them, list what we have, then call some of my contacts and see if anyone is interested. Okay with you guys?"

"I don't think that's cool at all. What do I get?" said Ernie.

"I don't really give a fuck what you think. No one has made a dime on this deal. You've got nothing to lose, and have no risk, so you're on the waiting list, just like the rest of us. Take it or leave it."

He looked at everyone. "Or maybe you guys would like Ernie to take care of this for you?"

"Hell no, we'll wait it out," said Scott.

17

After Ernie and the guys left the warehouse, August and Mickey loaded the bags back into the van. Mickey drove the van back to his house while August followed in his Porsche.

August was now living in the rear house; they carried the bags into his living room.

"You going to go through these now?" asked Mickey.

August looked at his watch. "I'm hungry; how about I take you to dinner? I'll work on this crap when we get back."

They had dinner at Admiral Risty's, a popular restaurant and bar located in Palos Verdes, overlooking the Pacific with a view of Catalina Island. Risty's is known for their marinated flank steak and prepared-at-your-table salads. Both of them frequented the restaurant, and the bartender, Danny Heller, had their drinks ready before they sat down. They were on their second drink when the manager, Wayne Judah, walked up. "August, your table's ready."

"Put the drinks on the tab?" asked Danny.

"I'll take care of it." August pulled out a fifty and set it on the bar. "Good seeing you, keep the change." They carried their drinks to the table, ordered appetizers, had a bottle of wine with dinner, and drove home.

Mickey asked, "You want me to help?"

"Nah, I'll take care of it."

It was a cold, damp night. As August unlocked the door, he got chilled. He threw some logs into the fireplace and lit it, then poured himself a little Blue Label on the rocks.

He moved the coffee table to one side, got a straight-back chair out of the kitchen, and set it in front of the roaring fire. Then he dragged one of the two-and-a-half-feet wide by four-feet high bags, weighing around fifty pounds, in front of the chair and sat down.

So let's see what these guys stole. He opened the first bag and started stacking the contents on the coffee table. *What the fuck am I going to do with these stock certificates?*

He picked up the first one: *150 shares of General Motors, I wonder how much this is worth?*

He reached behind him and grabbed the *Los Angeles Times*, finding the business section. *Let's see, General Motors is going for $81 dollars a share. That's around $12,000.* He started to check more of the stock certificate values, picking the companies he knew. *Three hundred shares of Exxon Mobil at $97, fuck, that's 29 grand. Westinghouse, five hundred shares at $47, that's $23,000.*

He went through fifty certificates, picked five more to check their value, and came up with a total of $100,200. He held them in his hands and looked at the six bags. *Fuck me, there has to be hundreds of millions of dollars in stock, and it's not worth a fuckin' dime to me or the guys.*

He looked at the roaring fire—then at the stock certificates. *Fuck it.* He was about to throw a certificate of five hundred shares of IBM worth $40,000 into the fire, stopped and looked at it, shook his head in bewilderment, and set it down on the table.

August poured himself another glass of scotch and started sorting out the second bag. He was about halfway through the bag; he was becoming so disgusted he felt like throwing the whole bag in the fire. But restraining himself, he grabbed another handful of certificates, and kept going through them, adding to the stacks on the table.

He continued to go through the individual certificates, but at a faster pace, knowing all of them would have to be destroyed eventually. He was halfway through the third bag, with another worthless document in his hand. He looked at the fire. *Fuck it!* He almost let it fly out of his hand, when he noticed it looked different from the rest of the certificates. He brought it closer to him—turning it, to get more light from the fire.

His eyes didn't fool him; it was a brand new one-million-dollar U.S. bearer bond with an expiration date of 2002, and right in the center, printed in big letters: "redeemable by the bearer." *Well—now this might have some potential. It does say redeemable to bearer.*

Now he began to look at the documents more carefully, hoping to find more of the same. His stomach was tied up in knots as he began to throw the stock certificates into the fire, along with the municipal bonds, while saving the few bearer bonds of various types and values. He didn't find another million-dollar bond in the third bag. It was almost too much to bear, throwing hundreds of millions of dollars worth of certificates into the fireplace stoking up the flames that created dancing shadows surrounding the walls and ceiling, witnessing August's despair.

He had three more bags to go through, and had to take a piss. He got up and headed for the bathroom, relieved himself, splashed his face with water and went into the kitchen, where he got some biscotti and a glass of milk and went back to work.

August opened the fourth bag, grabbed a stack of certificates and began to sort them out, finding nothing valuable, and tossed them into the fire.

He started going through the second stack; the whole living room flickered brightly from the roaring fire. About halfway through, he stopped, his eyes widened as he looked at another million-dollar bearer bond folded with paperwork attached to it. As he unfolded it and lifted the bond up to inspect it, his smile grew bigger as he noticed that the next certificate and the next were the same. The second stack proved to be much better; he found fourteen more million-dollar bearer bonds folded, with paperwork attached to each of them listing the broker, serial number, and the owner of the bond. August sat back after he emptied the contents of the fourth bag. He grinned, while looking at the growing stack, now at forty-one, one-million-dollar bonds. The flickering shadows grew brighter and more frantic—dancing with excitement.

It was five-thirty in the morning when he finished sorting the last bag, the fire roaring as he fueled it with another stack of certificates. He lay back on the couch with his hands behind his head and smiled looking at the coffee table where he had piled up 350 one-million-dollar United States bearer bonds.

He had separated everything, throwing the stocks and municipal bonds in the fire, getting rid of the worthless evidence. He estimated that he had burned up well over 300 million dollars worth of municipal bonds and stock certificates.

Now he began to examine the stack of bonds in front of him. All of them had sixty printed coupons on the bottom part of the certificate. Some bonds stated, payable at 6.9% per year, and most of them at 8.9%, redeemable for $69,000.00 and others $89,000.00 per year, obviously the higher the rate of interest, the higher the amount.

August made a rough calculation of the actual value starting with the purchase price of $350 million in United States Federal Bearer Bonds paid at a rate of 8.9% annually. He came up with an impressive $624 million in interest, added in the purchase price of $350 million, for a total worth $974 million, plus over $300 million for the stocks and municipal bonds, a grand total of $1.275 billion dollars. *This has to be the biggest heist ever!*

He sat there looking at the stack of bonds. *Now, what the fuck am I going to do with these?*

* * *

Papa Taracina, August's grandfather, lived on 17th Street in San Pedro, in a Victorian house that sat on the hill, overlooking Los Angeles Harbor. He was a fisherman on the Island of Ischia, Italy who immigrated with his wife to the U.S., settled in San Pedro, where he joined his friends and relatives that fished commercially off the coast of California.

When August was a kid, he spent a lot of time at his grandfather's home, along with his brothers, sister, and cousins, playing in the backyard.

Papa made his own wine that the locals called Dago Red, and the kids loved to help make it. He had a huge wine cellar, where he stored his wine in four sixty-gallon wood barrels. Nana also used the cellar to store her canned fruits and vegetables.

When not in use, August hid his plastic army men and other toys under the house, gaining access through a small door in the wine cellar.

As the years went by, August began to use this hiding place for drugs and cash. Who would ever question his frequent visits to his grandmother's after Papa passed away? Nana never questioned his visits to the wine cellar.

August rarely used his secret hiding place anymore and thought it was the perfect spot to hide the bonds. He went into his bedroom and pulled out two large stainless steel Halliburton cases that he used to move currency and contraband. He picked up three bonds that he planned to use as samples and put them in a hidden compartment under the living room carpet. He pulled out a couple of loose floorboards and stashed the three bonds there. August packed the rest in the cases and headed to Nana's house.

He buried the cases and stacked some old five-gallon "Sparkletts" water jugs, that Papa used in his wine making days, over the spot, and went upstairs to visit his grandmother.

18

The following morning, FBI,
Los Angeles Field Office

Special Agent Nick Cutler poured himself a cup of coffee, grabbed a bagel, and headed back to his desk. His phone rang as he sat down. He picked up the receiver. "Cutler."

"I need you to come to my office," said Paul Higgins, Assistant Special Agent in charge, Criminal Department.

"Can I finish my coffee and bagel first?"

"Bring it with you."

He got up and headed for his boss's office. Nick was a senior agent for the bureau, stood six-foot two, medium build, brown hair, dark brown eyes, and in excellent shape. Nick walked into his boss's office and took a seat. "So whaddya got?"

"You're going to like this one. We were contacted by Brinks. Yesterday at 0845, a Western Airlines plane was due to arrive at LAX. Brinks had a shipment onboard; they had one of their armored trucks waiting at the gate to pick it up.

"Flight 1757 departed from San Francisco International on time, but was delayed, due to heavy fog at LAX, and landed at 0915. The Brinks guard watched the plane pull up to the gate, watched the baggage crew open the cargo door, and secure the conveyor. The guard handed over the bill of lading, listing the six bags that were onboard, to one of Western's men.

"The Brinks shipment has priority and was to be unloaded

first, but the bags were not found in the bonded cage. A couple of Western's supervisors, Brinks guards, and airport police inspected the luggage as it left the plane and was loaded onto the bag carts. None of Brinks cargo was found on the plane, and the load of luggage was re-inspected before it was sent down the conveyors for passenger pick up. The Brinks supervisor that I spoke to said that they tried to trace the shipment; seems like it just vanished into thin air."

"That only happens in magic shows," chuckled Nick.

Higgins handed Nick a folder. "I'm appointing you the case agent on this one. The names and phone numbers of the people at Brinks and Western are in here. You'll need to talk to them to get more information. Who do you want to take with you?"

"I'll take Leo Panetta with me; he has a good nose for this sort of stuff."

"Good, keep me in the loop."

Nick stood, left his boss's office, headed back to his cubicle, stopped and went looking for Leo.

He found him in the lunchroom. "Hey, Nick, how's it going?"

"I just spoke to Higgins. How's your workload?"

"Busy as usual. What's up?"

"I just volunteered you to join me on a new one. It could be interesting."

"Yeah, like the rest of the shit I'm working on."

Special Agent Leo Panetta was a veteran FBI agent, now in his forties, married with three kids, bald, a bit on the heavy side due to too much pasta and vino, and known as a bulldog for his tenacity.

A four-year college degree is required before entering the FBI Academy, then, completion of a twenty-week course to become a field agent. A few joined the FBI with years of law enforcement experience. Leo was one of those guys who joined the New York Police Department out of high school, working his way up to sergeant, then became a detective in the Drug Enforcement Division. He met his wife, Sophia, through his cousin's girlfriend, and a year later, they got married. He got tired of pounding the streets and he hated the internal politics that he would inherit with a promotion to lieutenant. Still a young man, he decided to join the FBI; they were happy to have him, and he later transferred to the Los Angeles Division, where he developed a great reputation.

"So what did you volunteer me for?" asked Leo.

"Apparently, Brinks was waiting for a shipment at a Western Airlines gate at LAX. The plane was delayed by fog and eventually landed. When it arrived at the dock, the Brinks guards watched the baggage handlers open the cargo door and position the conveyor belt. Brinks cargo had priority, but the baggage crew never found the consigned cargo."

"Do they think it was stolen?"

"They really don't know at this time."

"What did they lose?"

"Six large bags, but they don't know what was in them."

"Could be hundreds of millions of dollars in those bags. Now that could be interesting."

Leo grabbed another doughnut. "Join me for some heartburn food?"

"Thanks, I already had a bagel; that's my limit. I'm going to make an appointment with the management at Western. Ten tomorrow, okay with you?"

"That's fine, just let me know."

Nick set up a meeting at 10:00 A.M. the following day, with Harold Green, the Vice President of Operations of Western Airlines, who recommended that a Brinks representative attend.

He looked at his watch; it was time to go home, not that he had anyone waiting for him.Nick was divorced and didn't have any children.

He graduated from Pepperdine University, received a degree in political science, and then entered law school. He married his college sweetheart, Kati Maguire, who was still enrolled at Pepperdine.

He never graduated, but got interested in law enforcement, after his cousin became a DEA agent. Kati wasn't thrilled about him leaving law school and later enrolling in the FBI Academy. After he graduated, he became a field agent. The hours were long and there were a lot of road trips.

Too many nights away, and the wife began to play. One Friday night Nick came home unexpectedly, finding no one there; her car was in the garage. The following morning, she was dropped off by some guy. After a long juicy kiss, she got out of his car. Nick and Kati were through.

Nick was handsome and rugged looking; he had no problem with women. Tonight he was going home alone. He stopped by his favorite Mexican restaurant, Maria's, got shrimp and beef fajitas to go, and headed to his apartment in Malibu.

19

It was seven-thirty in the morning when Nick stopped at a local donut shop, bought a couple dozen for the office, and a large cup of coffee to go. He got back into his Corvette and drove to the office, while eating a glazed donut for breakfast.

He dropped off the donuts in the lunchroom, headed for his desk and went to work.

Leo walked up to Nick's desk. "It's nine-fifteen, you ready?" asked Leo.

"Yeah, just give me a minute." He made a couple of notes to remind himself to finish some reports and got up. "Let's go."

They left their office and took the elevator to the underground parking level. They jumped into one of the bureau's Crown Vics, with Leo at the wheel. He pulled out on Wilshire Boulevard, turned left, took the 405 south to Century Boulevard, then a right, drove to Western Airlines Head Office, and parked in a visitor's space.

They entered the building, took the elevator to the fourth floor, and went through the door with "Executive Office" printed on it. Nick walked up to the receptionist and showed his credentials. "Nick Cutler, FBI, to see Harold Green."

"You have an appointment, Mr. Cutler?"

"Yes, at ten."

The receptionist got on the intercom: "A Mr. Cutler from the FBI is here to see you." She hung up and smiled. "Mr. Green will be out in a moment, please have a seat."

Fifteen minutes later, a nice-looking redhead, wearing a short skirt and a tight sweater, strutted into the lobby. "Good morning, gentlemen. If you would, follow me to Mr. Green's office."

She turned, sashaying toward the hall, knowing the two men were watching. Leo elbowed his partner whispering, "Shit, I'd follow her off a cliff."

Mr. Green's secretary opened the door, posing for the two agents who entered the office. The Vice President of Operations was seated at his desk, and the Brinks agent was seated across from him, with two empty chairs next to him.

"Thank you, Barbara," said Western's V.P. as he stood and came around his desk to greet them. As they shook hands, Nick introduced them. "I'm Special Agent Nick Cutler, and this is Special Agent Leo Panetta."

"Nice to meet you." He turned toward the other guest. "This is John Lucas, manager of the Brinks Los Angeles office." They shook hands as Green returned to his chair.

"John and I have been going over the—I hate to say this, but the 'disappearance' of the Brinks shipment on Flight 1757. We thought that the best way to proceed is to open this meeting as a question and answer session. You ask, and we'll tell you what we know."

Both Nick and Leo had their notebooks out. Nick started. "At this point, all the FBI knows is that a Brinks armored truck was waiting to pick up six bags consigned to Western Airlines on board Flight 1757, which was delayed because of foggy conditions at LAX. When the plane arrived at the gate, the cargo door was opened under the supervision of the Brinks guards. The six bags were not found on the plane. Did I get that much right?"

"Yes," said Green. "We also had the Brinks guards, airport police, and two of Western's people re-inspect all the luggage and cargo on that flight before it was released."

"Mr. Lucas, do you know what was in the bags?"

"At this point, we don't know what the bags contained."

"Do you know who the shipper was, and who it was consigned to?"

"The shipper was the Northwest Branch of the National Securities

Clearinghouse, located in Seattle, Washington. The consignee was their branch in Los Angeles."

"And I'll bet they won't tell you what was in the bags?" said Leo.

"Actually, they said the bags contained stock certificates, and municipal and federal bonds, consigned to them by various brokerage houses in the Northwest, including Canada and Alaska."

"So these stocks and bonds were sent to the Seattle branch from various stock brokerage houses, not to be cleared, but only to receive them, consolidate the load, and ship to L.A.?"

"That's the way it was explained to me," said Lucas.

"Sounds like every stock brokerage house in the Northwest will have to be contacted to determine what was actually shipped in those bags. Man, what a nightmare," said Nick. "Do you think the bags were stolen?"

"We don't know. Our men and the Brinks guards witnessed the loading of the bags in Seattle. The plane had one stop in San Francisco before arriving in Los Angeles. Cargo was off-loaded and loaded at San Francisco International," said Green.

"Any surveillance cameras recording the activity at the gate or baggage handling areas?" asked Nick.

"Unfortunately none," said Green.

"Has the Seattle clearinghouse been informed?"

"Yes, and I already received a call from their attorney and an insurance company."

"What did you tell them?"

"Basically, what we've told you. I asked them if they knew what was in the bags, the conversation suddenly became short, with their attorney saying he would call back."

Nick knew he wasn't going to learn any more from these guys. He pulled out two business cards and handed one to each of them.

"It appears that we all have a lot of work to do on this case. I'd appreciate it if I could have the names and phone numbers of the supervisors of Western and Brinks in San Francisco and Seattle, so our agents can have a word with them, informing them that we intend to talk to everyone connected to that shipment."

Green handed Nick a sheet of paper. "We assumed that you would want to contact them and already prepared a list for you."

Nick looked over the list. "Thanks, this will help speed things up." He folded the sheet of paper and slipped it into his coat pocket. "If you hear or think of anything that might be helpful, please give me a call."

They all shook hands, then the Vice President of Western walked them to the lobby. "Mr. Lucas and I are at your disposal; don't hesitate to call if you need anything."

"I'll do that, thank you."

They got into the Crown Vic and drove off. "So, whaddya think?" asked Nick.

"I think they have no fuckin' idea where the six bags are, and they're worried about a huge lawsuit and a major loss for their companies."

"Where do you think the bags are?" asked Nick.

"I think they're in San Francisco, whether they're lost or stolen, who knows? But if those bags were stolen, it had to be an inside job. How else would anyone know when a shipment was coming in?"

"I told you this case might be interesting."

"I'm not sure how interesting it's going to be, but it looks like we're going to have to travel to San Francisco and Seattle, and both cities have some great restaurants."

"Speaking of restaurants, I'm hungry. Why don't we stop for lunch before we go back to the office?"

* * *

After lunch, they drove back to their headquarters. Nick agreed with Leo that the Brinks shipment was somewhere in San Francisco and planned to arrange to fly up there the following day.

They rode the elevator up to their floor, and walked to Nick's cubicle.

"I think we should get some of our guys working L.A. before we leave. We don't want to leave one stone unturned," said Leo.

"Good idea. How about Rick Bender and Carol Straus? They just finished an assignment together and did a good job."

"Good choice; I was also thinking of Bob Moore and Leroy Jackson, Ken Lawry and Steve Baker. They always volunteer, and are very thorough."

"Sounds good. Why don't you contact them and set up a briefing for this afternoon, while I give a report to Higgins this morning."

Leo went to his desk, while Nick punched the intercom button. "Higgins."

"It's Nick. I just got back from a meeting with Western's Vice President and a Brinks official. Got a minute?"

"Hang on." A few seconds went by. "Meet me in the director's office."

Nick knocked on the door of James Warner, the assistant director in charge of the Los Angeles office; he was on the phone and waved Nick to come in. He took a seat next to Higgins and waited for the director to finish his call.

"Look, I have two of my best men working on the case; they had a meeting with the VP of Western Airlines this morning." Warner listened intensively. "Sure, I'll let you know as soon as I hear something . . . Yeah, I'll do that. Talk to you later." He hung up.

"That was Fred Thomson."

"Why's the Director of the FBI so interested in this?" asked Higgins.

"It has something to do with the bearer bonds in that shipment." He turned to Nick. "Whaddya got?"

"We had a meeting with the vice president and an official of Brinks. They have no idea what happened, and they don't know what was in the six bags consigned to Brinks. But the VP mentioned that the attorney representing the clearinghouse and an attorney representing their insurance company had contacted them."

"Maybe that's why Thomson is so interested in this case," said Higgins.

"Obviously someone got him excited. What's your plan, Nick?"

"I feel that something happened to those six bags while Flight 1757 was on the ground at San Francisco International. I'm contacting our offices in San Francisco and Seattle to open up a new case. We plan to fly up to San Francisco in the morning, as long as we can get reservations."

"After the phone call with the Director of the FBI, I think it would be more expeditious for you to use our jet. It's faster and you'll be able to move in and out of the airport quicker and on schedule. I'm sure you plan to go to Seattle after Frisco?" asked Warner.

"Absolutely, and wherever the case leads us. But before we leave, I'm putting a squad together to continue the investigation in L.A. Leo's contacting them; we're briefing this afternoon."

"Sounds like you have it under control. I'll have Susan make arrangements with our pilots; they'll be prepared to leave at your request. Get their pager numbers from Susan. Paul, keep me informed as we learn anything," said the assistant director.

Paul and Nick left Warner's office. "Stay on top of this one," said Paul.

"I always do," said Nick, as he walked away.

Leo was sitting in Nick's cubicle when he returned. "How'd it go?"

"Higgins and I were summoned to Warner's office. He was talking to Fred Thomson when I walked in. Apparently, this missing cargo has someone's feathers ruffled up enough to get Thomson involved; he's putting pressure on Warner. That's how we get to use the agency's private corporate jet for transportation while we're on this case."

"No shit? Traveling in style—I like it."

"I made contact with everyone. We're going to brief them at three o'clock."

Nick and Leo were in the conference room when the six agents entered separately. All six of the agents were in their late twenties, experienced, and still hungry to make their mark within the agency. Everyone knew each other and took a seat.

Nick described the incident and the meeting they had with the

VP and the Brinks official. "Leo and I are going to follow the trail of Flight 1757 back to San Francisco, then Seattle. While we're on the road, I want Carol and Rick to interview anyone associated, in any way, with this flight from the time that the tires hit the tarmac at LAX until it took off. Check with Brinks and Western about any of their employees' attendance, whether it changed, someone called in sick, bought a new car, unexpected vacations. Check all phone usage from Brinks and Western employees between Washington, San Francisco, and L.A. You guys know the drill.

"Bob and Leroy, I want you to review all documents, manifests, pickup and delivery bills of lading, at the airport and any freight forwarder with any cargo unloaded or loaded on that plane. If you need a subpoena to gain access, get one.

"Ken and Steve, visit all our informants; see if any of them heard anything.

"When all of you finish that assignment, we need to contact financial institutions that cash bearer bonds and see if there has been any activity.

"Any questions?" asked Nick.

"Who are our contacts at Western and Brinks?" asked Carol.

"Same guys we talked to this morning. They said they would cooperate with our investigation." Nick gave her the names and phone numbers. "Anything else?" He paused. "Okay then, get on this right away. Contact Leo or me if you find out anything, and if, for some reason, you can't find us, talk to Paul Higgins."

20

After August gained control of the bonds, he knew that he not only had to worry about the police, but also the low level gangsters that lived in the glamorous beach area.

Eddie Burger was one of the lowlife grifters who ran a crew of ex-cons that were always looking to rip someone off. If Burger knew August had $350 million in bonds in his possession, it could get ugly.

During the same time, George Jung was building his organization, becoming the largest cocaine smuggler around. They worked in the same area and frequented the same restaurants. They both hung out with some of the same guys, not good if you're trying to keep something a secret.

Jung and his associates had stash and money houses in Manhattan Beach, Hermosa, and the Palos Verdes area. Lots of men and women worked for him; some would sell their souls for a kilo of coke, and would certainly kill for $350 million, in fact, for a lot less.

There was also a clique of airplane smugglers; they called themselves Manhattan Airlines. The group originated from Riverside but it got hot—and not the temperature—so they moved to the Manhattan Beach area. They were notorious for being risktakers; the desert was dotted with used, stolen, and wrecked planes. Their M.O. was steal a plane, fly it down to Mexico, load it up, and fly it back, under the radar. Then they would land it on a deserted highway—unload the pot and get it to market.

August worked with them. He liked them; they were a ballzy

and trustworthy group, but who knew. In these days and times, the cocaine trade had guys turning punk and their old ladies turning tricks just to get high.

He did know one thing. He had 350 million dollars in bonds and needed to unload them as soon as possible.

He thought he could get twenty cents on a dollar, but even if he could get ten cents on a dollar, the $350 million could net him $35 million.

He'd be able to pay the boys half, give some to the rest of the crew and contacts, and make a cool ten million out of the deal. He felt that was enough money for him, based on the time it would take to make a deal with one of his contacts, the money he would have to spend, and the risks he'd have to take.

He visited one of his attorneys and asked him for advice, while he showed him one of the bonds. His attorney almost had a coronary. "Jesus Christ, August, where the hell did you get this?"

"Frankie, I've got a lot of those," August replied with a smile.

"How many?"

"Three hundred fifty."

Frank almost fell off his chair. "August, I don't have much experience with bonds and I'm fucking *positive* you don't. They're obviously hot?"

"Why do you think I came to see you?"

"Look, you get busted for smuggling marijuana, I can probably get you off, or you might get two to three years. But you get caught with those bonds, you're going to prison for twenty or more, and if I tried to help you, I'd be in the next cell. You want my advice? Get fucking rid of them as fast as you can. I love you, man, but, August, get that fuckin' bond out of my office!"

* * *

August immediately started to broker the bonds using a sort of cloak and dagger method. First, he made a call to some associates in the mafia on the East Coast, who showed some interest and wanted to meet.

He made a few more calls. They asked him how much he wanted per bond. He told them it was negotiable. Their response was always the same; they were not interested at this time.

August hung up the phone with a potential buyer, totally frustrated. He was always in control of his operations and finances, and knew exactly how much he wanted for the commodity he was selling.

He really had no idea what these bonds were worth in this very gray market, making it difficult for him to pitch the product. It also made him feel vulnerable, something he had never experienced. It was time to go to work, and follow Frank's advice: "Get fucking rid of them as fast as you can!" He also needed to figure out how to appease the guys, while he tried to sell them.

* * *

Three days had gone by since the heist. August knew Scott got off work at three. He waited until 3:45 to call Scott's house. He knew that the local police and the FBI would be investigating the robbery, and anyone in the baggage area would be a primary suspect and that their phones would be tapped, and/or bugged. So he hoped that Scott would catch on to a sort of coded discussion when he answered.

"Hello."

"Hey, been surfing lately?" asked August, hoping Scott would recognize his voice.

"Every day, I thought we'd see you at our local spot."

"I couldn't make it, but how about I buy you guys a beer at our local bar. Let's say seven?"

"If you're buying, we'll be there, see you later."

They both hung up; Scott's quick thinking impressed August, and Scott was proud of himself for picking up on the coded conversation. He called the guys about the meeting at the beach house.

August arrived at the beach house on time, but as usual, the parking sucked and he had to park a couple of blocks away. He took his time, enjoying the sunset as he walked down the hill to the Esplanade. He reached the beach house, took two stairs at a time and knocked.

Terry opened the door, and handed August a Coors. "Good to see you; come on in."

Before August could say anything, Randy blurted out, "So, how's everything going?"

August held up one hand, and then slid his finger across his lips, motioning to go out to the deck. The guys picked up on his signal. They stepped out on the deck and shut the door.

August sat down on a patio chair, and took a sip of his beer. "It took till six in the morning to go through the bags. The first two bags were full of stock certificates and municipal bonds that had no value to us. I was halfway through the third bag when I picked up a one-million-dollar bearer bond."

"Bearer bond!" Randy blurted out with excitement. "Anyone can cash them. My grandfather had some and left them to my parents. But his, I think, are worth ten thousand dollars each. My dad showed them to me; he said that whoever had possession of the bonds could cash the coupons in. They weren't million-dollar bonds, but they have to be similar."

"How many did you find?" asked Scott.

August hesitated, and then slowly looked at each of them. "Three hundred fifty of them." The guys' jaws dropped.

"Holy fuck!" said Scott.

Randy jumped up. "You gotta be fuckin' kidding me! We're rich!"

They all began to talk at the same time, giving each other high-fives, while August sat quietly."You don't seem that excited. What's wrong?" asked Scott.

"I showed one of the bonds to my attorney. Each bond and its coupons have serial numbers. Randy's correct, if you had possession of one of these bonds that you had purchased, inherited, or even stolen from someone, you could cash it in. But, these bonds were in transit somewhere, and all the serial numbers would have been recorded before they left the brokerage houses. My attorney's advice was to get rid of them as quickly as possible." August saw the disappointment on the guys' faces. "I made a few phone calls and I think these bonds are still worth something, not face value, but at a discounted price."

"Like what?" asked Scott.

"I really don't know, but maybe five or ten cents on the dollar. I've only had enough time to contact some of my friends, and one in particular, has some interest."

With a somber look on his face while shaking his head, "This is going to be a lot harder than I thought, and take a lot more time than I expected."

"How long?" asked Scott.

"I have no idea. I plan to fly to New York tomorrow. If that lead doesn't pan out, I'll move on. I know you guys are anxious but you just don't run around telling everyone that you have 350 one-million-dollar bonds for sale, or you'll get caught by the feds and go to prison or some gangster will rip you off or you could get yourself killed."

Randy began to pace back and forth. "You mean we pulled off a perfect robbery worth $350 million and we're not going to make a fuckin' dime?"

"Why not have someone go into a bank and try to cash one of the coupons?" asked Jeff.

August held up his hand. "Wait a minute. That's exactly what we don't want to do. These motherfuckers are on fire! The fucking feds will be looking for these bonds."

"Then what the hell do we do?" asked Scott.

"Here's what I think. I really have no idea what they're worth, or if I can move them. I'm going to give you $50,000 and I'll hold onto the bonds. I'm giving you the money so you have some security. If something happens to me, or the bonds, you'll make something out of this deal. But I don't want to be contacted; I mean it. I'll contact you. If I can't fence them, I'll give them back to you, and you can return my money. Does this sit right with you guys?"

The four of them looked at each other, and nodded in agreement. "Okay, that's good with us," said Scott.

"I'll contact Ernie and let him know what's going on."

"Scott, meet me at the car wash in Redondo on P.C.H. tomorrow at four o'clock. I'll be in the waiting room. As soon as I see you, we'll both go to the head and I'll pass you the money."

"I really don't know what to do with the money."

"You don't have any dogs, do you?"

"No, but I was thinking of getting one for the kids."

"Wait awhile. Put the cash in some Tupperware and bury it in your backyard. No one will think of looking for it there; even if your house burns down it will be safe. Okay, I'm going to be busy; I'll give you an update when I can." August stood. "You guys have to be careful. The FBI, and who knows who else, will be investigating the missing bags. You guys are prime suspects. Avoid talking about the heist; make no reference to stocks or bonds to anyone, amongst yourselves, or on the phone.

"If you think you're being followed, don't worry about it. It's their job to look into every suspect. Don't change your behavior in any way. Just continue doing what you normally do and you'll be fine.

"Eventually, you'll be paid a visit by the FBI. They'll have a bunch of questions. I think all of you should practice questioning each other and work on your answers. Keep them brief and precise. Remember, the more you talk, the better their chances of tripping you up. Just stay cool, and you'll be fine."

They shook hands and August took off. Randy looked at his friends. "We would have been totally fucked, if we didn't have that guy on our side."

21

Fourth day: FBI flies to San Francisco

Nick picked up Leo at 7:00 A.M. and drove to LAX, then to the government hangars. Nick parked his Corvette inside the hangar; Leo and Nick walked over to introduce themselves to the pilots, who were doing a final flight check on the FBI's Gulfstream.

"Think it'll be okay to leave my car in the hangar?" Nick held out his hand. "I'm Nick Cutler and this is Leo Panetta."

"Nice to meet you, I'm Captain John Carnes, and this is my co-pilot, Roger Owens. We're just finishing our flight check; I've filed our flight plan; we're fueled and ready to go. As far as parking your 'Vette in the hangar, I don't see any problem."

They grabbed their suitcases and boarded the Gulfstream. "Nice, in fact, very nice," said Leo, as he inspected the interior.

They took their seats and fastened their seatbelts. John received clearance for take-off, and a few minutes later, they were flying to San Francisco.

An hour and twenty minutes later, the FBI Gulfstream was taxiing down the tarmac at San Francisco International Airport to a government hangar. The plane came to a stop, and the jet engines were shut down. John came out of the cockpit. "Hope you enjoyed the flight."

"What's not to enjoy?" said Leo. "Comfortable seats, movies, fully stocked kitchen and bar; it's the only way to fly."

"Well, you'll be flying with us until you get back to L.A. We're staying at the same hotel and are on call."

"Great, let's get our luggage, rent a car, and check in. Leo and I have a briefing to attend to at one," said Nick.

They checked in at the Marriott Hotel, went to their room, dropped off their bags and went to lunch at the hotel restaurant. When they finished eating, Nick and Leo left the pilots and drove to the FBI office at 450 Golden Gate Avenue.

They entered the building, showed their credentials, and were escorted to a conference room where six men were seated. One of them stood and walked over to greet them. He shook Nick's hand. "Greg O'Riley, special agent in charge."

"Nick Cutler and this is Leo Panetta."

Greg shook Leo's hand. "Come on, I'll introduce you to my team."

"I had no idea we'd be briefing a team," said Nick.

"Neither did I, until my boss told me to put one together this morning. This is my partner, John Ling." He introduced the four other agents and Nick took the floor.

He went over the incident and the meeting with the vice president of Western and the official from Brinks. "After the meeting, Leo and I agreed that no one knew what happened to the six bags, and that the most logical place for them to go missing or stolen was at the San Francisco airport, while Flight 1757 was there."

"Did they have any idea what the contents were?" asked John Ling.

"They were told, by the attorney representing the Northwest Branch of the National Securities Clearinghouse, that the bags contained stock certificates, and municipal and federal bearer bonds received from various brokerage houses in the Northwest, including Alaska and Canada. Apparently, the clearinghouse did not know the exact contents of each shipment but only consolidated them into the six bags to be shipped to the West Coast Main Branch in Los Angeles.

"Brinks picked up the bags and delivered them directly to Western's Flight 1757 and witnessed the bags being loaded onto the plane at Sea-Tac. They were on the plane when it landed here; luggage and cargo were unloaded and loaded onto Flight 1757. There are no specific days or times that Brinks, Wells Fargo, or Loomis ship out cargo, which clearly points to an inside job. That is, if the bags were stolen."

"Don't you think, that as time goes on and the bags are not found or returned, it's more likely that they were stolen?" asked Greg.

"Yes, in fact, it's been forty-eight hours since they were discovered missing, add another four hours from the time Flight 1757 landed in San Francisco. Either the misplaced bags have been opened and the contents kept, because of their value, or it was a premeditated expertly planned heist. Either way, at this juncture, we're looking for stolen goods. Greg, were you able to arrange a meeting with Western's manager?"

"Yeah, we have a meeting tomorrow morning at nine-thirty."

"Good. We'll get authorization to interview anyone connected with that flight and to look at all the shipping manifests for all incoming and outgoing cargo and run a check on any freight forwarders dropping off or receiving cargo for that flight. Any questions?" Nick paused. "Leo and I will be flying to Washington tomorrow afternoon. If you think of anything, don't hesitate to contact us. Thank you for your time."

The agents stood and were about to leave. Nick thought, *If we're at the airport, why not leave for Washington after the meeting?*

"Greg, after our meeting at Western, Leo and I are going to leave for Washington, so we'll go over what we learned at the airport."

Leo and Nick left the building and headed for their hotel. "So whaddya going to do for the rest of the day?" asked Nick.

"Thought I'd take a ride on the trolley car down to Fisherman's Wharf, look around, and maybe buy something for the kids. You want to tag along?"

"Nah, the hotel has a gym. I think I'll work out for a while, take a steam bath, and relax. You decide where we're going to dinner?"

"They have some great Italian restaurants here, but I think we should do Chinese. I've always wanted to go to Tommy Toy's. One of my wife's girlfriends said it was the best Chinese food she's ever had and the presentation is artistic. It's a bit pricey but the company's buying."

"Guess we should take the pilots with us?"

"Not a bad idea. We are in their hands."

* * *

Same time, Western Airlines LAX

The guys were unloading the last bag cart from an incoming flight from Houston. "Hey, Scott, you going surfing with us this afternoon?" asked Randy.

"Yeah, as long as the waves are good."

"I checked them out this morning. Three to four feet and the weather's nice."

"Yeah, but the afternoon winds could blow them out."

"Man, you really sound bummed out. What's wrong?"

"What's wrong? Are you fucking kidding me? I haven't heard shit from August for two days."

"Jeez, give the guy some time. He said it wasn't going to be easy to unload that stuff."

"I know. I'm just disappointed. We were so fucking close."

Just then, Scott's supervisor, Wayne Harper, walked up. "What's so fucking close?"

Scott didn't even see him walk up, but he knew his voice. "My back is killing me so it's gonna be tough to finish this load."

Now Harper had a worried look. "You hurt yourself on the job?"

That certainly changed the subject. "No, I pulled a muscle moving some boxes in my garage."

He could see the relieved look on Wayne's face, knowing a workman's comp claim wasn't going to be filed.

"As soon as you're finished, a couple of FBI agents want to talk to you guys about the missing Brinks bags. They're waiting in my office." He turned and walked away.

August had warned them that they would eventually be

questioned, and they had rehearsed and synchronized what they were all going to say. Scott turned to his friends, who had heard the supervisor. "Iiiiit's show time."

They unloaded the last few bags and headed for Wayne's office.

There was a woman and a guy sitting with Wayne Harper, and four extra chairs had been moved into the office.

The guys walked in, and Wayne made the introductions. He looked at the two agents. "This was the crew assigned to unload Flight 1757. This is Randy Bowman, Jeff Holland, Terry Clark, and their foreman, Scott McCarran. Guys, this is Agent Carol Straus and Agent Rick Bender."

While they shook hands, Wayne explained, "They're here to ask you about the missing Brinks shipment. I'll turn the meeting over to them."

"Thank you, Mr. Harper," said Agent Straus. "So how long have you all worked for Western?"

They all started to answer at the same time; Scott held up his hand. "I've been here for eight years, and Randy, Jeff, and Terry, close to five."

"Have you all worked in the baggage department for that period?"

They all nodded; Scott said yes.

"Scott, you're the foreman, so why don't you answer the questions, and if any of you have anything to add, please speak up, including you, Mr. Harper."

Agent Straus pulled out her notepad and set it on the desk. "Will you tell us what you observed and experienced on the morning of February 4?"

"Our shift starts at 6:00 A.M. and we barely got to work on time because it was extremely foggy. There were many delayed flights, and some were being diverted to Ontario Airport. The planes that landed were backed up and waiting to dock as soon as they could. We were working as fast as we could to get the flights in and out, and expected to work overtime."

"Does that happen often?" asked Agent Bender.

"When planes get delayed, yes, but under normal conditions, no." Scott paused, waiting for another question.

"Go on," said Agent Straus.

"Okay. Our lunch break starts at ten and we were walking to the lunchroom when Mr. Harper came up to us and said he needed us to unload Flight 1757. So we went back to work, drove the bag tug and carts to the 737, and began to prepare to unload the luggage and cargo. A Brinks truck drove up next to the conveyor, and one of the guards walked over and handed me a bill of lading for six bags.

"The guard and I watched Terry and Randy open the cargo door while Jeff positioned the conveyor. I handed Randy the bill of lading, who gave it to Terry, before he entered the cargo hold with Jeff.

"We've unloaded cargo for Brinks, Wells Fargo, and Loomis before and knew they always had priority. Jeff and Terry began to pull cargo out of the bonded area, looking for the six bags consigned to Brinks, but never found them."

"So what happened after you didn't find them?" asked Carol.

"I called Mr. Harper, who came out with his boss, met the airport police, who, along with the Brinks guards, supervised while we finished unloading the plane. Then we took the cargo and luggage to the baggage handling area and they examined every single piece from Flight 1757 before we loaded them on conveyors headed to the waiting passengers."

"Is that it?" asked Rick.

"Yeah, that's it. After we finished we took our lunch break, then went back to work."

"Where did you go to lunch?"

"We bought lunch from one of the airport vendors. Ah, no— Randy and I went to McDonald's in Western's food court and Terry and Jeff got deli sandwiches, then we ate together in our lunch room."

"You have a very good memory Mr. McCarran," said Agent Bender.

"Not really. It's just that—it was an unusual day."

"Mr. Harper, you have anything to add?"

"No, I think Scott covered everything."

"Do you have the bill of lading for the shipment?" asked Carol.

Harper opened a file on his desk. "Here's a copy manifest for that flight, and the bill of lading." He handed the papers to her.

"Thank you. What is Western doing to try to locate the missing cargo?"

"We verified with our office at Sea-Tac, and the Brinks office in Seattle. The Brinks guards that delivered the six bags said they watched the bags get loaded on the plane.

"Flight 1757 left Sea-Tac, landed at San Francisco International where passengers, their luggage and cargo were unloaded and new passengers and their luggage and cargo headed to LAX were loaded onboard.

"Scott already went over everything that happened when Flight 1757 arrived at LAX. The FBI was brought in because we simply couldn't locate the shipment."

The two agents looked at each other, nodded, then stood and shook hands. "Thank you for your cooperation. I hope you won't mind if we call on you for anything else we might need."

"Not at all," said Harper.

The two agents left. "Thank you, guys." Wayne looked at his watch. "It's 9:45, take an extra fifteen minutes for your lunch break."

The guys walked out of Harper's office and headed for the lunchroom. With no one else in earshot, since they were forbidden to let anything slip, per August's orders, Randy chuckled, and then whispered, "You deserve an academy award for that performance."

22

Taking the bonds back East

First, August decided to take the bonds to someone he trusted and had done business with. He made a call to Billy Lamotta, a member of the Lamotta family that operated out of New York. Billy and August went way back; in fact, Billy married one of August's ex-girlfriends.

Billy, Sweet Willy, and August were partners in a smuggling operation with a group out of Morocco and Lebanon, and August still shipped loads of marijuana back to Sweet Willy from his West Coast operation.

He had to deal with them personally; he arranged to fly back to New York to meet with Lamotta. He slit the lining of his suitcase and slid in three one-million-dollar bonds, then sealed the edge, and packed his clothes in the same carry-on bag.

Mickey walked into the bedroom. "You ready to go?"

"Yeah, I'm ready, but I still don't know what the fuck I'm going to do when I get there."

Mickey drove him to the airport, taking the 110 to the 405 to the off-ramp on Century Boulevard. He pulled up to the curb at the American Airlines departure gates. "Take care of yourself, and call if you need anything."

"I will. Keep an eye on the operation."

"You didn't need to ask. Good luck."

August got out and headed for the counter. He paid cash for a first-class ticket, under his alias, leaving L.A. at 12:00 P.M., walked to Gate 32A, and took a seat. He started thinking about how he got involved in this caper, feeling a little unsure about bringing back these financial instruments, which he wasn't familiar with in the slightest, putting him far outside of his criminal comfort zone.

The attendant came on the P.A. system: "Flight 952 to New York City is ready to board, starting with the first-class passengers."

August got up and walked over to the attendant, handed his ticket to her, and boarded the Boeing 747. He found his seat, put his exceedingly valuable piece of luggage in the overhead compartment and took his aisle seat.

"Excuse me?"

August looked up at a gorgeous blonde, apparently taking the seat next to him. She had a carry-on. He had a hard-on. He smiled. "Need some help with that?"

She smiled back. "No, that's okay." She reached up and slid her bag into the compartment, while her short skirt slid up, giving August a good look; he almost got caught staring as she shut the lid. She sidestepped into her seat facing August, who was gawking at her cleavage, which was bulging from her low-cut blouse. She sat down. "Whew, feels good to sit. I've been running around all morning." She held out her hand. "Laura Stern."

He gladly grabbed her hand, not knowing who she was, he decided to use his alias. "Tony Lira."

"Leaving L.A., or going home?"

"Just going to New York for some business."

"How long are you staying?"

"Not sure, maybe two or three days."

"You like Broadway shows?"

He had no idea where this was headed, but unless she asked him if she was ugly, his answers would all be yes. "Yeah, I've been to a few."

"Well, if you find enough time, I'll give you a backstage pass and a front-row seat to see *La Cage Aux Folles*."

"Sounds like you have some good connections."

"I'm in the play."

"Really, what part?"

"I'm the fiancée of the son of one of the gay owners of La Cage."

They kept talking while the stewardess served them cocktails and hors d'oeuvres. The plane taxied down the tarmac.

The captain came on the P.A. system. "Hi, everyone, I'm Captain Paul Lamont. I'd like to welcome you and thank you for flying on American Airlines. We're on time and the weather looks good all the way to New York. The flight should take five hours and forty-five minutes, arriving at 8:45 New York time. Again, thank you for flying American and enjoy the flight. Attendants prepare for take-off."

The stewardesses went over the requisite ho-hum safety features and evacuation instructions, then checked everyone's seatbelts and took their own seats.

After the captain leveled off the plane, the stewardess came on the P.A. "Thank you for flying American Airlines, we'll be coming by with our menu to take your lunch and drink orders. After lunch, you can watch the first run movie *Lassiter*, starring Tom Selleck, who plays a jewel thief operating in London in the late 1930s." August chuckled to himself, *That's fucking perfect. Maybe I can learn something.*

After the movie, August dozed off. He awoke to Laura's voice and a nudge. He opened his eyes, looking straight into her blues. "What's up?" he asked.

"The stewardess just announced that dinner was going to be served. I thought you would want to know."

"Thanks, it's going to be late by the time we get into the city."

The stewardess walked up to their seats. "Would you like a cocktail before dinner?"

"I'll have a martini, with olives and onions," said Laura.

"Mr. Lira?"

"You have any good scotch?"

"Matter of fact, we do. On the rocks?"

"That would be fine. Thank you."

Drinks were served with an assortment of appetizers, followed by dinner and a good cabernet.

August and Laura kept each other company until they landed at JFK. They walked to the baggage claim area together; both only had a carry-on, so they stepped out to the curb.

"So, where are you staying?" she asked.

Billy Lamotta had reserved a suite at the Drake Hotel for him. "The Drake Hotel."

"I'm at the Regency; if you can make it, call me." She gave him a sexy smile. "In fact, call me either way."

August was about to hail a cab when Laura asked, "A limo is picking me up; you want a ride?"

"You mean I could limo to Manhattan with a gorgeous blonde, or have a guy wearing a turban, that can't speak English, and will probably get lost on the way?" He rubbed his chin and shook his head. "Jeez, I'll have to think about that."

They laughed, as Laura's limo pulled up. They entered Manhattan; the driver stopped in front of the Drake Hotel. August smiled and said, "It was great meeting you."

"Nice to meet you too." She leaned over and gave him a peck on the cheek. "Hope to see you again."

"I think you will."

The Drake Hotel, built in 1926, with renovations beginning in 1980, was located on Park Avenue and 56th Street, right in the center of all the action. It was the preferred accommodation for movie stars, famous singers, and musicians. August walked up to the counter. "Reservations for August Taracina."

The clerk looked it up. "Ah, here it is. Your suite has been paid in advance for three days. Will that be sufficient?"

"Yeah, I think so."

"Need help with your luggage?"

"No thanks, I only have a carry-on."

"Very well." He handed August the key. "Suite 2108; please call if you need anything. Good evening, sir, and have a nice stay."

August took the elevator to the 21st floor and walked to his suite. He inserted his key and entered. *Man, this place is big enough for a football team.* He opened the drapes. Not a tall building, but the view of Central Park and the surrounding area was excellent. *I'm going to have to invite Laura up here for dinner, and who knows, maybe more.*

He gave Billy a call. "It's August."

"Like the suite?"

"It's fantastic."

"Good, we'll meet there then. How about ten tomorrow morning?"

"Perfect, see you then."

The line went dead and August put the phone back on the cradle. It was too early to go to bed so August decided to go down to the lobby bar and have a drink. He took a stool at the bar. "What can I get you?" asked the bartender.

"Johnny Walker Blue on the rocks." He got his drink and turned around to scope out the action. There was a guy at the piano, played pretty well, but sounded like a worn-out drunk that smoked three packs a day, when he attempted to sing.

Most of the patrons were older and not one good-looking female in the bunch. He was on his second drink and could feel the booze and the time change. Anyway, he was tired, and getting bored, so he decided to go back to his suite. He took a shower and watched TV until he couldn't keep his eyes open, and then went to bed.

23

Fifth day: New York City

August woke up late because of the time difference. He called room service, ordered a full breakfast and a pot of coffee, then took a shower and got dressed. After he finished his meal, he poured another cup of coffee, turned on the TV, and watched the news, while waiting for Billy's arrival.

At ten o'clock sharp, there was a knock on the door. August cracked open the door, leaving the chain hooked. It was Billy, escorted by a couple of his bodyguards. He unhooked the chain and opened the door. Lamotta walked in and gave August a hug. "Hey, you're lookin' good, welcome to New York." Billy was followed by two large gentlemen who stood by the door while the two of them took a seat in the living room.

"You want a drink, or some coffee?" asked August.

"Little early for a cocktail, but I'd love a cup of coffee."

August poured two cups, handed one to Billy and sat down. "So you think you can do something with the bonds?"

"Like I said, we'll take a look at them and see what we can do," said Lamotta.

"You want to take them with you?"

"No fuckin' way; too much heat snooping around. Willy and I are having dinner at the El Cortelli. You know where it is?"

"Yeah, we had dinner together there with those wild stews, remember?"

"Vaguely, but that's before I met your ex-girlfriend," he chuckled. "Hard to remember any other women after that."

"You're a lucky man."

"Only one luckier is you; you knew Debra first."

"So how are Debra and the kids?" asked August.

"They're great. They're running all over the house. Just think, they could be running around yours," he chuckled.

"No, that's not me; I'm not the marrying type."

"They're both great. John just turned six and Sophie is four. Can you believe that?"

"I'm happy for you."

Billy was ready to leave. "We'll be there by six, bring the bonds. Come in ten minutes later and go directly to the restroom." He turned and pointed to one of the guys. "Tony will pass by you. If his left hand is behind his back, give him the envelope, and then join us for a nice dinner."

"Sounds easy enough. When will I hear from you if you're interested?"

Billy stood. "Sometime the next day."

August walked him to the door. They shook hands and hugged. "Good to see you, August." He turned and walked away, with the two big guys following.

August shut the door, locked it, sat down at the desk, and made a few phone calls to his men. Nothing was going on and no one, including the heat, seemed interested. He picked up the remote, then had second thoughts, picked up the phone and dialed the operator.

"Hotel operator."

"Yeah, connect me with the Regency."

"Regency Hotel, may I help you?"

"Yeah, I'd like to speak to one of your guests, Laura Stern."

The phone rang twice. "Hello."

"Laura, this is Tony Lira."

"Hi, I was just thinking about you. Going to have enough time to see the show?"

"Well, I'm busy tonight, but how about tomorrow?"

"That would be great! I'll make the arrangements. All you have to do is come to the theater and see the head usher. He'll take care of everything."

They said their goodbyes and August hung up, grabbed the remote, and turned on the TV. He watched a Dirty Harry movie, *Sudden Impact*, a golf tournament, then took a shower and got ready for the evening.

He opened his suitcase, carefully pried the lining open and pulled out the bonds, folded them, and put them in an envelope that he got from the desk drawer in his room.

He looked at his gold Rolex; it was five-fifteen. *Time to go.* He walked through the lobby and out the front door, and asked the valet to hail a cab.

Seconds later, he climbed into the backseat of the cab. "Where to, mon?" asked the driver, with a heavy Jamaican accent.

"El Cortelli restaurant."

"That in Little Italy?"

"Yeah."

August had to listen to this insufferably loud Reggae music until the driver pulled up to the El Cortelli. He couldn't get out of the cab fast enough, paying the tab and tip. He was ten minutes early so he took out a pack of Marlboros, shook out a cigarette, and lit it with his gold Dunhill. He took a pull, inhaled deeply and blew out a plume of smoke, along with foggy steam, as his warm breath hit the frigid air. It was a lot colder than he expected; he had only worn a light jacket.

He watched the traffic crawl by, horns honking, tires screeching, a guy rolling down his window, sticking his head out, and screaming and cussing at the car in front of him. The driver couldn't hear the asshole; his windows were shut. August smiled. *Only in New York.*

He looked at his watch, 6:08; he flicked his cigarette into the gutter, walked into the restaurant, heading directly to the bathroom. Tony came through a doorway, left hand behind his back. August placed the envelope in Tony's hand—the size of a catcher's mitt—he slid it in his jacket pocket, without anyone noticing, and kept on walking.

August entered the bathroom, took a piss and washed his hands, then joined Billy and Sweet Willy, who stood to greet him.

They hugged. "Good to see you; how's sunny California?" asked Willy.

"Hell of a lot warmer than here."

The waiter walked up to the table and began to hand out menus.

Billy Lamotta held up his hand. "Tell Carmine to make something special."

"No problem, Mr. Lamotta. Same wine as usual?"

"That would be fine. Thanks, Louie."

August turned to Sweet Willy. "How's Erica? I heard she wasn't feeling well; how's she doing?"

"Thanks for asking. It was touch and go for a while, but she's doing a lot better."

They talked about old times until dinner was served. Carmine outdid himself. They finished the evening with a glass of port.

"I'm done in," said Billy, as he glanced at his watch. "My driver should be outside by now; we'll give you a ride to your hotel."

The driver pulled the limo up to the elegant hotel entry. August shook hands with his friends.

"I'll call you in the morning," said Billy.

August went back to the lobby bar to check out the action. It was just as boring as the previous night. *Be nice to have Laura Stern with me right now. Maybe tomorrow night?*

He left the bar and took the elevator to his room. He opened the mini-bar and pulled out a bottle of Cognac, poured it into a wine glass, turned on the TV and kicked back on the couch.

24

August woke up at five, and couldn't get back to sleep. *Damn jetlag. Maybe I'll take a walk and have breakfast. Yeah, good idea.*

At 6:A.M., he left his room, took the elevator and walked through the deserted lobby, and out to the street. There was frost on the ground and he was happy he was wearing his overcoat. He walked over to 57th and took a stroll through Central Park.

New York was waking up. August lit a cigarette and sat on a bench. He watched this little old lady feed the pigeons, and the joggers and bikers getting their morning exercise. He took it all in, smashed his cigarette on the cement, and headed for Times Square.

The street sweepers and garbage trucks were moving through the soon-to-be-bustling city. The local merchants were opening their stores; trucks were making deliveries. It reminded him of the time when he worked for his father's restaurant in San Pedro, having to get up early to go to the fish market and the produce mart.

He began to walk back to the hotel. Traffic was already at a standstill, horns honking. The sidewalks filled up with men and women formally dressed, walking at a fast pace on their way to Wall Street, the New York Stock Exchange, banks, insurance companies; all of them possibly affected by this 1.25 billion dollar heist he was now involved in.

He stopped at a newsstand and bought the early edition of the *Times*, entered the Drake Hotel lobby, stopping at the concierge desk.

"May I help you, sir?"

"Restaurant open for breakfast?"

"I'm sorry; our restaurant is open for lunch and dinner only. Our coffee shop is open. It's very popular with the locals. If you turn left at the elevator, and go past the gift shops, you'll run into it."

"Thank you."

He found the coffee shop, took a table by the window, ordered breakfast, unfolded the newspaper, and relaxed.

August got back to his suite at nine. He spotted the message light flashing on the hotel phone. *Hmmm, awfully early for a response. Can't be good.*

He picked up the phone, hit the message button, and retrieved his messages.

"August, it's Billy, see you at quarter to eleven."

Next message: "Hi, it's Laura, I'm free for lunch, call me."

It was only nine-thirty so he grabbed the remote and turned on *Good Morning America* for the morning news. By ten-thirty, nothing was on TV except soap operas, so he turned it off and called Mickey in California.

"It's August, how's it going?"

"Going good."

"Any heat around the boats?"

"No, and nothing around home or the warehouses."

"Have you heard from Brian in Thailand about our new venture?"

"I just spoke to him a couple of hours ago. We're going to have to get a mule ready to deliver the down payment for the first shipment."

"I shouldn't be here too much longer. Contact Jerry and put him on call; we can trust him to go to Thailand for us. If Brian calls, tell him I'm out of town and that I will be back in a few days."

"Any luck?"

"Not yet, but I have a meeting this morning."

"Good luck. Talk to you later."

At twenty to eleven, there was a rap at the door. August walked over and opened it. "Buongiorno," said Billy, as he walked in with Sweet Willy, and another guy that August didn't recognize; behind them were his bodyguards. They sat down and got right to business.

"Hey, goomba," said Billy, "we'd like to do this, but you know—that Lufthansa heist caused a lot of heat to come down on the boys. It's hard for us to get them interested now."

The Lufthansa heist occurred at JFK on December 11, 1978. Five million in cash and $875,000 in jewels were stolen, making it the largest cash theft ever committed on American soil. People in the Lucchese family had accomplished that heist, but all the families were involved to some degree.

"The timing's bad; you'd have to sit on these for at least a year or so." Billy pulled the Drake Hotel envelope from the inside pocket of his overcoat and handed it to August.

"Not safe to walk around with this paper, for either party. Want me to hold on to this for you, Dage?"

"No, that's okay, I've got it taken care of," said August.

"I'll look in another direction to see if anyone's interested. In the meantime, I think you should pay a visit to the Jews and seek their advice."

"You know, that's a damn good idea. They control a lot of financial institutions domestically and internationally."

Bill and Willy stood—the meeting was over. They shook hands, hugged, and left the suite leaving August contemplating his next move.

Now that August knew he was free for the rest of the day, he gave Laura a call at her hotel.

"This is Laura."

"It's Tony, lunch still on?"

"Sure, I know a great place and it's close to my hotel."

"How about eleven-thirty? I'll take a cab to your hotel."

"Okay, I'll meet you in the lobby."

August hung up and called Ken in Florida.

"Ken, it's August."

"How you been?"

"I'm in New York; I'd like to talk to you and Slim."

"When would you like to meet?"

"How about tomorrow? Can you send up a plane to get me?"

"Remember the hassle the last time with the DEA? I don't need to go through that again," said Ken. "Aug, what's this all worth?"

"Beaucoup bucks."

"Cool. We'll have a plane pick you up at the same airport."

"What time?"

"Say, eleven tomorrow evening?"

August knew the drill. Ken was actually referring to morning. "Great, I'll be there."

"I look forward to seeing you; maybe we'll have time to go fishing."

"Yeah, and catch a big marlin." They just said, in code, that August was looking for someone or something and it was a big deal.

"Oh, one other thing, the pilot's a tall skinny guy and he'll be wearing a black jacket."

"I'll look for him; see you soon."

August now had the bonds in his possession. *Where should I stash these?* He decided to call the front desk and reserve a safety deposit box.

He took a quick look in the mirror; satisfied, he left the suite, took the elevator to the lobby, deposited the bonds in the security box, and went out and hailed a cab. August jumped into the cab. "Where to?" asked the driver in a Middle Eastern accent.

"The Regency Hotel."

The driver pulled up to the Regency right on time. "I'll be right back." He walked into the lobby and spotted Laura. She saw him and waved, then walked up to him and gave him a quick kiss. "I have a cab waiting," said August, a.k.a. Tony Lira.

They walked to the cab and slid into the backseat. "Café Pierre," said Laura. "You ever been there?"

"No, any good?"

"It's been there forever, and it's one of my favorites. You'll love it."

The restaurant was only a mile away; the driver pulled up, they got out, August paid the tab, and gave the cabbie a fat tip.

"Oh, thank you very much." He handed August a card. "My name is Rashid; call me if you need to go anywhere."

The maitre d' smiled. "Two for lunch?"

"Yes."

"Would you like to dine in the lounge?"

The woman pianist in the lounge was playing a Cole Porter song; it sounded great. August looked at Laura, nodded in agreement. "Sounds great."

They followed the maitre d', who showed them to a nice table, away from the bar and near the entertainment.

The pianist began to sing; Laura leaned over and whispered in August's ear, "That's Kathleen Landis, isn't she great? I come here whenever I can."

While Kathleen Landis sang and played Gershwin and Cole Porter favorites, they enjoyed a fabulous lunch and got to know each other better. August paid the tab, leaving a healthy tip. He pulled out the cabbie's business card. "I'll call Rashid to pick us up."

"Why don't we walk back? I'm so full that I'll have a hard time fitting into my costume tonight."

August gave her a look, from her shoes to her beautiful face. "I doubt you'll have any problems, but a walk sounds great. He extended his elbow; Laura hooked her arm in his and gave him a big smile. "Then let's go."

The Radisson was about a mile away; they took their time, enjoying the scenery, while window-shopping on the way. As they neared the hotel, Laura slowed down. "I hate to end our date, but I have to be at the theater by three." She turned and kissed him. "Maybe we can continue our date after the show tonight?"

"You can count on it. I'll see you after the show."

August didn't call Rashid; he just hailed another taxi and went back to his hotel. As he walked into his suite, the phone rang. He walked over and picked up the receiver.

"Hello."

"August, it's Willy. I'd like to talk to you alone. I think I can help relieve you of your burden."

"When can you be here?"

"How about in an hour?"

"I'll be here."

I wonder what Sweet Willy has in mind, and why didn't he bring it up during the meet with Billy?

Sweet Willy's real name was William Kelly. He was born in Belfast, Ireland in 1947, growing up in the Kelly clan, all members of the Irish Republican Army. The IRA's initial strategy was to use force to cause the collapse of the Northern Ireland administration and to inflict enough casualties on the British forces so that the British government would be forced, by public opinion, to withdraw from Ireland. This policy involved the recruitment of volunteers, increasing after Bloody Sunday, and launching attacks against British military and economic targets. The campaign was supported by arms and funding from Libya, and from some groups in the United States.

William fought alongside his friends and family, watching many of them die by the British military.

He was an entrepreneur; he began to smuggle arms and other contraband, and began to lose interest in the fight and the possibility of being killed. He decided to emigrate to the U.S. and increase his business, settling in New York City, building strong ties with the Irish and Italian mobs.

He quickly became a large and successful drug dealer on the East Coast, and a major customer of August's, who later gave him the nickname Sweet Willy, which stuck with him.

August was watching a National Geographic special on TV when Sweet Willy knocked on the door.

August looked through the peephole, then opened the door. "Have a seat. Want a drink?"

"Nah, I'm fine."

August sat in a wing chair facing Willy. "So, what's on your mind?"

"I'll get right to the point. You don't need to go to the fuckin' Jews. Look, Dage, I've got plenty of contacts—give me some time and I'll move those bonds for you."

"What about Billy? Is he part of this?"

"I see no reason to involve him."

"I'm not sure I like that, but how fast can you move them?"

"For that kind of money, it might take time."

"I don't have a lot of time. You have anyone in mind, Willy, let me know, but I'm not giving anyone an exclusive and I'm moving forward."

"Fuck, man, why deal with them? We've worked together for years. Just give me a little time and we'll both benefit."

"I don't think you understand. Billy and his goombahs didn't want to touch the bonds because they're too fuckin' hot. The feds and the treasury department, and who knows who else, are looking for them. I'm not going to sit on this bombshell and wait till it blows up in my face."

"So, you're going to see the Jews in Florida?"

"I've already made the arrangements."

"I'd appreciate it if you let me know how it goes."

"No problem. Like I said, no exclusive. If the Jews want them, fine, if not, the opportunity is open." August stood. "I hate to cut our meeting short, but I have a date tonight with a beautiful woman and I need to get ready."

Sweet Willy got up and they walked toward the door. "No problem, our meeting's over with for now; just let me know the outcome, and in the meantime, I'll start looking for a buyer."

As Willy walked to the elevator, his rage began to boil over. Alone in the elevator, he pushed the button for the lobby. On the way down he thinks, "Fuckin' August is out of his element, and fencing those bonds is going to be tough. That greedy fuck doesn't want to cut me in on the action. Fuck it! I'll wait. If the Jews turn him down, he'll be more motivated to let me in."

August got dressed and took one last look in the mirror; satisfied, he took Rashid's business card out of his wallet and gave him a call.

He took the elevator to the lobby level and waited for his cab. Rashid pulled up and August jumped in. "Thank you very, very much for calling me. Where can I take you?"

"To the Palace Theatre."

"Oh, going to see *La Cage*, very popular. I hope you have a ticket; that show is always sold out."

"I don't need a ticket; I've been invited by a beautiful woman who is in the play."

"You lucky man. Will you need me to pick you up after the play?"

"Yeah, and I'll need you tomorrow morning, if you'll take me to Teterboro Airport."

"No problem, what time do you need to get there?"

"Eleven."

"It's only twelve miles, but lots of traffic. I'll pick you up at 9:30. Okay?"

"That's fine. Don't talk about this tonight when you pick up the woman and me."

"I understand, Rashid's lips are sealed." He pulled in behind the string of cars dropping off people in front of the Palace Theatre.

The cars were moving at a snail's pace; August looked at the meter, pulled out a wad of bills, doubled the amount on the meter, and handed them to Rashid. "Oh, thank you very much."

August jumped out, walked to the entrance, and handed the usher the card he received from Laura. "Good evening, Mr. Lira, please wait here, I'll be right back." The usher returned with his supervisor who escorted August to the front row. He also showed him where to go after the play to gain backstage access.

The lights dimmed, the band began to play, and August sat back and thoroughly enjoyed the play. After three encores with standing ovations, the audience began to pour out of the theater while August gained access to the backstage party.

He ordered a scotch on the rocks from a waitress while waiting for Laura to change. She finally walked in strutting toward him, looking mighty fine. She gave him a kiss on the cheek. "Hi, Tony, did you like the play?"

"It was great, good story, funny as hell, and excellent acting. You were great and looked hot."

The waitress brought August's drink and Laura took a glass of champagne from her tray. They clinked glasses. "Here's to you, and the rest of the cast and crew."

Laura introduced Tony Lira to the stars, the producers, and the director who invited them to a party in his penthouse apartment. Twenty minutes later, they entered the penthouse already filled with the upper echelon of society.

They stepped out on the terrace, overlooking the lights of Manhattan, to have a smoke. "What a beautiful night," said Laura.

"Yeah, too bad it has to end."

Laura slid her hand behind his neck and pulled him close, kissing him long and hard. "It doesn't have to end unless you want it to."

August could feel "Augi Jr." stirring. "Well I certainly don't want to end it here."

"How 'bout we have our own party in my suite?"

"Junior" stirred some more. He hooked her arm. "I see no reason to stick around here any longer."

They stepped out to the curb, and to August's surprise, Rashid pulled up, grinning from ear to ear. He jumped out, ran around the cab, and opened the door. "Very nice to see you again."

"Thanks, Rashid, take us to the Radisson Hotel."

He shut the door, ran around, and jumped in. Ten minutes later, he pulled up in front of the hotel. The fare was nine dollars. August slipped him a fifty; Rashid's eyes popped open.

"Oh, thank you very much. Call me, call me anytime. I am at your service."

Laura inserted her card key and they stepped in. The door barely had time to close before they were at each other hot and heavy. A path of clothes and shoes led to the bedroom where they fell on the bed in the heat of passion.

August thought, "She's way too fine to just jump on her and fuck her. Slow down, make the moment last." He kissed her softly, and continued kissing her neck, then to her shoulders, and down to her breasts, stopping to play with her now hard nipples.

She moaned as she grabbed his head and pushed him down, holding him between her legs. She yelled in ecstasy, as she grabbed his hair and pulled him up; they kissed, tongues intermingling. He entered her and their bodies moved in perfect rhythm, as they both climaxed together.

They lay there panting, dripping with sweat. Laura wanted more and went down on him, fondling and kissing "Little Augi," who started to grow a lot faster than August could imagine. They traded positions as they fine-tuned their lovemaking, moving faster and harder. August thought he was going to have a heart attack as their orgasms took them to another planet.

They fell asleep in each other's arms, August waking up by the natural light from the windows. He looked at his Rolex; it was eight forty-five. Laura must have sensed his movement and rolled over on her side, facing him. He looked into those beautiful sleepy eyes. "Hi."

She smiled. "Good morning." Then she frowned. "You have to go, don't you?"

"Unfortunately, yes."

"Will I see you later?"

August shook his head. "I'm leaving town this morning." *Think. . . what do I say?* "When will you be back in L.A.?"

"In three weeks, then I'll have a week off."

"Maybe we can meet up there?"

"I'd like that," whispered Laura.

He dressed, got her home number, and reluctantly gave her his, but he couldn't resist seeing her again. He called Rashid, who said he would be waiting. They kissed; she hugged him tightly. "I really have to go."

She released her grip, and he left, shuffling backward, taking his last look at the beautiful woman he'd spent the night with, before he stepped into the hall and shut the door.

25

Rashid waited in front of the Drake, while August packed and checked out.

Traffic was heavy, and Rashid pulled up to the private plane area of Teterboro Airport at ten- forty. August spotted the pilot, not tall and skinny in black, per Ken's coded description, but short, stocky, and in white. Rashid got the luggage out of the trunk, and August handed him two one-hundred-dollar bills. "Thanks for being there when I needed you."

"You call me any time you're in New York. Have a nice flight."

While Rashid pulled away, the pilot walked up and held out his hand. "Nice to meet you, Mr. Taracina. My name is Rudy; we're ready to go." He waved him in, "Welcome aboard."

August climbed the airstairs and took a seat in a large leather chair. Rudy secured the door. "Want anything? Drink, coffee?"

"No thanks, I'm just going to put the headphones on, listen to some music, and get some rest."

"Enjoy the flight; if you need anything, let me know."

Rudy went back to the cockpit, radioed the tower, and ten minutes later they were flying to Florida. An hour into the flight the plane hit an air pocket, the jolt waking August. He got out of his seat, went to the head and took a leak. Then he went into the kitchen, got a Corona out of the fridge and took it to his seat.

He thought about the last year and how many things had changed. His operation was getting too much heat; he might be forced to shut down, at least for a while. And here he was, running all over the world trying to peddle a huge commodity that he wasn't familiar with, not having a whole lot of success.

He wondered if these fuckin' bonds had caused him to be less effective with his smuggling operation, making him begin to lose his edge. But the more he thought about it, the more he realized that it was just an era coming to an end.

He chugged down his beer, put on the headphones, and fell back to sleep.

* * *

While August flew to Florida, Special Agents Greg O'Riley and John Ling pulled up to the Marriott at 8:00 A.M. Pacific Standard Time, parked, went into the lobby, and called Nick's room.

"It's Greg, I'm in the lobby."

"We're all packed; see you in a minute."

Nick, Leo, and the pilots checked out; the five of them had breakfast in the hotel coffee shop. They squeezed into the Crown Vic and Greg drove to the airport, dropped off the pilots at the FBI's Gulfstream so they could refuel and register a flight plan, then drove to the Western Airlines office.

They entered the building and showed their credentials to the secretary. "We have a meeting with Harvy Stone," said Greg.

She picked up the receiver and pushed the intercom button. "Mr. Stone, Greg O'Riley from the FBI is here to see you." She hung up. "He'll be right out."

A portly, bald-headed guy dressed in a tailored dark blue suit hustled up to them and shook hands. "Harvy Stone, General Manager."

"Nice to meet you. I'm Special Agent Greg O'Riley, from the San Francisco office, and this is Nick Cutler and Leo Panetta, special agents from our Los Angeles office. Nick is the case leader in this investigation."

"Please follow me to my office."

They all sat down. "I'm aware of the incident regarding Flight 1757. So how can I help you?" Stone asked.

"The flight originated from Sea-Tac, stopped here, its final destination was Los Angeles International. We feel that San Francisco was the best locale for the theft," said Greg.

"You have got to be kidding. There's no way that could happen. There was no bonded cargo loaded or unloaded on Flight 1757 while it was here," said the General Manager of Western Airlines.

"Well, the FBI will determine that. I'll need you to provide us with the shipping manifests and passenger list before the flight landed, who disembarked and who boarded the plane. I'll also need a list of Western employees with even a remote connection to Flight 1757."

Nick could see that Stone wasn't too happy about all the demands, and butted in, "We'll also

need a list of trucking companies that picked up or delivered any cargo for that flight and any freight forwarders involved."

"Anything else?" Stone asked, in a perturbed voice.

Greg asked, "Do you have any surveillance cameras in the docking area?"

"No, only in the gate waiting and baggage claim area. But after this, I'm sure we will."

After the meeting, Greg drove back to the plane and parked. "Why don't we have our meeting onboard?" said Nick.

"Great, I'd like to see the interior," Greg said, as the four of them got out of the car.

As they sat down John Lee looked around. "Now this is definitely nice. So what do you want to talk about?"

"I've got this feeling that we're not going to find out anything from the information that we receive from Western or Brinks. Start putting pressure on your informants. Someone's going to brag about how they snuck these bags out, right under airport security," said Nick.

"Or they might hear about someone trying to sell the bonds," said Leo.

"I have to agree with you guys, but we still have to go through the process," said Ling.

"It'd be nice if we knew the exact contents of those bags," said Greg.

"Well, let's hope we learn something when we're up in Seattle," said Nick.

Sensing that the meeting was over, Greg asked, "Is that it?"

"Yeah, I guess so."

They shook hands. "Have a good flight, and I'll let you know if I hear anything."

John and Greg left and Nick stuck his head into the cockpit. "We're ready to go."

Two hours later, John got on the P.A. system. "We'll be landing in a few minutes, buckle up."

He received landing instructions and followed a United Airlines DC-10 into Sea-Tac International Airport, landed, and then taxied to a designated area for government planes. They opened the door and stepped down the airstairs. It was cloudy and drizzling—typical weather for the Seattle area. A black Crown Vic rolled to a stop next to them.

A guy, six-foot-two, with dark brown hair and built like a weightlifter, climbed out. "Hey Nick, traveling in style; you get promoted or something?"

They shook hands. "Nah, just a high profile case, Daryl. The boss doesn't want any delays."

Daryl worked in the Los Angeles office and was a friend of Nick's. They waited for the pilots to secure the plane, and then Daryl drove them into Seattle where they checked into the Monaco Hotel, which was a block from the FBI office.

"I set up a briefing with my squad tomorrow morning at eight," said Daryl.

Nick looked at his watch. "Why don't we have a meeting in my room, then I'll take you out to dinner."

"Just me and you?"

"Maybe you could arrange to have a couple of women join us?"

"That could be possible; how about tomorrow night?"

Nick chuckled, and turned to Leo and the pilots. "Dinner's on me tonight, but tomorrow you're on your own."

They took the elevator to the concierge level, where Daryl booked two rooms. "They serve complimentary cocktails and appetizers in the hospitality suite at five-thirty. I'm sure no one will be in there until then. Might be more comfortable having our meeting there," said Daryl.

"Sounds good, so let's put our bags in our room and get started," said Nick.

Nick told the pilots to meet them at five-thirty, and then they went to their room. "I'm sorry about booking only two rooms. I didn't know you had two pilots with you," said Daryl.

"It won't be the first time Nick and I have shared a room. At least it has two queen-size beds."

"Let's get to business, I want to take a shower before we go to dinner," said Nick.

They walked over to the hospitality suite. No one was in there so they took a corner table by the window. Nick went over the details of the missing bags, and the meeting they had with Western's V.P. and the Brinks official.

"Leo and I both think the bags somehow walked off the plane in San Francisco. But, it could have happened here."

"Certainly doesn't appear that it happened in Los Angeles."

"Well, no matter how or where they disappeared, the flight originated here and there's a lot of work to do. How many agents in your squad?"

"Twelve, including me."

"Good, because you're going to have to go to Seattle's clearinghouse to get records from every brokerage firm that sent documents, which were consolidated there, and find out what type of documents were sent, serial numbers, and their value. We'll need that information before the bureau will be able to trace any of the certificates and bonds being cashed."

"I wonder how many brokerage houses are involved?" asked Daryl.

"Six large bags weighing over fifty pounds each—I suspect

there's a lot of them," Leo said.

"You'll need to interview Western, Brinks, trucking companies, freight forwarders, and clearinghouse and brokerage firm employees connected with this shipment. Check phone records, unscheduled vacations, absenteeism. Hell, you know the drill," said Nick.

"Oh yeah, this is going to take some time. I think I'll split my squad into two groups, assigning eight agents to work the clearinghouse and the brokerage firms, and four, including me, following up on the employees and connected businesses."

"That's what I'd do," said Nick.

Hotel guests were beginning to come in for a drink, including the pilots, John and Roger. Leo looked at his watch, "Time for cocktails and something to eat." Leo stood up and walked over to the bar.

Later, they went out to dinner, got back to the hotel, and hit the sack. The following morning Leo and Nick were up at six, got ready, had the complimentary breakfast, then walked to the FBI building and met Daryl in his office. They walked over to the conference room and met the squad. Daryl and Nick shared the briefing. Nick left the details to Daryl.

Nick and Leo spent the day talking to the squad in L.A. and San Francisco, while Daryl assigned his agents.

At the end of the day, Daryl walked over to Nick. "Well, we got lucky. One of the girls I've been dating has a girlfriend visiting her and they're free for this evening."

While Nick was getting ready for his hot date, Leo and the two pilots went to the hospitality suite for appetizers and cocktails. Daryl walked in and joined them; Nick came in a minute later.

Daryl finished his drink. "Ready to go?"

"Are you kidding? He's been grooming himself since we got to the hotel," chuckled Leo.

"Yeah, and while you guys sit here and slop up drinks, we're going to party," said Nick.

"Pretty fuckin' optimistic. You know, she could be a dog."

"If she's anything like the girl I date, you'd be trying to hump her doggy-style," said Daryl, laughing as he and Nick walked out of the room.

Leo took the pilots to dinner at a sports bar restaurant, watched the Lakers beat the Celtics, and then went back to the hotel. He didn't see Nick until he walked in at six-thirty the following morning, with a shit-eatin' grin on his face.

"Looks like you had a good time," said Leo.

"Wow, that girl wore me out. I can hardly wait till we come back to Seattle. Hell, if we don't, I'll come up and meet her on my own. We ready to go?"

"We planned to leave here at six. Why the hell do you think I'd be dressed?"

"Pilots ready?"

"Yeah, they're in their room."

"Get them; Daryl's waiting for us," said Nick, while he packed up his bag.

Daryl pulled up next to the Gulfstream. "Have a good flight. Let me know when you're coming back up, I'll make sure Cindy invites Nicole over," he chuckled.

"I'm looking forward to it. Talk to you soon."

The pilots finished the preflight check; they boarded the jet and took off for Los Angeles.

26

Sixth day: August lands in Miami

August felt a hand on his shoulder, shaking him. "August, we'll be landing in fifteen minutes."

He must have been sound asleep and felt groggy as hell. "Thanks, Rudy."

The pilot headed back to the cockpit. August got up, went to the head, washed his face with cold water, then went to the galley and got a Coke out of the refrigerator, return to his seat and buckled up for the landing.

Rudy landed the plane, and then taxied to the executive airport. While Rudy shut down, the co-pilot opened the door. August grabbed his suitcase and climbed down the airstairs. He could see Ken and Slim sitting in a silver 450 SEL Mercedes, waiting for him.

All of a sudden, someone in a dark blue sedan drives up screeching to a halt, blocking his way to the Mercedes. Two guys jump out, holding their badges so August could see them. "DEA, you just get out of that jet?"

"Yeah," said August.

"So what's your name?"

"What's yours?"

"Don't be a wise ass."

"Wait a minute. I'm not the one being rude. You guys damn near ran me over, and came out flashing your badges. What's the deal?"

"Okay, let's start all over. I'm Agent Larsen and this is Agent

Roark. What's your name?"

"Tony Lira."

"I need to take a look in your bag," said Agent Larsen.

"You have a search warrant?"

"No, but we have the right to keep you here while we get one. Might take a few hours."

August set the suitcase on the tarmac. "Be my guest."

The agents knelt down and rifled through his bag, while August felt his ass pucker, knowing that the bonds were only inches from their hands.

They stood up; Agent Roark walked away from them and got on his mobile radio. August could see Ken and Slim watching, as he stood there for thirty minutes, while the agents talked on their radios.

August thought, "Maybe they think I'm a Colombian drug smuggler or something?"

Agent Larsen walked up to him. "Okay, Mr. Lira, you're free to go." The agent turned and got into the sedan with his partner and sped away, leaving August standing there with his suitcase wide open with three million-dollar bearer bonds hidden in the lining.

He shut the suitcase, walked over to the limo and got in. "What the fuck was that all about?" Ken and Slim laughed. "Fuck um, they're just a bunch of Keystone Cops, don't worry about it," said Ken. "Good to see you. How was your flight?"

"Great, I slept all the way."

"So, what's this big deal you want to talk about?" asked Slim.

"I really need to talk to your associates," said August.

"I hope there's something in this for Ken and me."

"There is, if the Jews are interested," said August.

"So what are we talkin' about?" asked Ken.

"Just tell them I have something they might be interested in that I need to unload."

"Well, you'll be staying at the Jockey Club, right next-door to their building, the Jai-Alai Club," said Ken. The driver pulled up to the entrance of the Jockey Club, a huge condominium complex.

"Why don't you check in and get comfortable. Go to the gym; take a steam, a sauna, and a facial," he chuckled, "and a massage with a happy ending. Whatever you want. I'll set up a meeting with the boys for some time this afternoon. We'll see you later." The driver left.

August walked up to the reservation counter and was met by a good-looking woman. "May I help you?"

"Yes, I'd like to check in."

"Your name?"

"August Taracina."

She typed in his name. "You're already checked in." She handed him a card key. "Your suite is on the top floor, number 26C. Sign for any charges at the club. Enjoy your stay."

August smiled as he headed for the elevator. *Should have known those guys would set me up, and they still don't know what I have.* He looked at his Rolex. *Think I'll take Ken's advice and go to the spa and order the works, including that happy ending.*

The Jai-Alai Club was owned by the Jewish Mob and the Teamsters Union and was the hangout for the guys. It was extremely private and when they wanted to have meetings, they held them away from their own premises. They knew the feds were monitoring and surveilling the place. Meyer Lansky, who died in January 1983, lived at the Jai-Alai Club in a suite. The notorious gangster was under surveillance twenty-four seven and the feds continued to watch the Jai-Alai Club after his death.

Now, completely content and relaxed, August sat on his balcony enjoying the view. The phone rang; he got up, went in, and answered it.

"It's Ken. These guys usually have their meeting elsewhere but they want to meet at the Jai-Alai Club at five. We're all going to dinner after the meeting. We'll pick you up at ten minutes to five."

"Great, see you then."

August got ready, carefully slit open the lining in his suitcase, and pulled out the bonds. On the way back to his room, he purchased a leather notebook from the lobby general store, and slid the bonds between the 8½ x 11 yellow notepad.

He took a last look in the mirror, left his suite and took the elevator to the lobby. A limo was already at the curb. August kept walking and climbed into the rear, joining Ken and Slim.

While Ken and Slim's driver took them next-door, the Jews were having the meeting room swept for bugs. Their technician left the room and informed Hal that it was clean so the group filed into the room and waited for their guest to arrive.

The three walked into the Jai-Alai Club's lobby and were met by one of the club's security men. "Good afternoon, I'll escort you to your meeting."

They followed this well-built, military-type guy to the elevator, and rode to the twelfth floor. The door opened and two more security men were standing there. They motioned for them to follow, stopped in front of an unmarked door, knocked, and then opened it.

August followed Ken and Slim into the room, the door shutting behind them. There were six guys sitting at a boardroom-type table. One of them stood and walked over to greet them. While shaking their hands he said, "Hey, Ken, how's it going? Slim, good to see you. August, never had the pleasure of meeting you personally, but we appreciate your contribution to our operation. Come on over, I'll introduce you to the guys."

Introductions were made; then Hal asked them if they wanted a drink. All nine of them got up, went to the bar, served themselves, talked a little, went back to the table, and sat down. There were a couple of platters of appetizers on the table, and the guys helped themselves.

"So, August, Ken and Slim asked for this meeting. They said you had something that we might be interested in," said Hal.

August knew he'd better not to be too ambiguous. He opened his notepad and pulled out the folded bonds. "About a week ago, I came into possession of some one-million-dollar bearer bonds. Obviously, they're hot, and I would like to unload them, at a large discount."

"How many of these bonds do you have?" asked one of the guys.

"Three hundred fifty."

That got everyone's attention, including Ken and Slim's.

"Can I take a look?" asked the president of an offshore bank.

"Sure." August, seated directly across from him, reached over and handed him the three bonds.

The banker carefully unfolded one of the bonds and studied it for a minute. "This was just issued, maturity date 2004."

"So what do you think?" asked Hal.

The president looked at August. "These aren't counterfeit, are they?"

"If they were, I would have told you so. As far as I know, they're the real thing."

The bank president said, "I think we should look into this further." He looked at August. "Mind if we keep these for a day or two?"

August knew they would want to have them examined. "No, not at all."

"What are you looking to get for these?"

"I'd like to get ten cents on the dollar."

"That's not unreasonable; we should be able to give you an answer around this time tomorrow."

That was the end of the meeting. Hal got on the phone and a minute later a bartender and a waitress appeared. Drinks flowed and the platters of appetizers disappeared. Hal announced that it was time to go to dinner. They took the elevator to the lobby; Ken, Slim, and August got into their limo, and followed the boys in their cars.

They caravanned out of the city in their Rolls Royces, Ferraris, and Mercedes. They turned onto a dirt road, making August a bit uncomfortable, considering the thoughts that dirt roads conjure in criminal history and crime literature. The dirt road ran next to a channel that eventually opened up into a bayou, with weeping willow trees, and tall reeds bordering the shoreline. The Venetian restaurant stood in the center of the grove of trees, at the water's edge.

They pulled up to the old establishment and parked alongside a Rolls and another limo. When August walked through the front double doors, it was like walking into Little Italy. There were four waiters catering to the patrons sitting around the huge, and only, table in the restaurant. A trio was playing one of Dean Martin's songs, "Return to Me." One musician played an accordion, another sang, while strumming his mandolin, the third kept the rhythm on his bass guitar. There weren't any other customers in the restaurant.

Hal motioned for August to take a seat next to an older man. August was in his mid-thirties and he thought the guy was at least in his seventies. "I thought the two of you might have something in common, since you're both from California," said Hal.

August turned to the older gentleman. While shaking hands, he introduced himself. "August Taracina; so what do you do in California?"

The older guy smiled. "I'm in the agriculture business, and my name is Ernest."

"What do you grow?"

"Grapes."

Ernest waved to a waiter, who walked up to him. "Why don't you pour some champagne, and uncork a few bottles of wine? It's over thirty years old and it needs to breathe awhile."

Corks popped on four bottles of 1955 Louis Roederer, Cristal Champagne. It was poured into the crystal flutes in front of all the guests. Several people made toasts. August was never into champagne, but after a couple of sips of Cristal, he had no problem accepting a second glassful.

It was a seven-course prix fixe dinner and August thought that every course topped the last one. They poured vintage 1950 Mouton Rothschild wine, made up of 85% cabernet sauvignon, 10% Cabernet Franc, and 5% merlot. August knew that this wine went for $500 to $1000 a bottle. The vintage they were drinking was over thirty years old. It had to have come from someone's private cellar because none would be for sale on the open market. August guessed that they went through a couple of cases during a meal he would never forget.

The following morning, August had a late breakfast at the Marina Restaurant, took a four-mile walk on the Esplanade, taking in the sunshine, admiring the yachts and the bikini-clad women.

He got back to his room at the Jockey Club at ten-thirty; the message light was blinking on his phone. It was Ken. "Call me when you get in."

August picked up the receiver and dialed his number. "Good morning. I presume you heard from the boys?"

"Just a few minutes ago. That's why I called. They want to meet at five for dinner."

"I walked four miles this morning. I'm headed for the gym just to burn off last night's feast, then get a massage. They say anything?"

"Not a word. We'll pick you up at ten minutes to five."

"See you later." August hung up, called the spa, made an appointment for an hour and a half massage at twelve, went to the gym and worked out. At eleven thirty, he took a steam, then a sauna, showered and headed to the spa's counter to check in for his massage.

He was greeted by a total fox, with long blond hair, a beautiful face, blue eyes, and an aerobics bodysuit painted on her awesome body. She smiled. "I'm Sandy. Ready for your massage, Mr. Taracina?"

He felt himself getting aroused. *Oh boy, I can hardly wait for the happy ending.* "Looking forward to it."

He followed her, unable to keep his eyes off her shapely ass. She opened the door to one of the private rooms where a massage table sat in the center. "Take off your clothes and get between the sheets; I'll be right back."

Forget the massage and get between the sheets with me!

Soft jazz played through the ceiling speakers, the room smelled of mint coming from a lit scented candle, which was the only light in the room. Ten minutes went by and he began to drift off, when the door opened. "Sorry for the delay, this is Ramona, our best masseuse. Enjoy your massage."

August was on his stomach and could only raise his head up halfway. All he could see was Ramona's three-foot-wide hips. He turned onto his side, and wished he hadn't, after he got a good look at her.

She said hello, in a low-pitched Eastern European accent, then she pushed him back on his face, poured some warm oil on his back, and started kneading out every tight muscle in his body.

At first, he was bummed out, no Sandy, and no happy ending. But after fifteen minutes, he knew he was getting the best massage ever.

After forty-five minutes, Ramona had August turn over onto his back. She started massaging his feet and worked up to his shoulders. He began to float into a black hole, leaving all negative thoughts behind. As he fell deeper into the abyss, Ramona's vigorous massage faded and slimmer fingers were rubbing his temples and head.

"Feel good?"

August recognized Sandy's voice. "Ohhh, yeah." Then his dream came true.

* * *

August was standing at the curb at quarter to five, smoking a cigarette. Five minutes later, Ken and Slim's limo pulled up. He dropped the cigarette onto the pavement, smashed it under his shoe, and slid into the limo.

"You look content."

"Best fucking massage I've ever had."

"So you met Sandy?"

"Did you have something to do with that?"

"Might have."

"I owe you one."

They laughed until the driver pulled up to the Jai-Alai Club. They were met by the same guy who escorted them to the same meeting room. This time Hal was the only one waiting for them.

Everyone hugged, poured a drink, and took a seat. Hal turned to August. "We spent all morning discussing our interest in the bonds. We are interested, but these bonds are new and extremely hot. It wouldn't be wise for us to take possession of them right now. We would like you to sit on them for a couple of years, and then we'd take them off your hands. Give the guys some money and tell them they're just going to have to wait it out. I can see by the expression on your face that you're not thrilled with our offer, but it is as solid as money in the bank. Think about it. If someone else steps up to the plate, we'll understand."

He held out his hand and they shook on it, while he gave August the bonds. "Now that our business is over, let's have another drink and go to dinner."

They took one limo to the hottest place in Miami, the Forge Restaurant. They passed a long line of Rolls Royces, Mercedes, Ferraris, and limos, and pulled in front of them. As the valet walked toward the limo, Hal got out. The valet stopped in his tracks. "Mr. Cantor, so good to see you."

They piled out of the limo and the guard at the front door allowed them to enter this swanky-to-the-max restaurant. The male patrons looked as if they were competing to see who could wear the most gold chains, while the women showed off all their diamond rings, bracelets, and necklaces.

August had been to the famous Buccaneer Club, and other popular restaurants in Miami, but this was his first time at Forge Restaurant.

August knew that with all the English oak paneling and Tiffany glass the prices for the haute cuisine would be steep. The elegant dining room featured high ceilings, ornate chandeliers, and European artwork. The atmosphere was elegant but not too stuffy, and he knew that the who's who of Miami society gathered there for dinner, dancing, and schmoozing.

They followed the maitre d' to their table and took a seat. As he passed out the menus, he said, "Our appetizers are mostly classics, from Beluga caviar to escargot. Stone crabs are in season and I highly recommend them, but as Mr. Cantor knows, The Forge is especially known for its award-winning steaks." He handed the wine list to Hal. "Your waiters will take your cocktail orders, and as you know, we have the most extensive wine list in South Florida, second only to Burns Steakhouse.

"I will make sure that we have a table and chairs ready for you and your guests in the lounge. We will ready your private locker in our humidor for your selections. Shall I have your favorite Cognac served to your guests?"

"That would be fine. Thank you, David," said Hal.

August was seldom intimidated, but these guys were so high profile, that it made him feel a little uncomfortable. He didn't like their offer and had no intention of holding onto the bonds for two or three years.

August still had the biggest hot potato around. He intended to unload the bonds as quickly as possible. Ken and Slim smuggled for them, and they set up the meet, so he had to be very diplomatic when he backed out of their offer. He thought it would be better to wait awhile, come back for a visit, tell them and thank them personally.

It was a perfect evening. The food and wine were excellent. They had a ball in the lounge, smoking Cuban cigars and drinking thirty-year-old port and Louis the XIII Cognac.

The following morning, August called Sweet Willy.

"How'd it go?" asked Willy.

"They were interested, but wanted me to sit on the bonds for a couple of years."

"So, are you going to give me some time to move them?"

"Hey, man, I already told you, there's no exclusive."

"You expect me to talk up this deal and get someone all pumped up, while you peddle them off to another buyer?"

"Look, Willy, there's not a big line of people waiting to snap these bonds up. It's going to take some time and I'm keeping all my options open. But I don't intend to have a bunch of guys out there brokering these things.

"At this point there are three parties that know I have the bonds. Two were potential buyers that turned me down and the other, is you. It's not an exclusive, but it's as close as you're going to get. If you have a solid buyer, let me know, and I'll fly out to meet them."

"Okay, August, I'll let you know. Thanks for calling." Willy hung up, lay back on his recliner and took a sip of his martini. "Fuck!"

August was packed and ready to get back to L.A. He met with Ken and Slim at the club's restaurant. They planned to bring in a load of marijuana from South Africa called "Durbin Poison." He said he'd let them know. They walked out of the Jockey Club; another car was parked behind Ken and Slim's Mercedes with two guys in it. "Tim and Jerry will take you to the airport and escort you back to Los Angeles on our jet," said Ken.

"Great, I can't wait to get back." They hugged and shook hands. "Thanks for everything," said August, as he jumped into the backseat.

Tim and Jerry were ex-cops from Los Angeles and ex-CIA operatives. After they got out, a mutual associate, Mr. Dillon, introduced them to Ken and Slim, who hired them to take care of their security.

They escorted everyone of importance and were in charge of any moneys to be picked up or paid out. The two guys would take control of any money or drugs when transported, but August kept the bonds hidden in his suitcase; the two guys never knew about them.

It had been a late night and August slept most of the way back to L.A. August's nephew was waiting to pick him up at the Santa Monica Airport, to drive him home.

As August got settled in, Mickey walked in. "How'd it go?"

"Not all that great. The boys from New York don't want them. They say they're too hot. The Jews in Florida don't want to pass up making a buck, but they want me to sit on them for two or three years before they can get me a good return for them. These fucking things are becoming a bigger hassle than they're worth. How's everything going on the home front?"

"Good and quiet, just the way we like it. You did get a visit from Jimmy Crittenden. He says he's got access to some tonnage of weed from Arizona that he'd like you to help him with."

"Yeah, okay, I'll page him tomorrow. I did get a page from Carolyn. I hope it's not about that fuckin' Belson. Why don't you call her for me? See what's going on."

27

Eighth day

After no success with the mob back East or the Jews, August decided to take a couple of days off to regroup, and figure out what to do next. He decided to give Scott a call.

"Hey, Scott, before you say anything, we need to meet."

"I understand, where?"

"Why don't you bring your family down to Redondo Beach Pier on Sunday? We'll have lunch."

"Where?"

"I'll meet you on the pier; see you at eleven-thirty." August hung up.

Scott wondered what all that cloak-and-dagger instruction was all about. Why bring the family? Then he recalled the meeting he had with the FBI, and figured out that August was just being careful.

It was a clear, warm Sunday. Scott pulled his Cherokee up to the tollbooth, grabbed a parking ticket, and drove into the underground garage at the pier. His kids were excited and dragged their parents through the shadowy concrete gloom and out onto the pier.

Scott told Karen that an old friend, Sal Marino, was meeting them there and wanted to take them to lunch. The pier was packed with people—tourists shopping in stores, buying fish and chips, corn dogs, and smoked fish from the open markets.

There was a long line in front of Quality Sea Food, hungry weekenders waiting to buy fresh steamed crabs, rent small hammers to crack open the shells, feast on the delicious meat, while sitting watching the crowds, enjoying the view and the cool ocean breeze.

The kids wanted everything but Scott told them he didn't want them to ruin their lunch. He promised to buy them anything they wanted for dessert.

August walked up to Scott, who immediately started to introduce his family. "Sal, this is my wife, Karen, and my kids, Kati and Josh. Say hello to an old friend of mine from high school."

"Hi, Sal," said the kids in unison.

"I haven't been down here in a long time but Tony's was a good restaurant. Why don't we have lunch there?" August scanned the area. It was packed with people, a good place to melt into the crowd. They walked into the renowned restaurant; August asked for a window table and the maitre d' showed them to one.

They ordered, while talking about the kids, and their excitement about the outing. Then August asked Karen, "I need to talk to Scott about something, maybe the kids shouldn't hear."

Karen being preoccupied with her kids, shrugged her shoulders, and waved them off.

The guys walked over to the bar and took a table. A waitress walked up. "Can I help you?"

"Two Coors on tap," said August. "So I'm sure you want to know how I'm progressing. I've been to New York and Florida to visit some people; I know they were interested. Both of them passed. I still have a few more ideas but this isn't going to be easy. How's everything on your side?"

"The FBI paid us a visit at work. It was routine but they were thorough. The meeting was held in my supervisor's office and I did most of the talking. I think it went okay."

"I had a feeling the FBI would have seen you by now. That's why I didn't want to discuss anything on the phone. If they have a team working on this—and I'm sure they do—they'll bug your phones or follow you around to see if you do anything to appear suspicious. That's why I had you bring your family with you."

"I'll be careful and remind the other guys to do the same."

"Good, we'll keep in touch." The waitress brought the beers to the table. August pulled out a ten. "Keep the change." He stood and grabbed his beer. "We'd better get back to your family."

They finished lunch, said their goodbyes and left. August said he had to go to the restroom and excused himself, letting the McCann family leave before him. They would not be seen together by any surveillance crew who might be loitering about.

28

Ninth day

August decided to call one of his friends, a business associate in San Francisco. Andy was an occasional mover for August, not the sofa and end table type with a "Starving Students" sign on his truck. He was a good guy, one who could be trusted implicitly.

He met Andy through his Pacific Northwest distributor, an old friend and business associate of August's in the seventies who ended up disappearing right after a large boat smuggle came in. His name was Mr. Dillon. He went out one day and never came home, never to be heard from or seen again.

Dillon was a smuggler with flare; a Southern California guy who moved to Marin County in the seventies. He gained notoriety when he was smuggling in hashish in the bottom of bear and tiger cages, coming from the Far East. He was one of the good ones who was robbed of his life at an early age.

After Dillon's disappearance, or perhaps murder (August bet the odds were much higher that he was murdered), August asked Andy to take over the territory. He would ship 1,000 to 5,000 pounds of marijuana, as needed, to Andy, who now effectively handled the Northwest corridor for him out of his warehouse.

He knew Andy was well connected; he told him about the bonds.

"I know these Chinese businessmen out of Vancouver, British Columbia. They're part of the Chinese Triad, in Hong Kong. They emigrated to Canada and used Triad money to set up legitimate companies there. They definitely have the money and the connections."

"Good, set something up. I'll be happy to fly up to Vancouver to talk to them," said August.

"No need to fly to Vancouver; they own an office building right here. Their trading business occupies the complete top floor. That's their 'legitimate' business, but the whole Triad operation on the West Coast reports to them."

"You trust these people?"

"Not the lower echelon, but I do trust one of the bosses, Young Lee. He's always been my contact with the Triad gangs; they're one of our biggest customers."

"Well, I guess it's time to meet him. Set up a meet and get back to me."

Later that day, August received a phone call from Andy. "I spoke to Young Lee; he wants to meet with us tomorrow at 8:00 P.M. for dinner at the Dragon's Breath Restaurant in the Chinatown district."

"Great, I'll get one of my friends to fly me up there in the morning."

"I'll pick you up; just let me know where and when."

"Thanks, Andy, see you mañana."

August called his close buddy, Tony Amana. "Tony, it's August, would you like to take a trip to San Francisco?"

Tony worked with August in the seventies, made a ton of money, and invested it safely, buying apartment buildings in the South Bay Area. He decided to retire from the smuggling business but still worked with August moving money around.

He owned a 1982 Beechcraft King Air Turbo-Prop, the Rolls Royce of private aircraft, financed by August, who preferred to keep the plane in Tony's name, but ready to use for business. It never transported drugs, only VIPs and associates.

"Sounds fun; when do you want to leave?" asked Tony.

"Nine A.M. that okay with you?"

"No problem. I'll meet you at the hangar."

August woke up at six, took a shower and got ready for the trip.

He pried open the floorboards and pulled one bond from his secret compartment. He opened his overnight suitcase, slid the bond between the linings, packed and left his house.

He got into his Carrera and drove to the Hot 'N Tot for breakfast, an institution on Pacific Coast Highway in Lomita. He chuckled, as he walked in, remembering the night the DEA agents, a.k.a. "the fishermen" followed him there. He sat at the counter and ordered a Denver omelet, and a pot of coffee.

After breakfast, he drove to nearby Torrance Airport, parked, and met Tony at the hangar. "She's fueled up and ready to go. I already filed the flight plan, so hop in and let's get going."

Tony started the port engine, then the starboard, and got on the microphone. "Torrance tower, this is Beechcraft King Air Alpha, Foxtrot 498, requesting take-off instructions."

"King Air Alpha Foxtrot 498, you're cleared for take-off after the Cessna now turning onto the runway."

As they cleared the hangar, they could see the Cessna taking off so they proceeded to the runway. Tony spoke to the air controller, revved up the twin turboprops, released the brakes, and sped down the runway.

They took off and leveled at ten thousand feet as directed, until they were out of the LAX air traffic zone, then Tony took her higher, to twenty thousand feet.

"You want to take it for a while?"

"Sure."

"It's all yours. Want something to drink, non-alcoholic of course."

"A Coke would be fine."

August thought about the upcoming meeting. He really didn't know these guys. It made him uneasy, and if that wasn't enough to make him uncomfortable, he still didn't know how much these bonds were really worth.

They were nearing San Francisco International. Tony radioed flight control and received landing instructions, made a perfect landing, then taxied to the private plane section of the airport.

They got out and secured the Beechcraft, then walked toward the parking area where August spotted Andy standing by his Mercedes, having a smoke.

"Andy, it's so good to see you," said August.

"Good to see you, guys. How was the flight?"

"Great, clear skies and no head wind," said Tony.

They shook hands and got into the car.

"I booked two deluxe rooms at the Ritz Carlton for one night; you can extend your stay if necessary, they're not busy. You want to have lunch before you check in?"

"Tony, you hungry?"

"Yeah, I had a light breakfast at six this morning."

"Let's go to Scoma's on the Pier. They have the best crab and Shrimp Louie in Frisco, and it's huge," said August.

They finished lunch and Andy drove them to the Ritz Carlton. "I'll pick you up at twenty to eight. Wear a jacket, no need for a tie."

Andy drove off, August and Tony checked in and took the elevator. "Andy and I have a dinner meeting at eight so you'll be on your own," said August.

"Hey, we're in San Francisco. I'll find something to keep me busy," Tony chuckled.

"I'm sure you will."

Their rooms were next to each other. As they walked up to their rooms, Tony turned to August. "See you in the morning."

August sat his overnight bag on the bed and started to unpack, hanging his blue blazer up to air and let the slight wrinkles smooth out. He looked at the lining of his suitcase. *Put the bond in the safe, or take it with me? Safer to leave it right where it is: in the open.* He picked up his bag, set it on the suitcase stand and left the rest of his stuff in it.

He took a shower, put on a terrycloth robe, compliments of the Ritz, and grabbed the remote. He began to channel surf and stopped at NBC afternoon news. The commentator was reporting another murder caused by the in-fighting that had been going on for months between the old and young Triads.

The news got boring so he turned on a movie that was equally boring, and fell asleep. He woke up at five-thirty, groggy as hell. *What the fuck do you expect? Pig out at lunch, drink too much wine, and then conk out for a couple of hours.* He stood, stretched, walked to the bathroom pulling off his robe, throwing it in the corner as he stepped into the shower, only turning on the cold water.

He toweled off and got ready for the evening. Not one to let dust collect under him, he grabbed his jacket and left the room. He took the elevator to the lobby and headed for the bar. There was a trio playing mellow jazz, almost drowned out by the hum of the conversation from the patrons. August scanned the area and spotted Tony, sitting alone at a table. He walked up to him. "Anybody sitting here?"

Tony smiled, "Yeah, that gorgeous, voluptuous blonde, the one from my dreams."

August chuckled, as he sat down. "Maybe you'll get lucky later."

The waitress walked up. "Would you like a cocktail?"

"Vodka martini, Gray Goose, if you have it, and another of what he's having."

The waitress brought their drinks; Tony raised his glass. "Salute."

They both took a sip. "Remember when we were flying a load out of Mexico and landed in that little airport outside of Palm Springs?" asked August.

"Yeah, you know, that was—twelve years ago. Where's the time gone? I'll never forget when I taxied the plane into the hangar and both of us closed the doors, as they slammed shut, one of the doors jumped the track, and started falling on us."

"Yeah, I remember you raising your hands to stop it, but the door was so heavy it smashed into your face and broke your nose."

"Well, I stopped it enough so that it missed the rudder by an inch; if it had hit, we would have been grounded, maybe in more ways than one."

"Yeah, but we did have to unload the plane, and I had to drive the load into L.A."

"Aw, poor boy. I had to fly that fuckin' plane back to Santa

Monica Airport by myself with a throbbing broken nose and blood all over my shirt, before I went to the hospital."

August frowned, as he examined Tony's face. "It's just a little crooked. You know I've always told everyone that you had a nose for this business."

They both laughed, and ordered another martini.

August looked at his watch; it was seven-thirty. He gulped his martini, pulled out a hundred and set it on the table. "I gotta go. Good luck fulfilling your dream."

Tony held up his glass. "Good luck with your meeting."

As August walked out of the hotel, he saw Andy's Mercedes at the curb, opened the door and slid in. "Ready for some dim sum?" said August.

"That and all the other dishes that go with it; I'm starved."

Andy drove from the hotel down Broadway to Chinatown. San Francisco's Chinatown is the oldest and largest Chinese district outside of Asia. It borders Union Street and North Beach, to Lombard Street and Grant Avenue. He turned on Stockton and pulled up in front of the restaurant. They got out and the valet parked the Mercedes.

They entered the Dragon's Breath Restaurant at eight sharp. The maitre d', a gorgeous Asian woman, walked up. "Good evening, may I help you?"

"We're meeting Mr. Lee Chung for dinner."

"Oh, Mr. Taracina, please follow me."

August looked at Andy quizzically. "How does she know my name?"

"They followed the maitre d' upstairs, down a hall to closed red double doors, bordered by two silent, sullen, Sumo-size guards. She whispered to one of them, turned and walked away.

"Please take your jackets off," asked one of the guards. "We are going to search you for weapons and wires. Please stand against the wall, facing out." The guards frisked them, checked under their shirts. "Now turn and face the wall and spread your legs." They did as they were told.

Apparently satisfied, they opened the doors, allowing entry. "Jeez, I thought these guys were friends of yours," whispered August to Andy, who looked at him wide-eyed, not expecting the disrobing exercise.

There were four Asian men sitting at a round ornate table with a lazy susan at the center. All four men stood, and the one that August assumed was Young Lee walked around the table to greet them. He held out his hand; August took it. "Mr. Taracina, so good to finally meet you."

"A pleasure, always good to meet the man in charge."

Lee turned. "Andy, how are you?"

"Great, thank you for meeting with us tonight."

The private dining room looked as though it was plucked out of an ancient palace in China and set gently in place. The room was adorned with Ming Dynasty vases, and original art, Oriental rugs and hand carved mahogany furniture.

"Please have a seat. I hope you are hungry. I've had my chef prepare a very special dinner for us this evening."

"It must be special. It's not very often I get frisked, when I've been invited to dinner."

"I'm sorry for any inconvenience, but we must take precautions—due to internal problems in our own organization. We have successfully operated in the United States for over 100 years. Now, the younger members, emigrating from China, have joined the other young gang members who now want more, if not total control of our operation in the States. This cannot be. We will not allow this to happen!" said Young Lee, with noticeable emotion.

"The youth have no respect for their elders, or even, amongst themselves. They have no patience. Greed eats them up, like terminal cancer," said Lee.

A waiter came out of nowhere, as if reading Young Lee's mind. "What would you like to drink?"

"Scotch on the rocks," said August.

"I'll have a Beefeaters and tonic," said Andy.

The waiter served a round of drinks; two others appeared with various appetizers, placed them on the lazy susan, then all three silently left the room.

August waited until Lee began to fill his plate with Chinese delicacies, and then helped himself.

"Compliments to your chef," said August.

Young smiled. "Thank you. So, Andy informed me that you have some new business to discuss with us."

This guy doesn't waste any time. "Yes, I do. I recently acquired 350 one-million-dollar United States bearer bonds. I'd prefer to dispose of them at a discount, rather than wait until they mature. I thought that a wealthy organization like yours could possibly capitalize on the purchase of these bonds."

"That is an interesting proposition; did you bring a sample with you?"

"No, I thought that if you were interested, we could meet tomorrow."

"A wise decision. We will meet at my office at 10:00 A.M.; that will give me time to discuss the proposition with my associates in Hong Kong. Now that we have taken care of business, we can enjoy the culinary artistry of my chef."

The waiters appeared, removed the empty plates, and placed numerous platters of gourmet Chinese cuisine on the lazy susan for everyone to share, along with the best Napa wines money could buy.

The evening was going smoothly; August was enjoying the company and the fabulous dinner. A man he had not yet seen before came through another door, briskly walked over to Young Lee, and began to speak rapidly in Chinese.

Lee's composed face abruptly changed to rage. He rattled off some instructions to this messenger, who bowed his head in respect, turned and virtually ran out of the dining room.

Now, visibly upset, Lee turned to the other three men and spoke, as if giving orders, then turned more sedately to August and Andy. "I'm sorry for the interruption. As I mentioned earlier, the younger men in our organization are causing trouble. It has escalated. I regret that we must conclude this enjoyable evening."

"I understand." August could see that Lee was anxious to leave, so he pushed back his chair and stood. "I want to thank you for a wonderful evening, sorry for the terrible chain of events and interruption to our meeting. Please tell your chef that tonight's cuisine is the best I've ever had."

They shook hands. "Thank you for your understanding; I look forward to our meeting tomorrow."

Young Lee walked them to the closed doors, opened one and spoke to the guards. "They will escort you to your car." He turned and joined the other three men.

When they finally got into Andy's Mercedes, he turned to August. "Fuck, when that guy spoke to Lee, and he blew up, I thought he was going to stab the guy with his chop sticks."

"The way he was moving his hands, I wasn't sure if he was going to stab the guy, or himself," chuckled August.

Andy pulled up to the Ritz Carlton. "Young Lee's office is a ten minute drive from here. I'll pick you up at nine forty-five."

August opened the door and slid out. "Sounds good; see you in the morning."

He went directly to his room, took a shower, and hit the sack.

The following morning, he called Tony who awakened to his phone ringing. Tony answered in a sleepy voice, "Good morning, August, what's up?"

"Obviously, not you. Meet me for breakfast in the restaurant."

"I'll be there in ten minutes."

Tony walked up to August's table and sat down. "How'd the meeting go?"

"Everything went well. You find the girl of your dreams?"

Tony cracked a smile. "Not exactly, but good enough for a one-night stand." They laughed. "When do you want to take off?"

"I've got another meeting at ten. Shouldn't take too long. Stick around, as soon as I get back, we'll check out, and have Andy take us to the airport."

Andy picked up August and drove into the underground parking facility of the Far East Trading Company building. They rode the elevator to the lobby, were directed to a guarded elevator, and took it to the executive office on the top floor.

The elevator opened to a luxurious lobby full of genuine Oriental art and statues. Another gorgeous Asian woman sat at the reception desk. She looked up. "Good morning, may I help you?"

"August Taracina to see Mr. Young Lee."

The receptionist stood and opened the door. "Please, they're waiting for you."

They walked into a large room even more plush than the luxurious lobby, with a breathtaking view of San Francisco Bay and the Golden Gate Bridge.

Young Lee and two other men were seated on a couch, facing another couch—reserved for them. August and Andy walked over. "Good morning, Mr. Lee, a most beautiful office."

"Thank you. I would like to introduce you to my Chief Financial Officer, Boon Low, and Tung Chiang, my investment banker." They all shook hands, then August and Andy sat down, facing the potential buyers.

"You are aware of our problems with the young Triad gangs. Our time is necessarily limited. I apologize for rushing. May we see the bond?"

"Of course." August pulled the envelope from his coat pocket and produced the bond, handing it to Lee, who carefully examined it, then passed it to Boon Low and Tung Chiang.

They talked to one another in Chinese; Boon Low handed the bond back to Lee.

"This is very impressive. Only a few people, or governments, would possess 350 one-million-dollar bonds.

"We have a very successful counterfeiting operation that produces bonds; not million-dollar bearer bonds, they would raise too much attention."

The head of the Triad operation in the U.S. handed the bond back to August.

"I am sorry; we are not interested at this time. But, it has been an honor to meet you directly. We have done business with Andy and Mr. Dillon for many years and value our relationship. In fact, I would like to speak to you about increasing the size of the shipments to us. They talked about terms and conditions, and agreed.

August was disappointed, not at all happy with the outcome. He was running out of options, spending too much time and resources, and not paying attention to his own operation at home.

"I thought they were going to cut a deal," said Andy, while driving back to the Ritz.

"Oh, I think they do want them. But they have big problems with the young Triad gangs, and are not going to enter into any more new business until they clean up their house first."

"Well, at least your trip up here wasn't a complete loss. We are going to increase our business with them," said Andy, as he pulled up to the hotel.

Fuck, I'm not sure I have any business right now.

August went up to his room and put the bond back into the lining of his suitcase and called Tony, who met him in the hallway. They rode the elevator to the lobby and checked out.

Andy pulled into the executive airport parking lot. "I've got a few ideas; I'll keep working on this."

"Please, because I'm running out of ideas." August shook hands. "Thanks for your help. Take care of yourself."

They got out and walked to the King Air. Tony had called ahead and the fuel truck was waiting for them. "Hope you didn't have to wait too long?"

"I just pulled up a couple of minutes ago," said the driver. "Ready to take on some fuel?"

A half-hour later, Tony was taxiing out to the runway, got clearance to take off, and was in the air three minutes after that.

29

Eleventh day: February 15

Nick was at his desk, going over all the reports from Greg and Daryl, when his phone rang. "Nick Cutler."

"Nick, it's Greg. Looks like one of our informants came through."

"Great, what did he have to say?"

"He heard from a good source that a Chinese gang had some bonds they're going to move."

"I knew this thing happened in San Francisco. The informant say anything else?"

"No, but he thought he could find out more information. My partner, John Ling, is meeting with him at seven tonight."

"I'll still be in my office working on these fuckin' reports. Call me as soon as you hear something, so I can make arrangements to get up there."

At seven, FBI Agent John Ling walked into this sleazy bar, his guy was sitting at a corner table, nursing his drink. He walked up and sat across from him. The waitress walked up and asked, "What can I get you?"

"Jack Daniels and Coke, and whatever he'd like."

His guy ordered another beer, and the waitress left.

"So, what do you have for me?"

"There's something big going down tomorrow night, at a warehouse down by the waterfront."

"That's a big area," Agent Ling said skeptically.

The waitress delivered their drinks. John took a sip, while his informant lit a cigarette and slid the matchbook to him. "I wrote down the address. The guy who told me this doesn't know what time this meeting is going down. He did mention that he thinks it's something to do with the Chinese Triad. They're bad motherfuckers, so be prepared."

"That's it?"

"That's all I know, and after I finish this drink, I'm going to disappear for a few days, so don't try to find me."

John left the bar, got to the nearest phone, and called his partner. After John filled him in, he immediately phoned Nick.

"Nick, I just received a call from my partner. Something big is happening tomorrow night. I have the address; the Triad gangs are involved."

"Maybe we'll wrap this up quicker than I thought. Get your team together; I'll see you tomorrow morning."

"Call me with your ETA and I'll pick you up."

Nick paged the pilot, made arrangements to take off at six the following morning, then he called Leo. "Better be important, my pasta's going to get cold."

"We're flying back to San Francisco at 6:00 A.M.; want me to pick you up?"

"What's happening?"

"One of Greg's partner's informants came through. It looks like the Chinese Triad has possession of Western's shipment of stocks and bonds, and is selling them, or they're going to buy them. There's a meeting tomorrow night; we'll be paying them a visit."

The following morning, Nick drove his Corvette into the FBI hangar, parking it in the same spot. Captain John Carnes and the co-pilot, Rodger Owens, were waiting for them.

An hour later, John landed the Gulfstream on the tarmac at San Francisco International Airport and taxied to the FBI hangar, where Greg and John were waiting for them.

They waited for John and Rodger to secure the plane, then the six of them squeezed into the Crown Vic, and Greg drove to the

Marriott. The pilots, Nick, and Leo checked in. The two agents put their bags in their rooms, then joined Greg and John, while the pilots settled in and waited for further instructions.

On the way to the FBI field office Nick asked, "So how is this going to go down?"

"I've put together a task force including the San Francisco Police, SWAT teams, detectives, and the FBI agents on my team. Since we now know the location of the meeting, we've had our agents driving around in unmarked cars surveilling the area, picking suitable spots to position our men.

"The SWAT team will have their snipers in position hours before the deal goes down.

We'll be in a delivery truck parked down the street. The truck is loaded with new technical stuff and cameras, so we can watch and hear almost anything."

"When are we going in?" asked Nick.

"The truck is already parked, not to cause any attention. The techs are already in the truck; we'll get dropped off at five."

"I'd like to take a look at the building and the area."

"No problem, John and I will take you two for a ride, and then we'll go to lunch."

They took the elevator to the underground parking level, jumped into an unmarked red Chevy Malibu, and headed for the waterfront. Greg drove down Third to Cargo Way, turned right on Mendel to Fairfax. "The building's two blocks away on the southeast corner." They drove past the delivery truck. "That's our truck, 'Napa Valley Trading.'"

Nick saw the truck, but was more interested in the building. As they drove up the street, they passed by a large roll-up door, and near the corner, a pedestrian door. Greg turned right; there was another roll-up door in the center of the building. The second story was lined with a few windows overlooking the street. "Seen enough?" asked Greg.

"Yeah, any doors in the rear?"

"One double pedestrian door. We can cover it from an adjacent building. The rest of the perimeter will be covered by the SWAT snipers, who are already up there conducting surveillance."

"Looks like you've got it covered. You taking us to lunch?" asked Leo.

"Jeez, Leo, is that all you think about?" chuckled Nick.

"That and retiring."

"Hey, Leo, you like Chinese food?" asked John Lee.

"Other than Italian, it's my favorite ethnic food."

"Good, we'll go to my cousin's place in Chinatown; it's not real fancy, but you'll love the food."

It took twenty minutes to get to the Shanghai Restaurant. It took two hours to eat, being fed and pampered by Lee's cousin. They waddled back to their car. Leo held his protruding stomach with both hands. "Best Chinese food I ever had."

They drove back to the FBI office. Greg and John went to their desks, while Nick and Leo called the agents in Seattle and Los Angeles for an update.

At three-thirty, Greg got a call from his techs. "A warehouse door just opened, a van and a Mercedes pulled in," said one of the techs.

"You hear anything?"

"Lots of Chinese. We'll need John to translate."

"We'll be there in half an hour."

Greg walked over to the desk where Nick and Leo were working. "What's up?" asked Nick.

"We've got some activity at the warehouse. I think we should get over there now."

Greg had another agent drive an unmarked car to the warehouse and drop them off behind the truck; they got in as quickly as they could.

Nick was impressed with all the surveillance equipment that was stuffed into the truck. John put on the headset and listened in. "I can hear them, but it's all garbled." John kept listening, while the rest sat and waited for some action.

It was starting to get dark and the images on the monitors were fading. John kept monitoring, only listening to a few conversations, none of any importance.

Greg was on the radio with the SWAT leader and the SFPD detectives. The street was dead quiet. It was nine thirty-five; they had begun to think this was a false call. Then the overhead door opened, two more cars drove in, and the door rolled down right behind them.

Greg's radio beeped. "I think we should move in," said the SWAT leader.

"Your guys all ready?"

"For the last five hours! Let's get this over with."

"Okay, at 0950 we move in."

Just as the task force was ready to roll, three vans and two cars appeared, flying around the corner, skidding to a stop next to the building. A squad of Chinese thugs jumped out with machine guns and charged the building. The task force followed them in, dodging and sprinting, taking cover wherever they could.

There was shooting going on in the building, as the team entered. Nick could see that these Oriental factions were firing at each other. Then the thugs spotted the agents moving in, and they sent a wall of gunfire at them.

The posted SFP snipers opened up, firing through the windows on the second floor, dropping several Chinese, and one mortally shot, the others going for cover as they attempted to retreat downstairs.

The nose-stinging stench of cordite flooded the air, as the gun battle escalated. Return fire began to diminish, amid moans, and the task force moved in with no resistance. In another minute, what was left of both factions dropped their guns and held their hands high above their heads.

There were bodies scattered everywhere, blood soaking aged, dusty wooden floors. Fortunately, the agents were all wearing bulletproof vests, and after a head count, the good guys had four wounded and no casualties. The other side suffered significantly, with three dead, nine wounded, and the rest banged up, missing teeth, or eyes swollen shut.

As the FBI team rounded up the gang members, the Triads began to yell at each other.

Nick asked John, "What the hell is going on?"

"Well, let's see what we stopped," said Nick.

"You're not going to believe this. We just walked into a shooting gallery. The young guys are members of new Triad gangs rebelling against the old Triad throng. We knew this was going on for the most part, but it was an internal faction war. This bust is going to have an interesting impact."

Greg was standing in front of the cargo door of a white Econoline cargo van, with a claw hammer in his hand. He yelled, "Hey, Nick, come over here. Let's see what we got."

Greg pried open the top of one of the cases in the van, revealing stacks of American Express Traveler's Checks. He picked up one of the checks and held it up to the warehouse lights. "There must be millions of dollars' worth of checks in these cases, and they look legit, but I'll bet a month's pay that they're counterfeit, and made in China."

Nick heard him, but his mind was elsewhere. *Would've been nice to find the bonds instead.* He patted Greg on the shoulder. "Congratulations."

After the coroner's deputies cleared all the bodies out of the warehouse, Greg, John, Nick, and Leo searched the whole building. Three hours later, they stood in the middle of the warehouse looking at all the contraband they found.

They had 20 thirty-five pound bales of marijuana, a large cache of weapons—hand guns, machine guns, and shot guns—and a few pounds of Semtex.

Hidden behind one of the file cabinets, they found $220,000, but to Nick's disappointment, no bearer bonds.

Greg shook his head. "Better get back to my office; we have one hell of a report to fill out."

30

Same Day

Karen called Scott at work and gave him a small shopping list of stuff for dinner. After work, he drove to the Safeway market on his way home. He pulled into the mall's lot and parked. As he jumped out of his Cherokee, he spotted a black sedan pulling into a spot in the next row. *Maybe I'm being paranoid, but that sure looks like an unmarked police car with two people in it.*

He casually walked to the market's entrance and went inside, but instead of shopping, he stepped to the side and watched the car that he recognized as a telltale Crown Vic. The two people were still in the car.

When he was halfway through the shopping list, he went to the front of the store and looked through the window. The Crown Vic was still there and the two passengers—whom he was certain were FBI agents—were still in their car.

Scott finished his shopping, went through the checkout line, and paid the clerk. He walked to his SUV, put the bags in the rear and shut the door. He jumped in and drove home with the black Crown Vic on his tail.

He pulled into his driveway, got the two bags of groceries, went through the back door, and set the bags down. Then he went straight to his garage, jumped on his bike, and rode down to the Strand, where the feds couldn't follow him and rode over to see the guys.

He carried his bike to the door and went in. "What's happening?"

asked Randy.

"We need to have a board meeting. Grab your boards, we're going surfing."

"But there are hardly any waves."

"That's not important; we need to talk."

They paddled out and sat up on their boards.

"So what's wrong? Is everything okay?"

"I thought it was until I spotted the feds following me from work, then to Safeway and home."

"Scott, August told us that we might see them following us. That it was almost a given, and that we should just act normally," said Randy.

"Easier said than done, until you have them following your ass. From now on, we have to act just like everything is normal."

"Hell, after they visited us at work, I haven't talked about it at all. You think they might bug our house?" asked Terry.

"Good question. Maybe we should assume they did, it would be safer," said Randy.

"We need to tell August," said Jeff.

"We can't. We have to wait until he contacts us. We're on our own. Hell, we pulled off the perfect crime. We need to ride this out."

An unexpected set rolled in; they acted normal and rode them in.

* * *

August was in the harbor area, checking his operation and the whites manufacturing setup. He was talking to Mickey when he got paged. He recognized the number, walked over to the phone, and called Andy.

"Andy, it's August, what's up?"

"I've been trying to get in touch with some friends of mine, but they were out of town until last night. I just spoke to them; they think they can unload the bonds, and are really interested in talking to you."

"Who are they?"

"They're international bankers who represent clients worldwide, and are experts when dealing with a variety of monetary instruments, including bearer bonds, securities, and lines of credit, domestically and internationally. In fact, the reason I couldn't get in contact with them, was because they were in Geneva working on another deal."

"Where do they live?" asked August.

"They have a house on the bay in Sausalito. They're both high profile international bankers and have contacts all over Europe, especially in Switzerland and Liechtenstein, and throughout the world. I think they've made most of their money by trading international currency and precious metals."

"Sounds good, when can we meet?"

"When can you be here?"

"I'm sure Tony wouldn't mind flying back up there. How about tomorrow?"

"They said the same thing, suggesting that we meet for dinner and get acquainted."

"I'll call you back with our ETA, and make reservations at the Ritz for two nights."

"Will do, talk to you later."

They touched down at San Francisco International at eleven-thirty. Andy was waiting, and drove them to the hotel.

"So, where we going to dinner?" asked August.

As Andy pulled up to the Ritz Carlton valet, he said, "We're meeting them at the Tadich Grill at seven. It's only a few blocks from here; I'll pick you up at quarter to seven."

August and Tony checked in. At 6:30, August left the bond in the lining of his suitcase and left the room. He was wearing Levi jeans, a long sleeve turtleneck shirt, and a blue cashmere sweater, with an Italian-made glove leather jacket in his hand.

He walked through the lobby and lit a cigarette, while he waited for Andy, who pulled up to the curb. August jumped in and a few minutes later, they pulled up to the restaurant. Andy handed his keys to the valet and walked in.

The Tadich Grill is the oldest restaurant in the city and the state, operating since 1849. It was founded by a Croatian family and began as "The New World Coffee Stand." It was also renowned for claiming to be the first establishment to grill seafood over mesquite charcoal in the 1920s.

It was a destination restaurant, and a local treasure, that evoked an Old World feel, capturing the history, ambiance, and flavors of San Francisco, and a long-time favorite of August's.

Steve and Linda Workman were already seated at the table when August and Andy arrived. They followed the maitre d'. The couple stood and shook hands as Andy made the introductions.

August was surprised to see how young they were. Steve was around six-one, well built, with black wavy hair. Linda was a fine-looking blonde with a hot figure. Basically, they were a young very good-looking couple, dressed in designer clothes, looking very successful.

August told them the restaurant was one of his favorites and that his father said it sort of brought back the old charm, being from San Pedro, where the Italians and Croatians traded recipes similar to Tadich's cuisine.

August remained as vague as he could about what type of bonds he had, their value, and how he had gained possession of them, but he admitted they were hot. That didn't seem to bother them.

The rest of the evening was spent getting to know each other, and after an excellent dinner, they agreed to meet for lunch the following day.

They met at Scoma's on the Pier, ordered shrimp and crab Louis, and two bottles of Cakebread Chardonnay from Napa Valley.

For the next half-hour, the conversation went from politics to sports. There was a lull and Steve put on his business face. "Before we go any further, I need to know what type of bonds you have."

August had no choice but to tell him. "U.S. bearer bonds."

"That's good, but because they're hot, it would be a bad idea to try to move them in the States. But we could put you together with some potential buyers in Switzerland or Liechtenstein."

"I assume we'd have to fly over there and show them what we

have to sell?"

"I could go alone and represent you, but I think it would be better if you were present."

August decided that his best chance was to go with them. "I agree. I guess the next step would be to show you a sample."

"Yeah, but not in a public place." He filled August's wine glass, and then his own. "Would you like to come to our house for dinner tonight? Andy knows where we live."

"Great idea, what time?"

"Say, seven o'clock?"

The waiter brought the bill. August grabbed it, took a quick look, peeled off three one-hundred-dollar bills and they left.

Andy picked August up at 6:15 and headed to Sausalito.

While driving over the Golden Gate Bridge, August asked, "Can we trust them?"

"Yeah, I think so. I told them that a person like you has a lot of influence and connections. You're not one to fuck with, because you could reach out and grab them if you wanted to. They know what I do for a living, and that you are basically my partner. They understand; it's not the first time they've been involved in a shady deal."

"Good, because I'm getting tired of fucking around with these bonds."

Andy turned off the highway and glided down the road to the water. He pulled into a gated driveway and pushed the intercom. August spotted a camera as the gate swung open. Andy drove up to the house and parked in front of a two-story Mediterranean-style villa. Steve and Linda came out the front door to greet them.

As they entered the house, August admired paintings by Chagall, Matisse, van Gogh, Monet, and other fine artists, hanging from the walls. Chinese art and beautiful Oriental rugs augmented the surroundings.

One item that intrigued August was a priceless saber-toothed tiger skull, sitting on the mantel above the huge fireplace. It was obvious that this young couple had done very well for themselves.

"You have a beautiful home," said August.

"Thank you, we love it here," said Linda.

"What would you like to drink? I have Johnnie Walker Blue, if you like," said Steve.

"On the rocks, would be great," said August.

"Same for me," said Andy.

Steve whipped up two Sapphire Blue martinis for himself and Linda, and poured a couple doubles of scotch over ice for their guests.

"It's a beautiful evening. Why don't we go out on the patio and enjoy the view? Would you like a cigar before dinner? I just got in some Montecristos from Cuba."

August and Andy both accepted and walked out on the patio overlooking San Francisco Bay and the Golden Gate Bridge, while Steve went to his humidor to get the cigars.

He came out with the ends snipped and traditional pieces of cedar to light the cigars, eliminating any fumes from a lighter. They fired up the cigars and sat around the outdoor bar, surrounding the barbeque and smoker, while a maid appeared with plates of hot hors d'oeuvres that she presented to each of them, then set them on the bar.

After ten minutes of light conversation, Steve got down to business. "So what exactly do you have?"

August knew it was show-and-tell time. He pulled the envelope out of his jacket inner pocket, opened it, pulled out the bond and handed it to him, while he said, "I have three hundred fifty of these."

Steve and Linda looked at the bond; August could see their jaws drop and their eyes bulge out, stunned at what Steve held in his hand.

"You're telling me that you have 350 million dollars in bearer bonds?"

"Yeah, you still think those Swiss bankers would be interested in them?"

He studied the bond. "It certainly looks real."

"I'm certain they are, since I know where they came from," said August. "How much do you think they'd be willing to pay?"

Steve paused for a moment. "I think we could get ten or maybe twenty cents on the dollar. I mean—hell, if they kept them till maturity they would be worth close to a billion dollars."

"I was hoping to get ten cents."

"They might pay ten cents, but then they could go for less," said Steve. "These guys are shrewd negotiators, and will try to squeeze every cent out of you."

"Well, for conversation's sake, let's assume I get ten cents. I think you should negotiate with the bankers for your share, your finder's fee."

"I have no problem with that; in fact, I'd prefer it."

August knew this amount of money could bring out the greed in anyone. He had made and dealt with a lot of money, but had never come across *anything* like this. But he knew just how dangerous this truly was and whether or not he could pull it off.

At a dime on the dollar, that's thirty-five million dollars gross, insuring that everyone down the line would make a lot of money, even Steve and Linda. The guys would make more than they ever dreamed of, and could definitely build that resort in Costa Rica, if they still wanted to.

First, he'd help the guys by setting up some offshore accounts with their shares, so that they could actually live off the interest and not touch the money for some time, keeping the heat off them, and him, at the same time.

Steve and Linda were excellent hosts, and lots of fun. They smoked their cigars, enjoyed the hors d'oeuvres, and had a couple more cocktails, while Steve barbequed some thick rib eyes and lobster tails for dinner. They shared a couple of bottles of cabernet with dinner and a thirty-year-old port with dessert.

Steve was ready to pack and head to Switzerland to cut a deal. He said he would arrange to leave the following day and began to make some appointments. Andy and August would fly over a couple of days later.

August finally felt that there was a chance to unload the bonds. If he got only five cents on a dollar, he'd be happy to get rid of them.

He knew that he had to bring three bonds as samples and decided that he needed a courier to carry them, and travel with him. His girlfriend had moved to Hawaii, and he really didn't want to involve her because he felt that their relationship was disintegrating, or was actually over.

Since Sandi left for Hawaii, August began seeing this gorgeous brunette, Candice, who worked at the Bare Elegance, another strip club owned by his buddy, Big Mac McKenna, located less than a few blocks from the strip joint.

August called Candice and asked her if she would come to Switzerland with him, and, of course, she was thrilled to go.

The following morning, Linda took Steve, Andy, August, and Tony to the airport, dropping her husband at the international terminal, and the others at the private executive plane gate. The King Air was already fueled and Tony called in his flight plan. An hour and a half later, they landed at Torrance Airport. Tony stayed at the airport to secure the plane. Andy threw his suitcase in August's trunk and then they drove back to San Pedro.

He dropped Andy at the Enterprise Car Rental to rent a nondescript sedan that they would use to drive to Mexicali, the capital of the Mexican state of Baja California, the following morning. Most of that day, August tended to his business, made sure everything was in order and talked to Mickey about keeping an eye on his operation.

"Make sure you go out and collect all the outstanding money. Too much exposure makes me feel uneasy."

"Don't worry, I'll make the collections and take it to the drop."

That evening, he called Candice and told her that he'd pick her up at 9 A.M. Andy was staying at August's house for the night, so the two of them went out to dinner, then drove back to the house. He packed for the trip, while Andy took a shower and hit the sack. August watched TV for an hour until he couldn't keep his eyes open, and turned in.

The following morning, August's driver, Tom Maxim, drove them to Candice's apartment. Her suitcases were packed and ready to go, but she left the largest one open on her bed, per August's instructions. He pulled the three bonds out of the inner pocket of his jacket, and using a new sharp box cutter, surgically slit open the lining and inserted the bonds, then sealed it with double-sided tape.

He examined his work. Satisfied, he shut the lid, spun the numbers on the combination lock, and carried it into the living room. He looked at Candice. "Ready to go?"

Andy and August carried her suitcases to the Ford Explorer, and loaded them in the back.

It took a little over two hours to reach the border crossing. August saw the line of cars. It took twenty minutes to reach the border, where they were waved through by the authorities.

Tom took the turn to Mexicali's Taboada Airport, pulled up to the departure gates, and dropped them off. August tipped a porter to unload the luggage, and while Andy and Candice followed the porter, August told Tom he would contact him about their return flight.

August paid cash for three one-way tickets to Mexico City via Mexicana Airlines. He had Candice and Andy go through customs together; he followed a few people behind them.

They landed at Benito Juarez International Airport. August had a porter load their luggage on a cart and follow them to the KLM Airlines counter. August, a.k.a. Tony Lira, used his credit card to purchase three one-way first-class tickets to Zurich.

They had a little over three hours to kill, so they joined other travelers in one of the restaurants, ordered a beer, and relaxed.

Their flight was announced; it was on time and boarding would start in ten minutes.

<h1 align="center">31</h1>

Fifteenth day: First trip to Switzerland

They flew to Zurich, via Lisbon, and landed at 11:30 A.M. Zurich time. They went through customs without a glitch and took a taxi to the Hotel Eden Au Lac, a five-star hotel on Lake Zurich.

They entered the opulent lobby and walked to the reservation counter. A formally dressed man stepped up. "Welcome to the Hotel Eden Au Lac. May I help you?"

"Reservations for Tony Lira," said August.

The clerk typed in the name. "Yes, here we are; Mr. Workman made your reservations. You have a one-bedroom suite, and a deluxe guest room reserved for one week. Is that acceptable?"

"We might stay a week, more or less, would we have any problems?"

"We are not full, and there should not be a problem. Are you paying with a credit card?"

August pulled out his wallet and gave the clerk Tony Lira's American Express card. The clerk swiped the card. "Please sign here. How many key cards do you need?"

"Three for the suite, and one for the adjoining room."

He handed Tony the key cards. "You'll find fresh fruit in your rooms daily, compliments of the hotel. The suite has a well-stocked bar, again compliments of the hotel, unless you wish for something beyond our standard inventory, which would be an additional charge. We have the finest French restaurant in Zurich, and we are centrally located to everything our beautiful city offers. I recommend that you take a walk on our famous Lake Promenade, located just steps out of the hotel. Have any questions?"

"Not at this time, thank you," said August.

"We have a concierge and room service available twenty-four hours a day, and a full spa service. If you require anything, please call. Enjoy your stay, Mr. Lira."

They followed the bellman to their rooms. He unloaded the luggage and August gave him a big tip. Candice was dancing around the suite; it was luxurious in every way. She walked out onto the balcony. "August come here, you won't believe the view."

August and Andy joined her; it was a magnificent view of Lake Zurich, surrounded by the towering snowcapped Alps. Candice put her arm around August. "Isn't it beautiful?" She took in a deep breath. "The air is so clean."

Andy knew it was time to leave the suite. "I'm going to unpack and contact Steve; I'll call you later."

Candice draped her arms around August's shoulders. "I feel all sticky and dirty after all that traveling. I'm going to take a shower." She pulled herself close, and whispered in his ear, "Want to join me?"

"I'd be crazy not to accept that invitation." August kissed her, then wrapped an arm around her waist, and escorted her to the bathroom.

The phone on the nightstand rang; August reached over and picked up the receiver.

"Hello."

"You sound like I woke you up. Sorry about that."

"Just taking a nap. What's up?"

"Steve just got back to his room and returned my message. He'd like to take us out for dinner."

August looked over at Candice, lying there naked and still asleep. "Candice doesn't know exactly what we're doing here. How about we meet Steve for cocktails in the hotel bar, discuss business, and then go to dinner?"

"Good idea," said Andy. It's four-thirty. How about six?"

"Fine, I'll meet you down there." August hung up the phone and lay on his back.

"Who was that?" asked Candice, in a sleepy voice.

"It was Andy. We're going to meet Steve in the hotel bar and go over some business, and then we're all going out to dinner."

"What time are you meeting?"

"Six."

"What time is it?"

"Four-thirty."

Candice slid her amazing body on top of him, gave him a kiss, and sat up, straddling his body. She looked over her voluptuous breasts, smiling. "Good, then I'll have plenty of time to fuck your brains out."

A half-hour later, they both lay there on their backs, totally spent. August rolled over on his side and gave Candice a kiss. "That nap certainly invigorated you."

"You invigorate me."

Uh oh, this is getting a little too heavy. He smiled. "I have to get ready." He gave her a quick kiss, and slid off the bed. He took a cool shower, and got ready for the evening. Candice was sitting on the couch in the living room, wrapped in a terrycloth robe provided by the hotel, watching TV. August bent over and gave her a kiss. "See you later."

"How long will you be?"

"About an hour."

"That long? Hurry, I'm starving after all that exercise this afternoon."

"I'll try to keep it short. Be ready by six-thirty."

Steve and Andy were sitting at a table when August walked into the bar. He joined them and ordered a scotch on the rocks.

"So, how's the progress?" asked August.

"The interest has been pretty positive. I've been able to set up morning and afternoon meetings for the next three days. Tomorrow morning we have a meeting at ten with the Older & Co. Privatbank

AG Zūrich, and the FSG Financial Group at one. Then, Banca Commercial Zūrich at nine the following morning, and a lunch meeting with Zūrich Investment Trust. The next meeting's at five— and they seemed to be very interested."

"What bank?" asked August.

"Bank de Priv'e Zūrich, one of my associates has done business with them. He said they were aggressive and had very deep pockets. I spoke to one of the owners, a David Zubriggen who invited us to dinner.

"Then, on the third day, we fly to Geneva in the morning. The first meeting is with Banque de Credit Genève, and after lunch, with Banque Lature-DuBois Genève.

"The following day I have to go to Liechtenstein for some other business. I'll be there for a couple of days. While I'm there, I plan to visit more private banks and see if I can drum up any interest, that is, if we need to."

August thought that, while in Geneva, he and Candice might take a road trip, perhaps rent a car, drive to Italy, and visit his relatives, since Steve would be gone for a few days.

"After we have the meetings in Geneva, I think Candice and I will take a few days, drive to Italy and visit some of my relatives."

"Sounds like a great idea. I'm going to need some time to talk to the bankers that we had meetings with. You might as well take four days off. If we have any takers, I'll set up the meetings when you get back."

August turned to Andy. "That sort of leaves you in the lurch."

"Andy can come with me to Liechtenstein," said Steve.

August was on his second drink and could feel the jetlag creeping in. "Anything else?"

"No, I think that covers everything."

"Good, because I'm getting tired and hungry. The hotel clerk said the French restaurant here is the finest in Zurich."

"I think it is and I've eaten there a few times. It's excellent. I had another restaurant in mind but we'd get back here late. I'll take you there when you get back from Italy."

August looked at his watch; it was six-thirty on the dot. "I'll call Candice and have her meet us. Why don't you two get us a table, reserved under Tony Lira?"

August called the room.

"Hello."

"We finished early. Steve was planning to take us to some fancy restaurant, but I'm exhausted and hungry, so we're going to eat at the French restaurant right here. You ready to go?"

"I'm ready, no need to come up, I'll meet you there, and I'm glad we're not going out anywhere because I need some rest."

"Table's under Tony Lira."

"Okay, Tony, see you in a minute."

Although the lobby was almost empty, the restaurant was teeming with people. Then he spotted the other door leading to the street where most of the patrons entered the restaurant. The maitre d' walked up. "May I help you?"

"Tony Lira. Two of my friends should be here."

"Yes, Mr. Lira, please follow me."

August took his seat. "Nice place."

"Better be, wait till you see the prices," said Andy.

Just then, the chatter from the throng stopped as heads turned toward the entrance, where Candice stood in a white low-cut dress that was virtually painted on her voluptuous body. As she followed the maitre d', all male eyes followed her and some got elbowed by their wives. The three men stood while the maitre d' slid in her chair; as the three men took their seats, the room went back to normal.

"You certainly know how to make an entrance," said August.

"I hope that was a compliment."

"Oh yeah, it definitely was."

They had a fantastic dinner. August could barely keep his eyes open, and called it a night.

It was around three in the morning when August was awakened by Candice sneezing. "You okay?"

"No, I feel terrible. I must have caught a cold from someone on the plane. I think I have a temperature and my body aches." She sneezed uncontrollably.

"You sound terrible; want me to call for a doctor?"

"No, that's okay. I can wait until morning. I'm going to sleep on the couch so I don't give it to you."

"If I was going to get it, I'm sure I'd have gotten it this afternoon. Get over here and come back to bed."

Candice slid in and pulled the blankets up close to her face. As soon as August fell back to sleep, she got up and went to the couch in the living room, where she lay sweating or chilled to the bone.

August found her curled up on the couch sleeping. He went back into the bedroom, shut the door, called the front desk and asked if they had a doctor that would make a house call. The clerk said they did, and would have the doctor call his room.

An hour later, the doctor finished his examination and gave her a shot of antibiotics. He turned to August. "She has a very nasty cold. I gave her a good dose of antibiotics." He handed August two envelopes. "Here are more antibiotics and a decongestant. The instructions are on the envelopes. She needs a few days of bedrest. Make sure she takes it easy, so she doesn't catch pneumonia. If she doesn't feel better by tomorrow night, give me a call."

"Thank you, doctor."

August went back into the bedroom and shut the door. He was dressed and ready to go. He opened the empty suitcase, carefully opened the lining, took out the envelope containing the three bonds, slid them into the inside pocket of his jacket, and then went out to the living room.

He looked at Candice. "Well, if you were going to get sick, better you're sick now, when I have business to tend to."

"I'm so sorry, August."

"Hey, no problem. Just get well. Day after tomorrow, we're flying to Geneva; then you and I are going on a road trip to Italy for four days."

"God, that sounds fantastic. I'll be fine by then." She chuckled, "I'll order some chicken soup from room service."

"Don't know when I'll get back."

"I'm a big girl. I can take care of myself. Good luck. If it gets real late, would you give me a call?"

"Sure, I'll see you later."

August joined Steve and Andy in the lobby, and followed Steve to his rented BMW. "So where is this Older & Company?" asked August.

"About a fifteen-minute drive."

"That would take us out of the city."

"As I mentioned before, we'll be doing business with private banks. They're small banks that use large financial institutions like Credit Suisse and UBS as their affiliates. They don't look like the banks you're accustomed to. The private banks might be located in elaborate small office buildings, large villas or chateaus, some with long driveways, with sophisticated security systems, gates, and security guards.

"You might drive by one, thinking you passed a private residence, but it could be an independent private bank that had a mere two or three hundred customers. They move and invest their money through their affiliates and all their deposits are under numbered accounts, some interest bearing. They also act as brokers, buying and selling commodities for their customers."

"Commodities, like bonds?"

"Bonds, gold, art, land, anything with value. Most of them have underground vaults for safe deposit boxes, art, and other valuable items. Because they are not regulated like the larger banks, they are known to lend money using these items including bonds, as collateral."

"Most banks would accept bonds for collateral," said August.

"That's correct, but not stolen ones."

"I see your point. What would they do with the bonds?"

"Probably cut a deal with one of their customers. Sell them at two or three times what they paid for them; hold them, promising to sell them later for a handsome profit. Which—, of course, they would receive a percentage of for their services."

Steve turned into a driveway lined with tall juniper trees, no sign of a gate or villa. The driveway turned left, then right, where they came up to an enormous ornate gate. There were no guards, but August was certain there were surveillance cameras everywhere.

Steve drove up to the intercom mounted on a steel gooseneck, and pushed the button.

A pleasant woman's voice answered in French, "Good Morning, may I help you?"

Steve Workman answered in French, "To see Mr. Rothenburg."

Twenty seconds went by. "Please drive in, Mr. Rothenburg's assistant, Jonathan, will be waiting for you."

As they drove to the mansion, they passed manicured lawns and beautiful flowerbeds. It was a bright and sunny day and the variety of flowers looked like rainbows bordering the winding driveway to the front of the two-story pillared entry, where, they presumed, Jonathan stood.

"Good morning, gentlemen. Mr. Rothenburg and Mr. Newhime are waiting for you in the meeting room."

They introduced themselves, and followed Jonathan into this stately manor. August thought the walls were made of granite, and the fifteen-foot double doors, held up with huge ornate brass hinges, were made of three-inch-thick red oak.

The opulent foyer had marble floors, statues and planters, original art on the walls, and a large coat of arms hung over the arched entry, to what August thought was the living room. They followed Jonathan through the perfectly appointed room, full of antiques, velvet chairs, tufted sofas, and crystal and ceramic lamps on hand carved tables. All this was under a twenty-foot ceiling with drapes flowing down the walls, partially covering the huge windows overlooking the manicured yard and array of flowerbeds.

Jonathan stopped at a set of double doors and opened one, walking into what looked like a library with a large table in the center. Previously seated, now standing to greet them, were the two managing partners of Older & Co. Privatbank AG Zurich.

"Mr. Workman, so good to see you."

"This is Tony Lira, and Andy Steel," said Steve.

The banker shook August's, a.k.a. Toni's, hand.

"Aaron Rothenberg, and this is my partner, John Newhime."

August shook hands with John. "Nice to meet you."

"Please sit down. Would you like a cup of coffee or tea?" They all ordered coffee. Rothenberg pushed the intercom button and ordered coffee all around and some Danish. Not ten seconds later, Jonathan came in with a tray, set it on the table, and asked, "Anything else, sir?"

"No, that will be all, thank you," said John. "So, Mr. Lira, Steve briefly told us about your business proposition. Before we go any further, we would like to have you explain your circumstances in detail, and answer any questions we may have."

"I'd be happy to. Around two weeks ago, I came into possession of 350 one-million-dollar United States bearer bonds with a maturity date of 2002, an interest rate of 6%, most of them at 8%. I would like to sell them at a discount, ten cents on the dollar." He paused, "I guess that's it."

Rothenburg was first to speak. "Mr. Workman said you had a large quantity of bearer bonds you were interested in selling. I had no idea how much. You want us to pay you thirty-five million dollars for these bonds. I don't intend to insult you but are they counterfeit or stolen?"

"To my knowledge, they're not counterfeit. They are stolen goods, and the nature of the theft ensures they are authentic."

"Do you have a sample with you?" asked Newhime.

August took out the envelope from his jacket, pulled out the bonds, and slid them across the table. The two bankers examined the bonds for a few minutes, and then excused themselves from the meeting room.

Ten minutes later, they came back in and sat down. "Mr. Lira, we checked all of the U.S., Swiss, and Interpol reports about any bonds stolen recently, and there hasn't been one incident. Can you explain this to us?"

"The FBI and police have yet to determine whether the bonds are lost or stolen; there's no way they'll ever know without finding the bonds."

"Well, we are interested, but we need a few days to determine what we're willing to offer you. We'll contact Steve and set up another meeting when we're ready."

"That will be fine," said Steve. "I'll be in Zurich for two more days, and then I have to go to Liechtenstein for two to three days for some other business."

Rothenburg slid the bonds back to August. "That's fine; just call us when you get back."

The meeting ended and the three left Older & Company and went to lunch. Steve pulled up in front of a small two-story building in the financial district of Zurich, the FSG Financial Group. They entered the building and walked up to the receptionist, who escorted them to the boardroom where they met the president, Carl Zubriggen. August, a.k.a. Tony Lira, went through the same pitch and was asked the same questions.

The president examined the bonds; he seemed very interested. Then, all of a sudden, he went cold, and said he wasn't interested. They thanked him and left for their hotel.

They went to their rooms. August found Candice bundled up in bed. She looked up. "Hi."

"How're you feeling?"

"Crappy; my temperature hit one hundred and three this morning. I got up and took some aspirin and a cool shower to bring down the temperature. I just checked; it's gone down to 99 degrees."

"Maybe you're on the mend."

"God, I hope so." She gave him a sexy smile. "I want to be at one hundred percent for you when we go to Italy."

Eighty's just fine. Hundred percent might give me a coronary. "Sounds like you're getting better."

August ordered dinner through room service. He had veal chops and Candice had some more chicken soup, and half of August's dessert.

The following morning, August joined Andy and Steve, who drove to their first meeting with

Banca Commerical Zūrich, housed in a villa on a country road outside of the city. August went through his pitch; the managing partners examined the bonds, and passed on them.

The lunch meeting with Zūrich Investment Trust was more productive and the president, Albert Acklin, was interested. After lunch, they drove back to his office; Acklin looked over the bonds and agreed to have another meeting with Steve and August when they got back.

It was after four o'clock when the president of Zūrich Investment Trust walked them to their car. It took half an hour to drive to the Bank de Priv'e Zurich. The driver took a private road up to the gate; he hit the intercom button.

"Can I help you?"

"Steve Workman to see Mr. Zubriggen and Mr. Grunfelder." The gates opened and Steve drove through. The grounds were more natural than manicured.

They drove along the tree-lined cobblestone road and stopped in front of an old, somewhat enchanting chateau. August spotted cameras all the way from the entrance to the chateau and knew they were under surveillance. As they walked toward the entrance, the front door opened and two well-dressed men walked out to greet them.

Steve shook hands with one of them. "Steve Workman."

"David Zubriggen, nice to meet you. This is my partner, Hans Grunfelder."

"This is Andy Steel and Tony Lira." The bankers shook their hands, and then they followed them inside. August thought the décor was like the setting of a ski lodge in an old movie.

None of the furniture or artwork were props; they were the real thing and very expensive.

They went into Zubriggen's office, very masculine, beautiful oak paneling, leather chairs and a sofa. They took a seat. Hans Grunfelder turned toward August. "So, Mr. Lira, Steve informed us that you are in possession of a large amount of U.S. Bearer Bonds?"

Fuckin' bankers get right to the point, don't they? Well, then so will I. "Yeah, I just so happen to have 350 one-million-dollar bonds that I'd like to unload at a substantial discount."

"Are they counterfeit?" asked Hans.

"As far as I know, they're authentic, but they are hot." August didn't leave out anything, except how they were stolen. Then he handed them the three bonds. The two bankers carefully examined them. David went to his desk drawer, pulled out a magnifying glass, and set one of the bonds on his desk to take a closer look. He asked Hans to join him outside for a moment. "We'll be right back."

Five minutes later, the two bankers returned and took a seat. "Mr. Lira, what is your price?"

Fuck'um. "Why don't you make an offer?"

"We'll need a few days to make some inquiries and decide what the bonds are worth. Is it possible for you to leave one of the bonds with us?" asked David.

August looked at Steve, who turned to the bankers. "I need to speak to my client in private."The bankers stood. "We'll be in the living room; take your time," said David.

As the door shut behind the bankers, August said, "I wasn't sure if I should let them keep the bond. Not that I don't trust them, but if the serial number got back to the feds, we could be in deep shit."

"I forgot to tell you that I told the bankers we've seen, that you are a lifelong friend and not one to be fucked with, and if they did, you'd have them killed."

August laughed. "I wondered why all of them seemed a little nervous."

"I wouldn't give a bond to all the bankers we've met, but my friend vouches for these guys and thinks they might be willing to deal."

"Andy, tell them to come back in."

The bankers took their seats.

"We're going to Geneva tomorrow, and then I'm going to Italy for a few days. Steve will be in Liechtenstein during the same time. When we're back in Zurich I'll have Steve call you." Tony slid one of the bonds across the table. "I can't expect a receipt for a stolen bond."

"It will be safe here," said Hans. "Do you have dinner plans this evening?"

"No, I haven't thought about that yet," said August.

"Good, I hoped you would join us. We made reservations at the best restaurant in Zurich."

"In that case, we accept."

After a fabulous dinner, August got back to his suite late. Candice was bundled up under the covers fast asleep. It had been a long day and he was exhausted. He took a quick shower, then slid into bed and immediately slept.

Candice was already out of bed when August woke up. He put on a hotel terrycloth robe and walked into the living room. He found Candice dressed and sitting at the table, reading the paper. Room service had left a cart, one plate still covered, and a pot of coffee on the table. She looked up and smiled. "Good morning, I hope your breakfast is still warm."

"Looks like you kicked that cold."

"I feel great, and I'm ready to go." She poured coffee into a fresh cup and handed it to him. "When are we leaving for Geneva?"

"We're leaving at nine-thirty. He looked at his watch; he was surprised he had slept until eight. "We should be at the airport an hour before we take off so we better hurry. He walked over to the cart and took off the cover. "Eggs Benedict, perfect."

* * *

They arrived at Zurich International Airport at quarter to nine, checked in their luggage at the ticket counter, and headed for the gate. They took off on time, and fifty minutes later, touched down at Geneva International. Steve had made reservations at the five-star rated Des Bergues Hotel.

They checked in; Candice went shopping with Tony Lira's credit card, and the guys went to their first meeting with Banque de Credit Genève. They met with the president of the bank, Olin Halsek. Tony Lira went through his pitch; Halsek wasn't interested.

After lunch, they met Jacques Lature and Pierre DuBois, the managing partners of Banque Lature-DeBois Genève. They spent most of the afternoon there, negotiating a price for the bonds. They offered two cents on the dollar. August pushed for five. The bankers stood firm; Tony told them he would get back to them.

They got back to the hotel and went to the bar. They got a table and ordered drinks. August took a sip of his favorite scotch. "Well, at least we got an offer, not that I'd take it."

"Neither would I," said Steve. "We'll get better offers."

32

Before August went back to his room, he got recommendations from the concierge for some good restaurants and for a Ferrari rental for their road trip. She contacted the rental agency and reserved the car.

"I've reserved you a new 1984 Red Testarossa. It will be delivered at eight-thirty tomorrow morning."

August slipped her twenty dollars. "Perfect, thank you."

Candice wanted to paint the town, but August felt that she was pushing herself, for his benefit. Another night's rest would guarantee her full recovery, and he could use the sleep.

"You know, you were a pretty sick girl. I think we should take it easy tonight."

She pouted. "If you say so. I'm starving; can we at least go out to dinner?"

"There's supposed to be an excellent restaurant within walking distance of our hotel. Do you care if Steve and Andy join us?"

"That's fine, as long as we go early, and you're right, I could use more rest."

They met Andy and Steve in the lobby and walked to the restaurant. The food was excellent, and after the second bottle of wine, August could barely keep his eyes open. He paid the tab, they walked back to the hotel, said their goodbyes, and went to their rooms.

August and Candice got up at seven, got dressed, and packed. They had breakfast in the hotel, and checked out. The red Ferrari was parked in front of the hotel. The bellman loaded their luggage into the trunk and behind their seats. They got in, August turned the key, and the $100,000 Testarossa with a 4.9-liter, 12 cylinder, 390 horsepower engine came to life.

Candice opened the road map, gave directions as August shifted into first, and took off.

They took E-62, around Lake Geneva to Lake Lugano, and stopped to have lunch at a lakeside restaurant. They spent the night at the Hotel Villa De Este at Lake Como, and had a romantic dinner. After that, they strolled the ancient cobblestone streets, taking in the sights and stopping at a local coffeehouse for some espresso and a light dessert. They took the boardwalk back to the hotel, stopping to look at the moonlight glittering off the calm waters of Lake Como, then arm in arm, strolled back to their room, satisfied each other's lust, and fell into a deep slumber.

They flew through Milano, stopping in Pisa and Florence where they spent time sightseeing, touring the beautiful cathedrals, The Duomo, and museums full of magnificent art and statues, such as Michelangelo's "David." They had a late lunch then took off for Rome.

They arrived in Rome and checked into a hotel. The next day, they toured the city, marveled at the Sistine Chapel, and visited the Trevi Fountain, St. Peter's Cathedral, and The Coliseum.

The following day, they drove to Naples and took a ferry to the island of Capri, where they stayed at the Royal Pagono Hotel, spending the day at the hot springs and visiting the Blue Grotto Azure. The next morning, they took a ferry to Ischia to visit the gravesites of August's ancestors on his mother's side. All were involved in the fishing industry, long-lining for tuna and netting mackerel and calamari.

The Festival of Saint Joseph was being celebrated that evening. All of August's family was celebrating the engagement of one of his younger second cousins, Consetta, and her future husband, Jovanni. The accordions and mandolins played all night, as they sang and danced. Candice and August joined the children, cousins, aunts, and uncles in a traditional line dance as the beat to the music increased to a crescendo, taking their breath away.

The next day, they went to the island of Procida to visit his relatives on his father's side. He was amazed to see that all his uncles looked like his father, and his cousins looked like himself.

It seemed like half of the island joined in this party, one of the best August had ever attended. He hadn't seen them in years, and danced with his aunts and cousins, while all the men stood in line to dance with Candice, who was the hit of the party.

They drove back to Geneva, returned the Ferrari and took a train to Zurich, enjoying the scenery and gaping at the homes and chalets scattered around the countryside.

They checked back into the Hotel Eden Au Lac at 11:00 A.M. Steve had left a message at the desk. Steve and Andy had gotten back the day before yesterday; Steve was busy setting up meetings, and he should call him ASAP. As soon as they got to their suite, August called Steve, hoping he was still in his room.

He answered on the first ring.

"It's August, sounds like you've been busy."

"Liechtenstein wasn't very productive, but we have a few takers and more meetings with some new prospects. Why don't you come over to my room and we'll go over everything, then we can all go to lunch?"

"Good idea, what's your room number?"

"Fifty-one; see you in a few."

"I'm going over to Steve's room to talk about business, shouldn't be too long. We'll go to lunch when I get back."

"Great, it'll give me time to unpack and clean up." Candice headed for the bedroom, and August left the suite. Steve's room was down the hallway. He knocked, and Andy opened the door. "How was your trip?"

"We had a great time; toured Florence, Rome, and Naples, and then we visited my relatives in Procida and Ischia, where we partied and ate all day and night. I just wish I had more time to visit with them. So, fill me in."

"We have our second meetings with Older & Co., Zürich

Investment Trust, and Bank de Priv'e Zurich, which I still think is our best prospect. I also set up meetings with three more banks who showed some interest. One was recommended by one of the owners of a bank that I visited in Liechtenstein. Our first meeting's at three this afternoon, then three more tomorrow, and two the following day."

"What's your take on the banks we've already visited?"

"I think the bankers are trying to legitimize the bonds. They understood they were hot but authentic. Currently they're not listed as stolen, which confuses them."

"That's because the feds are still not sure what happened to them, and have no proof that they were actually stolen. They're still visiting all the stock brokerage houses throughout the Northwest and Canada that shipped the stocks and bonds to the clearinghouse in Washington. Hell, they probably don't even have a clue about what's missing, or how much they're worth," said August.

"They might by now but nothing has come up on the radar yet, at least not in Europe," said Andy.

"Well, let's hope we get a solid offer. I'm going to get cleaned up before we go to lunch. I'll call you when we're ready to go," said August. He turned, walked to the door, and let himself out.

After lunch, they regrouped and Steve drove to their first meeting with a new bank, AEG Privat Bank Zürich. They met with the managing partners, William Burkhart and Peter Halsek.

The meeting went well; they said they would have an offer on the table the following day.

Steve wanted to take everyone out to dinner at his favorite restaurant, the Château Beaujolais, a small very old restaurant located on the hillside overlooking Lake Zurich. Steve had invited them the first night they arrived in Zurich. August was burned out from the road trip, but accepted.

It was a fantastic evening with gourmet food, excellent wine, a beautiful atmosphere, ending up on the balcony smoking Cuban cigars, except for Candice who smoked a small cigar recommended by the maitre d'.

They enjoyed a snifter of Cognac, smoked their cigars, and then drove back to the hotel.

The following morning, they went to their first meeting with Older & Co. The partners, Aaron Rothenberg and John Newhime, offered two cents on the dollar and were prepared to cut a check or wire seven million dollars U.S., upon receipt of the bonds.

August already had an offer of two cents on the dollar from Banque Lature-DuBois in Geneva and decided that seven million was not enough. At this point, he wasn't about to burn any bridges and told the owners of Older & Co. that he would think about it, and get back to them.

The afternoon was spent with two new prospects. The first wasn't interested. The second meeting with the partners of Privat Banque Krieger-Dutch lasted until six. They were definitely interested, but said they needed some time. They intended to resell the bonds to one of their clients.

The following day's morning meeting was with Zürich Investment Trust. The president, Albert Acklin, talked for almost an hour about the risks and the possibility of being unable to convert the bonds. "Mr. Lira, after giving this much thought, I am willing to offer you two cents on the dollar. That's seven million dollars."

August was ready to tell him to go fuck himself, but bit his tongue. "That's a lot of money, but I was hoping to get more. I have a few more offers coming in; Steve will stay in contact with you."

"I can only keep this offer open for three days, after that, we'd have to renegotiate."

August was almost ready to jump across the table and strangle this greedy motherfucker, but kept his hands to himself, as he clutched the arms of the chair, his hands turning white.

They went to lunch. Steve chuckled. "I thought you were going to smack him."

"If I had a gun, I would've shot that fat greedy fuck."

That got them all laughing, while they enjoyed their cocktails.

At two o'clock sharp, they drove down the tree-lined cobblestone road and again stopped in front of the old and somewhat enchanting chateau that housed the Bank de Priv'e Zurich.

David Zubriggen and Hans Gruenfelder met them at the door. They went back to the same room and sat in the same seats. After a little chitchat, they got down to business. David slid the million-dollar bond across the table. "Mr. Lira, after due diligence, we can offer you . . . two cents on the dollar," said Zubriggen.

August didn't react the same way that he did with Albert Acklin, with whom he had bad vibes. He liked these guys. *Can't blame them for giving a low-ball offer.* "I was hoping for more." He pulled out the envelope containing the two other bonds, stuffed the third one in, and put it back in his inner coat pocket. "We'll be leaving for the U.S. tomorrow morning. If you decide to reconsider, contact Steve." He now knew that the bonds had some value, and was sure he could get more. "I have some business I need to tend to back in the States. I intend to come back to Zurich in a week or two. Steve will let you know when. No matter what happens, I enjoyed your company and would like to take you and your wives out to dinner when we return."

They stood and shook hands. "I look forward to seeing you then," said Hans.

The two bankers walked them out, said their goodbyes, and Steve drove them down the cobblestone road. "It's got to be a fuckin' conspiracy. I think all these bankers are in on it, and somehow those assholes plan to share in the profits," said August, half-heartedly. Then he cracked up, with Steve and Andy joining in.

Steve got serious. "There's one thing for sure. These guys know you don't have a lot of options and are going to work you over the coals. But I still think that if we're patient, we'll get a better offer."

"I think you're right, and they really haven't had enough time to find an interested buyer," said Andy.

"I think you're both right. We'll wait a week or two and come back. As for tonight, let's go out and have a good time."

On the twenty-ninth of February, Steve and Andy flew back to San Francisco, and Candice and August to L.A.

33

Nick was at his desk, leaning back on his chair, looking at the stacks of reports he needed to review before he prepared his summations to his boss. There were over thirty field agents assigned to this case, and other than the action in San Francisco with the Chinese Triad, no one had heard or found out anything pertaining to the Western Airlines robbery.

It was 9:00 A.M.; he needed a strong shot of caffeine before he tackled the boring part of his job. He got up, went to the bathroom to take a leak, washed his hands and splashed his face with cold water, went into the lunchroom and poured himself a large Styrofoam cup of coffee and headed back to his desk.

At 11:30, Leo walked up. "Wanna go to lunch?"

"Thanks, but I need to finish this report. Higgins and Warner are bugging my ass to get it done."

"We're going to Louie's. Want me to bring you back something?"

Nick reached into his pocket and pulled a five out of his money clip; he handed it to Leo. "Get me a large meatball sandwich. Thanks for thinking of me."

Leo left and Nick dove back into his paperwork.

An hour later, Leo brought Nick his sandwich and a large Coke. Nick was starving; he unwrapped his sandwich and took a bite.

"How's it goin'?" asked Leo.

Nick swallowed, and took a sip of his Coke. "Thanks for the drink. I'm starting to understand why this robbery is so fuckin' important. I've kept a tally of all our field agents' reports concerning the consigned stocks and bonds sent to the Washington clearinghouse. We're talking about a billion dollars or more."

"I knew this was big, but over a fuckin' billion dollars! That makes this the biggest heist ever."

"That's not the topper. So far, I've listed over 250 one-million-dollar bearer bonds in this shipment. Not too many people can write a check for a million-dollar bond. I'll bet these bonds are the reason Higgins, Warner, and the director of the FBI are pushing for answers."

"This may go further than the FBI, maybe to the treasury department, or even the White House," said Leo. "Can I give you a hand?"

"Thanks, maybe I'll be able to go home tonight." Nick showed Leo the process. Leo slid a chair over and got to work, while Nick finished his meatball sandwich; then he jumped in too.

By six o'clock, they finished and sat back. They ran the totals of the various types of documents.

Nick looked at the figures. "Let's see, there are 350 one-million-dollar U.S. bearer bonds paying an interest rate of 6.9 to 8.9%, maturity date 2002, 100 million dollars in mutual bonds, and over 250 million dollars in stocks, at the current value.

"The interest paid on the bearer bonds could be as much as $620 million, and the municipal bonds, $80 million. When you include the interest paid on all the bonds, through maturity, and the market value of the stock, the total is $1,400,000,000."

Leo shook his head. "No wonder they're having a fit. This is the largest robbery in, not only U.S. history, but the whole world. I read that our federal budget deficit is around twenty billion dollars. That means the amount stolen could add seven percent to our deficit.

"That amount could fuck up our whole economy."

Nick stacked his papers, putting his report and three copies on top. "Well, I guess it's time to see Higgins."

Nick picked up the phone and pushed the intercom button.

"Higgins."

"It's Nick; I finished my report."

"Meet me in Warner's office."

Nick stood. "Thanks for helping me out."

"No problem. I'm going to stick around. We'll go out for a drink after you're finished."

Nick knocked on Director Warner's door. Warner waved him in; Nick sat next to his boss, Paul Higgins.

"Well, whaddya got?" asked Warner.

"It's been twenty-five days since the robbery. We have over thirty field agents working on this case and have followed up on every lead, interviewed anyone associated with Western Airlines, Brinks, airport personnel, freight forwarding companies, the Washington clearinghouse and all the brokerage firms involved.

"We have run surveillance on everyone closely related to the robbery, from baggage handlers to Brinks guards. We've set up an 800 number for anonymous tips, and have squeezed our informants dry.

"So far, we have nothing. It's as if these stocks and bonds just disappeared into thin air.

"I now have all the information from all the brokerage houses that sent the documents to the clearinghouse consigned to the stolen shipment. I've run totals on the stolen certificates. Municipal bearer bonds total $100 million, stock certificates, $250 million, and 350 one-million-dollar U.S. bearer bonds. Interest on the municipal bonds is $80 million, and a whopping $620 million on the bearer bonds, for a total of $1,400,000,000."

Nick knew there was a lot more to this case than his bosses had told him, and it was time to put the cards on the table.

"Not many people can afford to buy million-dollar bonds, except wealthy individuals, banks, or other governments. Almost four weeks have gone by, and we're no closer to solving this case than day one. I need all the help I can get. I feel you've held back information that might help us get these securities back."

The director of the L.A. office leaned back in his chair. "I'm not sure that the information that was held back will help, but I think you deserve to know everything.

"In 1983, the total budget deficit was 20 billion dollars. If someone were to dump a billion dollars, the equivalent to 5% of the budget deficit, there could be major financial repercussions. That's why the treasury department contacted the FBI.

"Bearer Bonds, issued from 1983 and earlier have no recorded ownership and could be sold or redeemed by the person or organization in possession of them. They are registered by a serial number to prevent counterfeiting.

"But, what if another country held a large sum of counterfeit or stolen bonds, and wanted to cash them in? Our government would have to honor them, or face political embarrassment.

"So the legislature passed a law that stops the issuing of bearer bonds, which is replaced by the issuance of 'registered bonds' that lists the purchaser electronically. The bearer bonds that were stolen were being recalled by the treasury department and had already been replaced with 'registered bonds' in order to meet 1984 requirements, listing those who purchased them.

"Now, if the stolen bonds were sold to another country, our government's exposure would not only be the new 350 registered bonds already issued, but the 350 stolen bonds as well.

"Forget the stocks and municipal bonds. The total liability at maturity of 700 one-million-dollar bearer bonds is close to 2 billion dollars, increasing the budget deficit by 10%.

"We need to get those bonds back!"

"I think we should contact Interpol. Those bonds could already be on foreign soil," said Nick.

"Good idea, take care of it. Let us know if you learn anything; we're getting a lot of heat from upstairs."

Nick sensed that the meeting was over and stood.

"One more thing, I've been ordered to keep a lid on this. We don't need the media to find out about this story," said Warner.

"There was a small article in the *Times* the day after the robbery. It was on the ninth page and only mentioned a robbery at Western

Airlines. I haven't seen anything since."

"Good. Make sure all the agents involved keep it zipped."

"Anything else?"

"No, just keep us in the loop."

Nick left the director's office and headed for his desk. Leo was still there leafing through the reports. He spotted Nick. "How'd it go?"

"Let's get the hell out of here. I'll fill you in over a drink."

* * *

After returning from Switzerland, August spent a couple of days with Mickey, going over his concerns with one of the Butler brothers. He was causing a rift with the crew, complaining that his cut was too small and that August got paid too much for what he does.

Bill Butler had a reputation for being a hot head and a bone crusher. August took Diz with him, had a little talk, and worked things out.

It was dark when August pulled into his driveway. He got out of his Porsche. The March winds were howling, dropping the temperature farther. The wind created an eerie whistle through the surrounding trees, causing a chill to run down his spine.

He heard something behind him. He spun around, as he grabbed the Berretta 9 millimeter automatic from the small of his back. The sound seemed to have come from the side of the garage. He moved toward the garage, gun extended in both hands. He reached the front corner of the garage, leaving only the space between the garage and the property wall.

He didn't hear another sound. He dropped to his knee and peeked around the corner. He stared eye level with a large coastal raccoon who hissed indignantly at him. Startled, he damn near pulled the trigger. He chuckled to himself. *How the hell would I explain firing my gun, to my neighbors, and possibly, the police?*

He pulled out his keys and started to unlock the front door, and saw it was ajar. He stepped back and moved to the side of the house, and again pulled out his gun. He went to the back door; it was wide open. He thought, "Someone's been here and is already gone, or he's stupid enough to leave doors open, giving me a warning."

Not taking any chances, he cocked his Berretta and stepped through the back door. It was dark; no lights were on in the house. About halfway through the kitchen, he stopped and listened. He moved to the light switches, one turned on the kitchen light, and the other the living room.

He turned on the kitchen room light, fanning his gun back and forth, expecting someone to jump out shooting—nothing. He turned on the living room light, and entered the living room, which had been ransacked. He headed for the bedrooms and the bathroom, turning on the lights as he went through them.

The place looked like a tornado had gone through it. He went to the front door; the lock was busted out. He got a chair, secured it under the knob, then walked into the kitchen and shut the door and locked it. He opened a cabinet and pulled out a bottle of scotch, got a glass, some ice, and poured a stiff drink.

He took inventory to see if anything was missing. The end table sat on the corner of the Oriental rug. He moved it and pulled back the rug to see if anyone had found his secret compartment. He took out his pocketknife and pried up the loose oak boards. Nothing had been tampered with. He put everything back in place, then sat down, and took a good pull of scotch. *This has fuckin' Eddie Burger's prints all over the place.*

August reported the incident to the guys. He questioned Burger's involvement in Carlito's murder and no one could pin Burger for the hit. August sent Diz and the Nieto brothers to pay a visit to Eddie and some of his men. They caught them off guard at the Bare Elegance. Diz told Eddie that he'd better not have been involved in the ransacking of August's house, while Flea Nieto pulled out a measuring tape and measured Eddie's height, as they stood in the parking lot. One of Eddie's men asked, "What the fuck is he doing?"

Chuck Nieto said, "Measuring him for a body bag."

As Chuck, Flea, and Diz laughed, Eddie said, "Fuck you!" in a serious tone.

"No, fuck you! You fat piece of shit. I got a bullet with your name on it," said Diz.

"You're not the only one that has bullets. Tell August he's not the only one that's runnin' shit around here."

Diz said, "Yeah, the only thing that you're running around here is your fuckin' mouth," as Diz, Chuck, and Flea turned and left.

* * *

A week had gone by since August returned home from Switzerland. Mickey and he were watching the 1982 NBA Champion Lakers play against the '83 NBA Champions, the Philadelphia 76ers, on TV.

James Worthy took the ball up the court, shot, and missed; Kareem Abdul Jabbar got the rebound and passed the ball to Magic Johnson, who took a shot, making three points. The fans yelled, including August and Mickey.

The phone rang. August got up to answer the phone, and Mickey turned down the volume. "Hello."

"I think it's time we plan to fly back," said Steve.

"When do you want to leave?"

"How about Saturday? Andy will fly with me."

"Meet you there, same hotel?" asked August.

"Sounds good to me. I'll call you tomorrow to exchange flight numbers and times of arrival."

"I'll make arrangements in the morning." August hung up, and then called Candice.

"Want to go to Switzerland?"

"When!?"

"Plan to leave on Saturday. Think you can make it?"

"I think so. I'll start working on it when I hang up."

"I'm going to make reservations tomorrow morning, so let me know."

34

Saturday, March 10
Second trip to Switzerland

Candice and August flew from Tijuana Airport to Mexico City where they boarded an Iberia Airlines 747 to Europe at 1:30 P.M., landing at Zurich International at 11:30 Sunday morning.

They disembarked, walked to the baggage claim area, and found the carousel where their luggage would come out.

The baggage started to dump off the conveyor; they spotted their suitcases, pulled them off the carousel, and headed for customs. August had Candice go in front of him and take her own suitcase (with the bonds hidden in the lining) through customs. She handed the official her passport. "Your reason for coming to Switzerland?"

She gave him a sexy smile. "A vacation."

He took his lecherous eyes off her cleavage, quickly glanced at the passport, and back to her cleavage. Then he looked up as if he was verifying the passport's picture, stamped it, and handed it back to her. "Enjoy your stay."

August, a.k.a. Tony Lira, handed the customs official his passport. He thumbed through the stamped pages. "You certainly travel a lot, Mr. Lira."

"Business."

"Yes, and I see you were in Zurich ten days ago."

"Yeah, I had to come back to close this deal."

"What kind of business are you in?"

August didn't like where this was headed. "I'm in the entertainment business."

"Would you please take your luggage and go to the table?" He pointed, "Over there."

August set his suitcase on the table; another official opened and searched it, not finding anything of importance. He asked to see his driver's license and to empty out his pockets. August did as he was told; the official waved him through, and walked away.

As he adjusted his clothes and shut the suitcase, he thought, "Man, am I glad I sent Candice through by herself. We would have been fucked if they searched her suitcase. I wonder why the customs guy didn't notice that she was here ten days ago. Had to be that sexy body and her good looks. Hell, she has the same effect on me."

To his surprise, Candice was standing next to Steve and Andy, who were both holding signs with "Mr. Lira" on them. They all tried to keep a straight face as August walked up to them.

"Mr. Lira?" asked Andy.

"The one and only," he growled.

Steve was about to say something serious —but started to crack up; the rest joined in.

"What are you doing here?" August asked.

"Plane was delayed, so we thought we'd wait for you. I already rented a car; it's parked outside," said Steve.

August and Andy put the suitcases in the trunk of the Mercedes 500SEL, climbed in, and Steve pulled into the traffic. "How come it took so long for you to clear customs?" asked Andy.

"They gave me a hard time, and then they searched my suitcase."

"You think they suspect anything?"

"Mr. Lira does a lot of traveling, and was in Zurich ten days ago. Maybe that raised a red flag. I can tell you this much, if we have to come back here again, we're flying over in a private jet."

Steve pulled up to the valet parking at the Hotel Eden Au Lac, where they checked in, went to lunch, made plans for the meetings starting Monday morning, went to the spa for a massage, compliments of the hotel, then had an early dinner.

The first meeting was with a new prospect, Privat Banque Krieger-Dutch. The owners, Hans Krieger and Karl Dutch, were not only hospitable, but also very interested in the bonds. Hans was examining the bond and looked up. "I'm sure you have talked to other bankers of private, independent, clandestine, and holding banks. Many have only a few customers with enormous amounts of money, and other valuables, like art, jewelry, and precious metals—held in their vaults. Some of these riches go back as far as deposits made during WWII by Nazi Germany.

"Our fathers started this bank in 1936; we have customers from all walks of life, and throughout the world. If we purchase these bonds, we would sell them to one of our customers who would be willing to sit on them. We want to purchase these bonds and are willing to pay two cents on the dollar for them."

August was stunned. *You mean I sat here listening to how great their bank was, and they offer a measly two cents on the dollar.* He tried to keep his composure. "This is the fifth offer of two cents on the dollar that I've received. The reason I returned to Zurich was to inform my first four prospects that I will not accept two cents on the dollar for these bonds; my counter offer is ten cents on the dollar, not a penny less."

Hans looked like he was going to choke. "Would you excuse us for a moment?" The two bankers stood and left the room.

"I didn't expect you to ask for ten cents," said Steve.

"Fuck'em. Let them come back with another offer."

They came back and took a seat. "We were able to speak to a couple of our clients, who are interested. Our counter offer is five cents on the dollar." He held his hand up as if to stop August from responding. "I know you have other bankers that you're meeting with. Our offer is good for the next forty-eight hours."

"We will have an answer to you by then," said August as he stood to leave.

They had lunch with Aaron Rothenberg, and his partner, John Newhime, of Older & Co. Privatbank AG Zurich. They were on their dessert when John Newhime started to get down to business."We have increased our offer to five cents on the dollar," said Newhime, who had this smug look on his face as if he expected Mr. Lira to jump out of his seat and take the offer.

"Well, it looks like five cents on the dollar is now the benchmark for the value of the bonds. As I informed the bank that just offered me the same amount, I want ten cents on the dollar for the bonds, not a penny less."

August could see the disappointment on the banker's face, who hesitated for a moment before he spoke. "I'm sorry but this will be our final offer. If you should reconsider, please give us a call." He stood, followed by his partner and the three of them. They shook hands and left.

That afternoon they visited two more new prospects—both passed on the deal. They got back to the hotel; Steve had a message on his phone from Jacques Lature a managing partner of Banque Lature-DeBois Genève, who thanked them, but was not willing to increase their offer.

"Well at least we don't have to go back to Geneva," said August at dinner. "Who're we seeing tomorrow?"

"Our first meeting is with Albert Acklin, the president of Zūrich Investment Trust. Then we have a five o'clock with Bank de Priv'e Zurich. Last time we met, you extended a dinner invitation to David Zubriggen, Hans Grunfelder, and their wives. I took it upon myself to invite them to dinner this evening."

"I'm glad you did. I still think they are our best bet."

They met with Albert Acklin the following morning. Five cents on the dollar was the most he was willing to offer.

At five o'clock, they met with David and Hans. Drinks were served, then appetizers, and then they sat down and got to business.

"We have a client that is willing to buy the bonds from us. He's willing to buy them for seven cents on the dollar, so the best I can offer at this time is five cents."

August was about to blow them away then thought, *What the hell, give it one more shot.* "Look, I want ten cents on the dollar. That's thirty-five million to me." He locked eyes with Zubriggen.

"You take care of Steven's share and I'll take care of Andy and all the expenses. I've received a better offer than five cents and I'm returning to the States tomorrow. The prospective buyer is flying into Los Angeles on Monday to discuss the terms.

"I hope you consider my offer. But let me be clear. I'm not interested in flying back here to negotiate. If you decide to accept my terms, contact Steve and we'll fly back with the bonds.

"I hope we can come to terms, I like you guys, and trust you implicitly. If the buyer doesn't come through for some reason, maybe we can do business."

"I'm glad you're keeping the door open; the price we would pay is predicated on what our buyer is willing to offer for the bonds. Things could change tomorrow.

"Enough business, let's have another drink, pick up our wives and go to dinner," said Hans, as he stood up and walked toward the bar.

"First, I have to pick up my girlfriend at the hotel; I'll give her a call so she can get ready."

"Fine, we'll pick you up at your hotel in one hour."

The guys entered the lobby; Candice was sitting in the lobby, nursing a martini. She spotted them and stood. She was wearing a skintight black dress with a halter-style top that showed off her hourglass figure.

August caught himself gawking, as well as his friends, and every other male and jealous woman in the lobby area.

They went into the lobby bar and had a drink. It was time to meet up with the bankers and their wives. As they walked out the lobby door, a black Mercedes limo pulled up.

David Zubriggen and Hans Grunfelder introduced their wives, who were immediately a little jealous of Candice because their husbands couldn't take their eyes off her cleavage.

August thought that the restaurant and dinner was one of the best, and after a couple of cocktails, even the bankers' wives loosened up and all had a good time.

The following day, they got up early, packed, and left for Zurich International Airport.

35

August got back from Switzerland and dropped Candice off at her apartment. She was extremely beautiful, but it was getting a bit heavy with demands and expectations; he wasn't interested in settling down just yet.

August went home and checked on his operation. He was tired, needed a break, and space to think. He drove down to the marina, got on his Viking, forty-six foot yacht, *BLACK FIN*, motored to Catalina, grabbed a mooring line in Emerald Bay, and tied off his boat. He changed into swim trunks and dove into the crystal clear water.

It was early spring and the water temperature was in the low sixties, giving August an electrical jolt, as he hit the flat, glassy sea. There were only a few yachts moored in the picturesque bay, giving him plenty of room to swim, as he tried to get accustomed to the bone-chilling temperature.

He swam up to a sixty-foot Hatteras sportfisher and hung onto the swim step to catch his breath.

"You're pretty adventurous, to take a dip in that cold water."

August looked up toward the sound of the woman's voice, seeing this very attractive blonde, smiling at him.

"It feels great, why don't you join me?"

"No way, I'll stay right here and enjoy the sun."

"Suit yourself, I better keep moving, because it's a lot colder than I want to admit."

She laughed, as August pushed off. "See you later."

Thinking, "God I hope so."

He climbed out and lay on his deck, soaking in the rays, listening to the waves splash against the hull of his yacht, the seagulls squawking, and the seals barking. He could feel his mind clearing, enjoying the simple things of life, instead of the crazy pace he had maintained for the last few months. He took a deep breath, exhaled, and dozed off.

The wake of a passing yacht hit the hull, jarring August, who woke up abruptly. The sun had moved well toward the west. He knew he had been soaking in the rays far too long, and was probably sunburned.

He felt a little groggy so he dove off the bow, swam to shore, and walked on the beach. He looked over at the Hatteras, where the girl he'd met gave him a wave. He waved back and kept walking.

After combing the beach for an hour, he swam back to his yacht, took a quick shower, and changed into a pair of shorts and a Hawaiian print shirt.

He went into the galley, poured himself a drink, twenty-year-old Glenlivet scotch on the rocks, pulled a cigar out of his humidor, snipped off the end, climbed up to the bridge, and sat in the captain's chair. He took a sip, then a pull from his cigar, while looking out at the Catalina Channel. It was a beautiful afternoon, infinitely clear; he could see the Palos Verdes Peninsula.

August thought about his life as he passed through the continuum of time and space, now and then entering a time warp, capturing whole chunks of his past. He was aware of what was going on because he'd been there, and controlled his destiny. Now he was faced with an unknown. There wasn't any guarantee he could pull this complicated caper off, so he knew he had to rely on his instincts and experience to get him through. He made a commitment to those surfer dudes, and had to do something with these bonds, not to mention his own investment.

August realized, that after coming back from Switzerland the second time, having unsuccessful meetings with the bankers, the New York Mafia, the Jewish Mob, and then the Chinese Triad, moving the bonds was not going to be as easy as he had anticipated.

He spent several months of his time and money, traveling, fronting his friends, and even advancing fifty-thousand dollars to the surfer dudes so they felt secure.

The most August had been offered was five cents on the dollar from the Swiss bankers, grossing him 17.5 million dollars. There were many people involved that would have to be paid their share. He calculated his expenses. After paying off everyone, he'd net a couple million, if he was lucky.

He sat back and looked at the figures, musing, "A lot of money. But, I could make that much on a large load of marijuana with less risk, and I know and trust my guys and my customers."

On the other hand, in the time it was taking to move these bonds, many new, untested, and perhaps dangerous people were becoming involved, increasing his risk exponentially.

Sure it had cost him some dough, but hell, he had made around 350 grand on the pot smuggle caper with the guys. So he was satisfied.

He asked himself, "Who would benefit by having the bonds? Who wants them the most?" He took a sip of scotch, enjoying the warm sensation, as it flowed downward. Then it hit him. "Son-of-a-bitch! The fucking government! Who else would want these bonds more than the government? Fuck, at maturity, Uncle Sam would lose close to a billion dollars. I'll bet they would pay out a big reward to get them back. Now, how the hell could I contact them and approach the issue without them throwing me into prison?"

His glass was empty so he left the bridge, climbed down the ladder to the deck and went into the salon. "That's just not going to work. I'm going to have to find the right person. There has to be somebody out there who would take charge of them. But the longer it takes to unload them, the more exposure I get. And my gut feeling is that I've had enough."

He poured himself another drink, grabbed a jar of cashews, and headed back to the bridge.

"I need a go between,—yeah, why not one of my attorneys?

Frank almost threw me out of his office—I'll ask Alan. He's good and I can trust him, and he actually has the balls to do this. All he has to do is open up some dialogue with the FBI and see what they're willing to pay.

What if they're not interested? The fucking feds would be all over Alan's ass, and probably mine too. Nah, he's too smart; I'm sure our asses would be covered somehow. But, if that doesn't work, what then?"

He relit his cigar and took a pull. As he blew out a plume of smoke, he flashed back to his meeting with Young Lee as he said, "We counterfeit bonds, but not million-dollar bearer bonds."

"Why the hell didn't I think of that? I guess that could be another option." He thought of the Swiss bankers. "Those greedy mother-fuckers, they knew that they had me bent over when they first offered me two cents on the dollar. What if I sell them counterfeit bonds? Would serve those fuckin' bankers right. Now, how am I going to . . .? Shit, why didn't I think of Jim and Dusty before? They could possibly do this. If the feds take back the bonds and pay the guys a reward, my obligation to them would be settled. Then I'll go back to Switzerland and get mine."

In 1971, August got busted by the DEA for smuggling marijuana by plane and was sentenced to five years in the Terminal Island Federal Prison, with a melancholy view of his old Palos Verdes playground.

During his incarceration, he met Jim and Dusty, who were doing time for counterfeiting. After they all got out, August stayed in touch with them.

They ran a printing company located in the San Fernando Valley and were still in the counterfeiting game. August planned to give them a call as soon as he got back to the mainland.

He was so excited, as the potential solution unfolded, that he thought about casting off and leaving the island that very afternoon.

"Hello, *BLACK FIN*, anybody on board?"

August jumped off his chair and looked over the stern. There was the lovely lady that he met briefly on the Hatteras, and a couple, in a small Boston Whaler.

"Hi there," said August.

"We're going on a cocktail cruise. I noticed you were alone. Want to join us?"

Slim and Dusty can wait till tomorrow. "Sure, sounds fun."

"It'll have to be BYOB, unless you want a martini."

"No, that's okay; I've already started drinking scotch. I'll just pour a fresh one." He ran through the salon to the galley, filled his glass, grabbed the jar of cashews, and headed for the stern. He opened the door, stepped out on the swim step, handed the jar of nuts to the guy, and climbed aboard the Whaler, sitting down next to this beautiful woman, whose name he still didn't know.

He held out his hand. "I'm August Taracina."

She smiled. "Cindy Alden; this is my cousin, Tina, and her husband, Joe Stephano." They shook hands.

"I usually like to know the man's name before I hold his nuts," Joe quipped, with a chuckle.

"Good one. Nice to meet you," said August. He turned toward Cindy. "Thank you for inviting me. It's a beautiful afternoon for a cruise."

They motored through Emerald Bay and Crystal Cove, then into Twin Harbors, having a great time. Joe invited August to join them for dinner on his yacht, where they enjoyed the evening together. August had been with plenty of women—but for some unexplained reason, he really felt a good, solid connection with this one.

"So, what do you do when you're not on your yacht?" asked Cindy.

"I'm in importing and exporting."

"What about you?"

"I'm a dental hygienist; I work and live in Long Beach."

They talked for another hour. It was getting late; Joe offered to take August back to his yacht. His time was up and he had to make his move. "Maybe I could see you when we're back on the mainland?"

"Maybe you could." Cindy walked over to the galley counter

and got a notepad and a pen. She gave him her number and lightly kissed him on the lips. "I had a lot of fun, and I'm glad we had time to get to know each other."

"Me too. I'll call you."

Joe and August jumped into the whaler. Joe started the motor and took him back to his yacht.

"Thanks for inviting me along tonight," said August.

"I enjoyed your company, but thank Cindy; she's the one who wanted you to join us."

Joe pulled the Whaler alongside the stern of August's sportfisher. He climbed onto the swim step. "Thanks for the ride."

"You're welcome. I think we'll be seeing you again," said Joe, smiling, as he pulled away and headed back to his yacht.

I'm sure we will, if I have anything to say about it. August looked over at the Hatteras; Cindy was looking his way and gave him a wave. He waved back, as their eyes locked onto each other's. Neither moved until Joe pulled alongside his yacht, then Cindy gave him a little wave and walked into the cabin.

He thought Cindy was absolutely great and planned to take her out. Little did he know, with all the bond strategy and planning on his mind, that down the road, the woman he had just met would become his wife.

36

The following morning, August was up at six, fired up the throaty twin diesels, released the mooring lines and headed for San Pedro, and a new business venture.

He pulled into his slip and secured the lines, then hooked up the shore power and phone connections.

Jim and Dusty were a couple of 1960 throwbacks, still reliving the hippie life-style, but they were really excellent at their clandestine trade. Before they got busted and did time in the California Federal Penitentiary, they counterfeited IDs, and provided all the background documents for entire organizations. These documents were required to get passports and drivers licenses. They also printed all of the betting cards for the bookies in the area.

August knew these guys could, possibly, counterfeit the bearer bonds, and gave his old cell mates a call.

"Valley Printing, this is Jim."

"It's August; you have time to meet with me today?"

"If I didn't, I'd make time. How's it going, buddy?"

"Great, I think I have something for you."

"How about one o'clock?"

"See you then."

August went to his house, opened his secret compartment under the rug, and pulled out one of the three bonds he used as samples for the Swiss bankers. The rest of the bonds were still buried in the watertight Halliburton stainless steel cases underneath Nana's house.

He jumped into his car, took the 110 north to the 405 west, took the 101 north and then the off-ramp to Coldwater Canyon Road, turned left, then right on Burbank Boulevard.

He pulled his Porsche to the curb in front of Valley Printing, got out and headed for the entrance. He walked up to the counter; Jim was at his desk and looked up. He was a Camel- smoking, tall skinny guy, around fifty with long shaggy hair, wearing thick lens, horn-rimmed glasses. He was an expert line drawing artist, an excellent printer and engraver.

"Hey man, what's happening?"

"Been busy, that's why I wanted to talk to you two."

Jim stood and walked over to August and shook hands. "We gonna need some privacy?"

"It would be a good idea."

Jim went to the front door, locked it, and turned the open sign to the closed side. "Let's go see what Dusty's up to."

Dusty was slumped over a workbench, busy, toiling meticulously, wearing highly magnified glasses. "Dusty, we have a visitor," said Jim.

Dusty flipped up the magnified glasses, as he turned to greet August. Dusty was a light-skinned, green-eyed black man around fifty-five. Dusty and Jim lived together in a small house not far from their job. They had a large detached garage in the backyard, where they stored a lot of old printing equipment that they refurbished and used for their little counterfeit operation.

He got up and they shook hands. "How's it hanging, Italian stallion?"

"So, what have you been working on?" asked August.

"The tickets for the Olympics. We've been doing real good with them. I'm in the process of making up some new plates for the next run."

"Aren't the seats numbered?"

"Yeah, but we're not printing those. We're doing field tickets, and wholesaling to guys that are moving them on the street. There's no numbers, but they're a bitch to duplicate because of the hologram on them. We have to run them through the printer three times to layer the ink. They're coming out perfect and we're making a good profit."

"Well, that's why I want to talk to you guys. You're the best counterfeiters I know, not that I know a lot of them. But I've seen your work and I think you can do this for me."

He pulled the sample out of his jacket and unfolded it. "I want you guys to print this." He held it up. "Think you can do it?"

They stared at the bond in shock and amazement; the room fell silent for thirty seconds. "Can we do it?" Jim took the bond from August, walked over to the workbench, and held it under a bright light. Dusty and Jim studied it for a minute. "Think we could keep it overnight to make sure?" said Dusty.

August chuckled, "No fuckin' way." They all laughed.

"You know the government is having big problems with the advent of high quality copy machines being used to counterfeit all sorts of documents. But those documents are nothing like this bearer bond which is three dimensional.

"Not too many people that can match them and there's only a handful who could reproduce them perfectly. Can we do it? I don't know, but we can sure give it a hell of a try. It's not going to be easy; in fact, it would be the hardest thing we've ever tried," Jim said.

Dusty studied the bond again. "Going to have to do a little research on the printing process first—we've done currency before, and I know this is similar, but I want to check out the ink.

"I think our biggest obstacle will be reconstituting the paper. How many pieces do you have?"

"Three hundred fifty of them."

Jim whistled. "Fuck me! That's a lot of dinero."

"How many can you do in a relatively short period of time?" asked August.

"I'm pretty sure the ink and paper used for the bonds is the same ink and paper our government uses to print currency. If I'm right, we have to retrieve all the ink off existing dollar bills, and then reconstitute the paper. The ink we can do, but the paper—I think I know someone that might be able to pull it off."

"What kind of time frame are we looking at for something like this?"

"Hell, August, I don't fuckin' know. After we do our research, maybe we should do a small run first. Let's say, we do twenty of them."

Jim re-examined the bond, set it on the table, measured it, and then made a few calculations on size and thickness. "We'll need a minimum of fifteen one-dollar bills per side. I'd say we should start with twenty a side to be safe. Dusty and I will retrieve the ink from the bills. Then we have to separate the colors and oils so that when we print, we can layer the different colors, making them exactly like the original bonds.

"Now you have a full process of alchemy going on, but the next thing is to process the paper from the blank dollar bills to re-create material exactly like the original bonds were printed on."

"Who's this friend you were talking about?" asked August.

"Her name is Sunny Rain. Who knows what her real name was before she became a flower child. She's an artist who creates her own paper and parchment to paint on. She uses an ancient art form to make all sorts of elegant paper from rags and used material. She'd take this material, process it, stretch and press it, making paper just like they did in the old days."

"Can she be trusted?"

"I don't intend to tell her what we're going to use the paper for. We'll take the dollar bills, shred and pulverize them, bring her the raw material and a small sample of a blank dollar bill so that she can produce paper of the same thickness."

"You never answered my question. How long will it take to do them all?"

"I really need more time to give you an answer to that. I just went over the first part of the process, which only gives you the raw materials. To make exact duplicates, we need to make plates for the front and back of each bond, with different serial numbers, then run the bond through the printer three times. It's going to be a long and slow process, and we'll need to study that bond very carefully."

What the hell. "Would it help if I leave it with you?"

"I didn't want to ask, but, yeah, it would help a lot, unless you want to move in with us for a couple of days?" chuckled Dusty.

"You think that by doing twenty first, it will slow down the process when you do the rest?"

"On the contrary, I think it will help speed up the process. We'll know exactly how many dollar bills we're going to need, and if we should do them all at once, or not. We have to see how the ink is going to hold up, and how much paper pulp Sunny can handle at one time. The best guesstimate I can give you is that we'll probably be able to do fifty at a time."

"Where do you intend to do the work?" asked August.

"We do small stuff in our garage, but we're going to need . . ." He turned and pointed at the equipment. "We'll do the printing here, but we'll need a place to do the ink separation and paper preparation."

"I'll find a place. Let me know what else you need. I'll cover all the expenses," August responded.

"Talkin' about money, what's in this for us?" asked Jim.

"It's a little premature to really know how much I can make from these bonds. I'll figure out the minimum for your time, and a percentage of what I'll get from this deal. Is that okay with you?"

"Shit, you trust us with a million-dollar bond; I know you'll take care of us," said Jim.

They shook hands to seal the deal. August left and the two counterfeiters went back to work.

37

It took forty minutes to get back from Jim and Dusty's place. Now that he was optimistic that the bonds could be counterfeited, he was anxious to contact one of his attorneys and have him call the feds. While he drove home, he thought about all the lawyers that had represented him or were just friends, deciding which one could or would do this.

Coming back on his boat he thought that Alan Cohen would be the best man for the job, and, after going over the selection once again, August stuck with him. He had all the prerequisites to pull something like this off. He was experienced, shrewd, had the balls, and was greedy.

As soon as he got home, he called Alan's office and set up an appointment at two that afternoon.

He went into the kitchen, and made a sandwich. Satisfied with his creation, he grabbed a beer, and took his full course meal to the table.

After a satisfying lunch, he made a few phone calls, checked up on his operation, and then drove to Century City, in Los Angeles, to see Alan.

He turned off the 405 at Santa Monica Boulevard, turned right toward the Wilshire District, and right on Century Park East. He pulled into the Century Plaza Tower 1 underground parking facility and found an end space—less chance for some asshole dinging his doors—and pulled in.

He rode the elevator to the thirty-second floor and entered the

Law Offices of Cohen, Preen, & Littcomb. He walked up to the receptionist, who looked up and smiled. "May I help you?"

"August Taracina to see Alan Cohen."

The receptionist pushed the intercom button. "Your two o'clock appointment is here." She looked up and batted her eyelashes. "He'll be right out."

"Thank you."

Alan opened the door to the lobby. "August, come on in." They shook hands, and headed for Cohen's office. Alan took a seat at his plush desk; it sat in a corner facing the unobstructed view of Wilshire Boulevard to downtown Los Angeles. August sat in one of the two leather chairs facing him.

"So, what can I do for you?" asked Cohen.

August didn't want to beat around the bush; he pulled out a one-million-dollar bond and slid it to Alan, whose eyes widened as he stared at it. "I'm in possession of three hundred fifty of these."

Alan studied the bond, and then raised his head, eyes and mouth wide open. "You're telling me that you have 350 one-million-dollar bearer bonds in your possession?"

"Yeah, they're hot, and I've been around the world trying to unload them."

Cohen studied the bond. "They're bearer bonds, so why not hold on to them, clip the coupons, and cash them in?"

"All the bonds came from various brokerage houses and I'm certain the serial numbers have been listed."

"Can I ask how you came into possession of these instruments?"

"It's not something you need to know at this point. The fact of the matter is, I have them, have a plan to get rid of them, and this is where you come in."

"If you want me to help you, I need some information to work with. When were the bonds stolen?"

"A couple of months ago."

"Where?"

August paused. "At LAX; they were consigned to Brinks."

"No shit! How come it's not all over the news or in the papers?"

"I really don't know why at this time. The way this heist went down, the feds still may not know whether the bonds were stolen or misplaced."

"So what do you want me to do?"

"I've spent over a month trying to sell these bonds with no success. Everyone I've contacted knows they're hot and aren't interested at this time. The longer I keep them and try to move them, the greater the risk factor multiplies. I want you to contact the FBI and negotiate a deal to return them to the government for a reward."

"You've got to be kidding me."

"No, I'm serious. I want you to contact the feds, tell them you have an anonymous client that's in possession of these bonds, and wants you to negotiate with the government on a contingency basis."

"I don't want the fuckin' FBI on my ass!"

"The government's exposure is around $900 million at maturity. I think they'll be happy to cut a deal."

Alan leaned back in his chair, rubbing his hands together in thought. "You might be right; the feds don't make deals, but I'm sure Brinks insurance company would like to get off the hook. How much are you looking to get out of this?"

"It's a little premature; let's see what the insurance company wants to settle for."

"This is about the craziest thing I've ever heard of, August. But it just might be doable. Give me a couple days to do a little research and think about this. I'll let you know."

"Look, Alan, you can't breathe a word of this to anyone, not your wife, definitely not your girlfriend, and not even your boyfriend."

"Fuck you," said Alan.

"Yeah, but if you fuck up, you'll end up a cellmate sweetheart in Leavenworth." August and Alan laughed, but not too heartily.

They stood, Alan walked August out to the lobby and shook hands. "Talk to you soon," said Cohen.

"Fine, I look forward to hearing from you."

* * *

While August rode the elevator down to the parking garage, a mile away, FBI Special Agent Nick Cutler was sitting in the office of James Warner, the assistant director in charge of the Los Angeles Field office, along with Cutler's boss, Phil Higgins.

Warner addressed his men. "It's been a week since the director of the FBI ordered us to develop a task force. Our attorneys have consulted with the Attorney General; we now have agents from the treasury department, and the FAA getting involved.

We don't have any leads and our first briefing with them is an hour from now. Either of you have any idea what the hell we're going to tell them?"

Higgins turned to Nick. "You're the case agent."

"The only thing we can do is go over, in detail, what we've done in the past month. We've squeezed our informants dry and haven't received one valid lead. Not one certificate has shown up for sale in the U.S., four days ago I informed Interpol to be on the lookout."

"You hear anything from them?" asked Warner.

"I spoke to Eric Hodel, director of the Swiss Interpol office. Interpol believes the best opportunity for someone to unload the bonds would be through offshore banks or private banks in Switzerland or Liechtenstein, and their agents have been alerted."

"Having these guys running around our office, meddling in our investigation, is going to be a cluster-fuck. I don't want Thomson on my ass, so do the best you can to be civil."

Nick and Paul sensed that the meeting was over. "Anything else?" asked Higgins.

"That's it. Let me know how the briefing went."

They left the assistant director's office and headed for their respective offices.

* * *

August pulled out of the Century Towers, headed to Wilshire Boulevard, and turned right toward Central Los Angeles. He took the Harbor Freeway south to Exposition Avenue, then right on

Flower, and right on East Jefferson.

Earlier, he had set up an appointment with a realtor to look at a building to rent for Jim and Dusty to work in. Although all the printing would be done at their shop, they needed a space to separate the ink from the dollar bills and prepare the pulp for Sunny Rain, the paper wizard, with a name like a foxy TV weathercast girl.

August pulled up behind the realtor's car that was parked in front of the building. They both got out and introduced themselves. Previously, the building housed an x-ray equipment distributor selling and maintaining x-ray equipment for doctors and hospitals. There was still a bunch of old equipment and miscellaneous tables and chairs in the warehouse space.

August was only interested in leasing by the month and only a few buildings were available. The space would be fine for their needs; he rented it under one of his aliases, paying for three months in advance. He knew they would be long gone, before the three months expired, leaving no trace of what they used the building for, or who had rented it.

* * *

The following afternoon, August gave Alan Cohen a call. "Law Offices of Cohen, Preen, & Littcomb."

"This is August Taracina; I'd like to speak to Alan Cohen."

"One moment please." There was a pause. "Mr. Cohen's speaking to another client. He wants you to hang on."

"No problem."

Thirty seconds later, Cohen got on the line. "August, sorry to keep you waiting."

"So, what's the verdict?"

"I did some research, reviewed some prior cases; I think we can do this. But August, you and I know that after I speak to the feds, they'll be pounding on my door. It's a lot of money, but not enough to lose my law practice."

"There's no rush, Alan; before we pull the trigger, we need to make sure we're on target."

"This is a monster move," said Alan. "If we pull this off, it will be the biggest deal of the century. But when we set this in motion, there's no turning back, and my only defense will be attorney-client privilege."

"I still have to work out some details on my side, so I'll contact you when I'm ready."

"I'll be waiting for your answer."

"Thanks, Alan, I'll talk to you later."

38

Now that August had Alan Cohen working on the deal with the feds, he could concentrate on getting Jim and Dusty started. The next morning, he drove to Encino to see the talented craftsmen.

August walked in; Jim was on the phone and Dusty waved. "How's it going?"

"Real good. Let's wait for Jim to get off the phone."

Jim hung up, turned toward August, and said, "Well, buddy, we think we can definitely do this."

"I hoped you could, so I rented a building for you both to work out of. Think you could meet me there tomorrow after you close up?"

"What's the address?"

"201 East Jefferson."

"How about four-thirty?" asked Dusty.

"I really need to get started on this. How much do you need to get going?"

"How many bonds are we going to start with?" asked Jim.

"What do you think?"

"We still think we should start with twenty, and work out the logistics. If everything works out, we should be able to do fifty at a time."

"Fine, what do you need?"

"We need about six grand for equipment and supplies, a couple of thousand for Sunny Rain, and a thousand one-dollar bills for the ink and paper for the first test run."

"I'll get started on the dollar bills; see you tomorrow at four-thirty."

August decided to visit his old friend, Big Mac McKenna, because a strip club would have tons of one-dollar bills, many fished from G-strings, but serviceable, none the less.

The following day, he pulled back the rug in his living room, pried up the loose oak floorboards, revealing his hidden compartment. He pulled out a bundle of hundreds, counted out eight grand, put the rest back, secured the boards and flipped the rug back in place. He drove to the Jet Strip Club, walked in and stepped up to the bar. The bartender looked up. "August, how's it going?"

"Hey Mike, where's Big Mac?"

"He's up in his gym working out."

August climbed the stairs and walked in. Big Mac was on his back bench-pressing what looked to be three hundred fifty pounds. He grunted as he finished and set the bending bar on the rack. As he sat up, sweat dripping across his muscular body, he spotted August. "Hey man, how's it going?"

"Good. Sorry to interrupt your workout."

"No big deal. What's up?"

"I need eighteen thousand in one-dollar bills, a thousand now and the rest in a few days." Big Mac laughed. "What do you need that for? You're not going to pass these off as bundles of hundred-dollar bills and rip someone off, are you?"

August chuckled, "Nah, I'm just paying off some asshole, all in ones."

Big Mac laughed. "That's why I love you, man. You always did like to get the last jab."

He stood, stretching his muscular frame, grabbed a towel and wiped off his face. "Let's go to my office."

Mac opened his safe, pulled out ten bundles of 100 one-dollar bills, put them into a brown paper bag and handed it to August. "I'll put in an order for the rest at my bank."

August pulled out ten one-hundred-dollar bills and handed them to him. "Thanks, Mac, I owe you one."

"Nah, you don't owe me shit, brother."

Big Mac stood. "Got two more sets of ten to do, don't want to cool off." They shook hands. Mac walked back to the gym, August left the club, put the bag in the trunk with the other cash, jumped into his Porsche, and headed for downtown L.A.

Jim and Dusty were parked in front of the building. They all got out, shook hands; August unlocked the front door and handed the keys to Jim. They walked around. "This housed an x-ray equipment distributor," said August. "All the fixtures were left intact, like the sinks and counters, and a few tables and chairs in the rear room."

"This is perfect," said Dusty.

"I've got a thousand one-dollar bills and eight grand for expenses; I'll have the rest of the dollar bills in a couple of days. The bags are in my trunk. I'll give them to you when we leave. "When do you need the bonds?"

"Jim and I think we should only keep what we intend to print for each run; twenty the first time. If everything works out, we'll give you back the originals and the counterfeits, take fifty more and go through the same process, until we're finished. We'll start buying what we need and get set up. I'll let you know when we need the first twenty bonds."

Dusty handed the original bond to August. "Won't need this until we're ready. We should be ready to extract the ink by tomorrow night. Then we have to separate the colors and oils so that when we print, we can layer on the different colors, making them exactly like the original bonds.

I'll be shredding and pulverizing the bills and getting them ready to extract the ink. Then we'll take the pulp and deliver it to Sunny. We gave her the specs; she will reconstitute the pulp to the exact thickness and texture of paper that we ordered.

"After the paper dries, we cut it to the exact size of the original bonds. At that point, we'll need the original bonds to proceed."

"So how do you actually print these?"

"Using modern lithography, we'll use a photographic process

to produce flexible aluminum printing plates for each side of each bond with a different serial number. The plates have a brushed texture and are covered with a photosensitive emulsion. A photographic negative of a bond is placed in contact with the emulsion and the plate is exposed to light. To print an exact duplicate of one bond that is three dimensional, we'll need separate plates for each color. For perfect duplication, these plates can only be used once. Sloppy tools make for sloppy merchandise.

"After development, the emulsion shows a reverse of the negative image, which is thus a duplicate of the original (positive) image. The plate is then chemically treated so that the positive image is receptive to printing inks. The plate is affixed to a drum on a printing press. Rollers apply water, which covers the blank portions of the plate, and ink, which adheres to the positive image areas where the type and pictures appear.

"If this image were directly transferred to paper, it would create a positive image, but the paper would become too wet. Instead, the plate rolls against a drum covered with a rubber blanket, which squeezes away the water and picks up the ink. The paper rolls across the blanket drum and the image is transferred to the paper. The image is first transferred, or *offset* to the rubber drum, and is known as offset printing.

"There's one more procedure. After the bonds dry, we have to perforate the redeemable coupons at the bottom. We located the machine that does that at Allied Printing, a real antique. They used it to print the old S&H Green Stamps in the sixties."

"How much will it cost you?"

"Five grand and we can pick it up tomorrow."

"Great, I'll bring you the money."

Dusty noticed that August was getting a little bored. "Sorry, man, I guess you really don't need to know all this, but we can't hurry this process."

"That's all right. I had no idea what this process entailed. I'm here to help in any way to get this done as clean and quickly as possible."

"We're going to stick around, take inventory of all the stuff in here, clean up the place, and see what we can use. No need to stay if you have something else to do."

"All right then, come out to my car and I'll get you the cash."

39

Jim delivered the pulp to Sunny Rain, who reconstituted the paper. Two days later, Jim picked it up and cut it to size. Jim and Dusty held the paper to the light. As they marveled at the craftsmanship, Jim remarked, "We're fuckin' good, but this bitch is a magician."

Jim called August to bring the first twenty bonds to the L.A. office. He drove to Nana's house for a visit, picked up the twenty bonds and delivered them to the counterfeiters.

Jim and Dusty used the equipment at Valley Press to produce the aluminum plates and the offset press to print the counterfeit bonds. The ink had been separated and the consistency tested.

It was Saturday morning when Jim gave August a call. "Thought you might like to come up to see the progress."

"Where are you?" asked August.

"In the valley and we're ready to rock and roll."

"Does that mean I should bring the second batch?"

"You catch on quick, buddy."

"Don't stop for me. I'll see you in a couple of hours."

Jim told August that if everything went as planned, they would be ready to print by the sixth day. He already had the fifty bonds ready to go. He jumped into his car and drove cautiously to Valley Printing.

August pulled up to their place of business, grabbed the two grocery bags and headed for the door that had a closed sign on it. Jim opened the door. "Did I miss anything?" asked August.

"Your timing couldn't be better; come in, we're ready for the final print."

August took a seat and watched as the two pros went to work. Two hours later, the three of them stood and admired their work. In front of them were twenty perfectly counterfeited one-million-dollar bonds.

Jim carefully picked up one by the edges and handed it to August. "Be careful, the ink isn't completely dry."

August held it up to the light. He couldn't believe how perfect it looked. "You guys did a fantastic job." He handed the bond back to Jim, then pulled three crystal champagne flutes out of the bag, a bottle of Dom Perignon, popped the cork and filled each glass.

"Salute!"

* * *

Before his sixth and final trip to Nana's, August set up a meet with Alan to give him the go- ahead to contact the feds. They met at the Cheese Cake Factory in Marina Del Rey, close to Alan's residence, for dinner.

"So, we ready to do this?" asked Alan.

"That's why I wanted to see you to go over the details and get started."

"Okay, first I need to know more about the robbery."

"Like I said, no one knows how the goods came off the plane. Just after the incident, the feds didn't know if the goods were stolen or the shipment was lost, but by now I'm sure they think they were stolen.

"The shipment originated in Washington State. The plane stopped in San Francisco to pick up passengers, then landed in LAX.

"Brinks pulled their truck up to the conveyor next to the plane, watched the cargo doors open and gave their bill of lading to the baggage employees to retrieve their shipment of six large bags containing stock certificates and bonds. The bags were not on the plane, as if they had vanished into thin air."

"I guess you're not going to tell me how your friends pulled this off."

"Maybe later. Anyway, the stocks and municipal bonds were destroyed because they had no value to them. They kept 350 one-million-dollar U.S. bearer bonds and intended to sell them.

"These guys are not pros. In fact, they never stole anything before. They're just normal working stiffs. We had done a little business earlier, and they asked me to help them unload whatever they ended up with."

"Why didn't they steal a shipment of cash or gold?"

"They could only confirm that there was a shipment consigned to Brinks onboard. Brinks, Wells Fargo, and Loomis never identify what's consigned to them."

"It sounds to me like the shipment was stolen in San Francisco," said Cohen.

"I agree, and I hope they continue to think that way. But after you contact them, it's going to point to LAX, and they'll have agents scrambling all over the place."

They went over a few details while they finished dinner. August picked up the tab, and they left. While walking to their cars, Alan stopped and faced August. "Are you sure you want to go through with this? You're a smuggler, not a thief."

"Yeah, I have my end covered. How about you, pal?"

"I'm good. This isn't going to be easy, and from this point on, my ass is going to be under a microscope, so I hope you have everything worked out."

"The only item I have to work out is to get the bonds to your office, but I think I have the solution; I'll let you know." August pulled an envelope out of his coat pocket and handed it to Alan. "This bond will let the feds know you're for real."

"After I contact the feds, I'll call your pager from a payphone on my early morning walk."

"Sounds good, I'll be waiting for the call."

* * *

Sunday, April 1

It was a quiet, restful Sunday morning, August and Mickey were kickin' back on the couch watching professional basketball on TV, when the phone rang.

"Hello."

"August, it's Alan Cohen. Can you meet with me tomorrow?"

"Where are you calling from?"

"The marina."

"Sure, where and what time?"

"Meet me at my gym at two. Check in at the spa's counter. I'll be in the steam room."

"Sounds good, see you then."

The following day, August fired up his Carrera and headed for Marina Del Rey. He walked up to the counter. The receptionist saw him enter. "Good afternoon, may I help you?"

"I'm here to use the gym; Mr. Cohen made arrangements for a guest pass."

She looked at the appointment book, then handed August a towel and a key to a locker. "Enjoy your workout."

August found his locker, took off his clothes, wrapped the towel around his waist and headed for the steam room, where he found Alan pouring water over the heated coals, steam billowing out around him.

"Isn't it already hot enough in here?" asked August.

"Good timing. I just got here and the only other guy just left."

They both sat down on the tiled seat. "So, what's up?" asked August.

"I've been in contact with the feds. When I mentioned bearer bonds, I was put through to Special Agent Nick Cutler, who said he was the case agent. He came to my office with his partner, Leo Panetta. They pushed me around a little, trying to get me to reveal my clients' names. I reminded them of attorney-client confidentiality. They threatened to charge me with conspiring with felons.

"I told them there was no proof that my clients were felons, and that I didn't know their names or their identity. They finally backed down and allowed me to continue.

"I related. . . that my clients told me they possessed six bags that were consigned to Brinks, containing stock certificates and bonds. They destroyed the stocks and municipal bonds because they had no value to them. They have in their possession 350 one-million-dollar U.S. bearer bonds. They want to return them for a reward, but if the government is not interested, they will try to sell them.

"At first, they laughed and I laughed with them, because of how ludicrous this actually sounded. Then Nick held up his hand, we stopped laughing, and he asked me if I had any proof."

"You show him the bond?" asked August.

"No. After you gave me the bond, I realized that if I show the feds an actual bond before we made a deal, they could arrest me for possession of stolen goods, then force me to reveal my clients' identities. So I took a picture of it. After the two agents examined the photo, Agent Cutler, asked if he could use a phone. I pointed to the phone on the coffee table, and told him to use that one.

"He called the assistant director of the L.A. field office, went over the basics, listened, and hung up. He asked me why they contacted me. I told him that I asked the same question, and the clients told me I was referred to them but wouldn't reveal by whom.

"He said they would consider my request and get back to me. He called back that afternoon and set up a meeting at my office the following morning. He told me the government doesn't pay rewards for stolen bonds, and then started to put on the pressure for me to cooperate with them.

"I reminded them of attorney-client confidentiality again, and suggested that Brinks and their insurance carrier would love to settle this enormous loss and should be contacted. Two days ago, Nick called me back. He told me that Brinks was insured by Lloyds of London and they were interested in settling. I told them I would have to wait for my clients to contact me because I didn't have their phone number. But as soon as I heard from them, I would pass on the information.

"Now that I knew they were interested, I let them stew for

twenty-four hours, and set up another meeting in my office.

"I told them my clients would settle for 1% of the face value of the bonds. Upon verification that the bonds are authentic, Lloyds of London would give me $3.5 million in unmarked hundred-dollar bills and the U.S. Government would hand over four letters of immunity, releasing my clients from all current or possible future charges in this matter, and I would fill in the names, after the transaction was complete. I explained that I would take my fee from the proceeds and the rest would go to my clients. Agent Cutler said he would get back to me.

"That's what I was going to report to you today. This morning Agent Cutler called me. He said the FBI will provide the letters of immunity, and that Lloyds of London accepted the offer. I couldn't fuckin believe it!"

"That would net the six of us around $580,000 each. That's one hell of a payday. When do you think you can close the deal?"

"Agent Cutler said the representative from Lloyds of London told him it would take at least a week to ten days to put everything together and that he'd call me when they're ready to meet."

"I'm sure the guys will be thrilled with the settlement. I'll work out the details and we'll do this."

"I'm done for the day; want to have a drink to celebrate?"

"I think, from this point on we shouldn't be seen together. There's no doubt in my mind that there's a couple of agents sitting in their car watching this place as we speak."

"Yeah, I'll bet you're right."

August stood. "If I stay in here any longer I'll shrivel up into a prune. Let's leave at different times. I'll talk to you later."

* * *

By 3:00 P.M., August was on his way back to San Pedro, then changed his mind and took the 405 west to Manhattan Beach to talk to the guys. At three-twenty, he parked a block away from their beach house. He got out, locked his car, and walked down to the

Strand and over to their house. The surf was up and in perfect form, and the odds were good that the guys planned to go surfing as soon as they got home.

August loved to surf, but lately, he had little time for sports. He watched the surfers, longing to join them. *I'm sure the guys have another board and trunks I could use.*

As predicted, Randy parked his car in front of the beach house and Scott was right behind him. They got out of their cars, spotted August standing on the Strand, and waved him up. He waved back and walked up to the house.

"So what's up?" asked Scott.

"A lot. You guys going to ride some waves today?"

"Hell yeah, look at the surf," said Randy.

"You have an extra board?" asked August.

"You never said you surf."

"You never asked."

"We all have extra boards. Take your pick."

"I didn't bring any trunks."

"No problem. Let's get going, before it gets dark."

Fifteen minutes later, the five of them paddled out through the breakers and waited for the next set of waves. August picked the third wave rolling in, positioned himself, spun his board around and paddled. As the wave began to crest, he was on his feet, dropping down the face of the wave, turning left to stay ahead of the break crashing behind him.

It had been a while and he decided not to try any radical turns, but just enjoy the ride. As the wave broke over his head, the spray of water and air rushing by his face was so exhilarating that he let out a yell, as he kicked out of the wave and paddled back out.

They rode a few waves and were sitting on their boards waiting for another set to roll in. "So, what's happening?" asked Scott.

August looked around. There weren't any other surfers within earshot. He motioned for the guys to move in closer to him.

"I've spent a couple of months and a lot of money flying all over the world trying to unload these bonds. I got one offer, which was so low that I laughed in the guy's face and walked out.

"When I got back from Switzerland the second time, I had an idea. I wondered who would want these bonds the most? I realized that the government would, and maybe give a reward for their return.

"I contacted one of my attorneys and asked him to look into it. I did not give him your names, just that you had possession of 350 one-million-dollar bearer bonds that were originally consigned to Brinks. He did some research and we decided to go for it, so he contacted the FBI."

Randy interrupted him. "Jeez, August, we could go to jail!"

"Please, let me finish. The feds came back and told him that they don't pay rewards for stolen bonds. My attorney suggested that they contact Brinks and have their insurance company make a settlement. He didn't even call me, because he knew that they were quite interested. The FBI agent contacted him, and said that the insurance company was interested in settling. He told the agent that you wanted 1% of the face value of the bonds and four letters of immunity for the crime."

August saw that this got their full attention. "I just paid a visit to my attorney, and then drove here to tell you the good news. Brinks insurance carrier, Lloyds of London, accepted the offer and will settle for 3.5 million dollars. You will be receiving four letters of immunity from the FBI."

"You think it's a good offer?" asked Scott.

"Man, it's the only reasonable offer I had."

"How much does the attorney want?"

"This is one hell of a settlement. I suggested that we split the money equally. The attorney, not only negotiated a good settlement, but got the feds to give you letters of immunity. He did that on his own, and he definitely deserves a full share."

"What's going to happen when they find out what our names are?" asked Scott.

"It's not going to happen. My attorney will receive four letters of immunity concerning the total shipment with no names listed for the perpetrators. He will hold them in safekeeping as an insurance policy for your protection."

"I think I might want to keep them myself," said Scott.

"I'm sure that can be arranged; I'll talk to him about it. If this proposition is good with you guys, we'll get it done.

"I told you I would do my best to try to sell the bonds and was not successful, but this is one hell of a deal, and you should go for it. I do expect you guys to return my fifty grand, and my attorney will handle the rest. If this is all acceptable, my attorney is ready to move forward. I'll deliver the bonds to the attorney, and figure out the best way to get the money to you."

Randy was smiling from ear to ear. "That's fucking over $500,000 each." He looked at his friends. "With that kind of money we could build our hotel and have money left over."

They all agreed, and then surfed until the sun dropped over the horizon. As they walked through the sand back to the beach house, Randy whispered to August, "Take a look up the street. There are the two agents that have been tailing us."

* * *

A couple of days went by. August went to dinner with some local friends, and got home at nine o'clock. He turned on the TV, and decided to have a drink. He poured two fingers of Blue Label on the rocks, and headed back to the living room, when the phone rang.

"Hello."

"It's Steve; I've been trying to reach you all day."

"What's up?"

"The bank accepted your offer."

August was speechless. "You there?" asked Steve.

"Yeah, yeah, I'm here. I guess we'll be going back to Switzerland. Thanks for making my day."

August had already decided that he would accept the banker's initial offer of five cents on the dollar. Seventeen-and-a-half million was a big payday, but 35 million dollars was beyond his wildest dreams.

* * *

Ten minutes later, his pager went off. He recognized the number and called Jim and Dusty. "How's the progress?"

"We'll be doing an all-nighter; can you meet us at the shop at nine?"

"No problem, see you then."

August pulled up in front of Valley Printing at 9:00 A.M. sharp. He knocked on the door, and Jim opened it. "Just in time. The ink is dry and they're ready for pick up."

August followed Jim to the workshop where Dusty was stacking the bonds. Now that we're finished we can go back to our normal work."

"I really appreciate you getting this all done so quickly."

"Yesterday, we compared the original with the counterfeits. We even used a magnifying glass and couldn't find a flaw. These have come out finer than any hundred-dollar bills we've seen. These fuckin' bonds are flawless."

"You guys are truly Michelangelos at your trade."

"Why, thank you, August. I hope we make what you could sell one of his works for," Dusty chuckled.

"I think you'll be happy with your share," said August.

"You've always been a fair man and don't worry about that office on Jefferson. We'll be going back there tonight, cleaning it up, and wiping down the whole place for prints. We did change the lock on the door so we'll change it back to the original. That way none of us have to go back there."

"August, before you leave, we have a little surprise for you," said Jim, who pointed at a crate sitting on the floor. Jim opened it. "To print a perfect duplicate you can only use a plate one time. If we made an error or the equipment malfunctioned, we'd lose that bond. We made an additional set just in case, and we never made a mistake. Now you have another full set of unused plates. They might come in handy in the future. Don't you think?"

August picked one of the plates up and took a good look, and smiled. "You know they just might. I can't take these with me right now. Okay if you keep them for a couple days? I'll pick them up later."

"No problem, just let me know and I'll have them ready."

"You guys are the greatest. I'll contact you as soon as I get back in town, and settle up with you." They shook hands, hugged, and August left with the last original and the counterfeit fifty one-million-dollar bonds and drove back to Nana's house.

40

Alan Cohen arranged a deal with the feds and the guys agreed to it. August was confident that the counterfeit bonds would pass inspection.

The stage was set—commitments made. There was no turning back. Before leaving to go to Switzerland, August needed to return the original bonds to Alan Cohen.

It was time to put his ingenious plan into action. He drove to his old friend's surf shop in Hermosa Beach. John was just a local surfer dude who worked for August, until he saved enough money to start shaping surfboards, and eventually opened his own business. August pulled up to John's Surf Shop, and walked into the store. John was with a customer, saw August walk in, smiled, and held up his hand, one finger up, signaling one minute.

The guy bought a wetsuit and left. John came around the counter and gave August a hug. "Good to see you, man."

"How's it going?" asked August.

"Great, business is booming, I just got engaged, and I even joined the local Chamber of Commerce." Reluctantly he asked, "So, what's new with you?"

"A lot."

"What can I do for you?"

"I need you to make two surfboards that look the same, but one with a hidden compartment in it."

Although John would have done anything for August, he was relieved because all he had to do was alter a surfboard. "How big a compartment?"

"About 14 by 72 inches."

"Too long. How about two compartments one on each side of the stringer.

"That's fine."

"Need to be waterproof?"

"No, it just needs to look like a normal board."

"When do you need them?"

"As soon as possible."

"I just finished shaping a couple of long boards; I could have them finished in a couple of days."

"Man, that would be great."

They talked for a while, reminisced, then a couple of surfers walked in. "I gotta take care of business, and close up early, so I can work on your boards."

"Can I use your phone?"

"Sure, it's right over there."

They shook hands. "Thanks a lot, John."

It was quarter to eleven. August paged Alan Cohen, who left his office and went to a payphone near the elevator. They agreed to meet at the Jonathan Club for lunch at noon. Alan was already seated when August arrived. "So what's up?" asked Cohen.

"I need to get the bonds to you and I didn't think it would be a good idea to carry two large Halliburton cases to your office."

"So what do have in mind?"

"You still surf, don't you?"

"Whenever I have time."

"Well, I'm going to have two new boards delivered to your office. One of the boards has a couple of hidden compartments big enough to hold the bonds. After you make the trade with the feds and Lloyds of London, you can put the cash for the four guys and the letters of immunity in the compartments. You keep our shares, and I'll settle up with you later. That way the board won't be too heavy to carry. I'll make arrangements to pick that board up and deliver it to the guys, who surf almost every day."

"What's the other board for?"

"A present from me, and a good decoy that we can use if the feds get too close."

"How the hell did you come up with this?"

"You surf, I surf, and your new clients surf. That's the only thing we have in common."

"You're a fuckin' genius. The special for the day is oso buco. I took the liberty of ordering one for each of us."

"One of my favorites. Now who's the genius?"

* * *

August waited three days, and then called John. The boards were ready. He had borrowed Mickey's Ford Aerostar van and drove to the Surf Shop to inspect them. A fine lookin' woman was working the counter. "Hi, can I help you?" she asked.

"I'm looking for John."

"You must be August?"

"Yeah, is he here?"

She reached across the counter and they shook hands. "Nice to meet you. I'm Vicky Caldwell, John's fiancée. He's in the rear working on your board. Why don't you go on back; he's waiting for you."

August walked back into the rear of the shop. John was standing over a surfboard that was lying on a couple of sawhorses, and an exact duplicate, leaning against the wall behind him. "Hey, August, you're just in time. Both boards are ready to go. Can't wait to show you how the lids work."

August walked up to John and shook his hand, then looked at both of the boards. "Nice colors."

"Thanks, that's how I was able to conceal the compartment. Can you see anything, like seams?"

He knew that if he examined it carefully, he would find them, but no one else would look that close. From three feet away he couldn't see a thing. "Looks great. You did a fantastic job."

"The way I painted the stripes causes an illusion, making it look flat and smooth, but there's a seam between the blue and green stripe and a slot to pry the lids open. The lid opens from both rails and they're secured in the center. Each lid has three snaps to hold it shut." John opened one side and lifted it up. "There are no hinges, it just uses the fiberglass's flexibility; be careful not to open the lid too far."

John secured the lid. "They're ready to go."

"How much do I owe you?"

"You're kidding. If anything, I owe you. Look around; if it wasn't for you, I wouldn't have a pot to piss in. Now I have a successful business and I'm getting married."

"She's quite a catch. When's the big day?"

"In three weeks; didn't you get the invitation?"

August shook his head. "I had to move, no forwarding address."

John walked over to a workbench, wrote out the date, time, church, and address where the reception would be held, and handed it to August. "Here's the information, I hope you can attend."

While John was writing down the information, August pulled out a wad of one-hundred-dollar bills and palmed them. John handed him the handwritten invitation and August handed him the cash. "This is your wedding present; have a nice honeymoon."

John glanced at the cash; he knew it had to be at least five grand. He slid it into his pocket. "Thanks a lot, man. That's exactly what I'm using it for. We wanted to go to Hawaii but we're already over our budget for the wedding."

"Glad I could help. There's one more thing. I have one favor to ask."

John thought, *Ooh oh, here it comes.* "Sure—what?"

"I'm going to take the board with the compartments home and bring it back here."

"August, I'm not into dealing or delivering drugs anymore."

"It's nothing like that. There will be no drugs hidden inside; I just want you to deliver the boards to my attorney's office in Century City. It's on the 32nd floor."

August could see the relief on his face. "No problem; just give me his name, address, and tell me when you want them delivered."

"I'll be back in an hour or so; could you deliver them this afternoon?"

"No problem. I'll have one of my employees come with me so that we only have to make one trip to his office."

"Good idea, but have your guy stay in the lobby while you show the attorney how to open the lids."

John picked up the surfboard with the hidden compartments. "Come on, I'll carry it to your car."

"Thanks for getting this done for me so fast."

They walked into the store; John couldn't wait to tell Vicky. "We're going to Hawaii for our honeymoon."

"John, we can't afford it."

"We can, after you see August's wedding gift."

She ran around the corner and gave August a big hug. "I hope you can make it to our wedding?"

"I plan to, unless I'm out of town for business."

John and Vicky walked him out. August opened the rear door of the van. John slid the board in and shut the lid. They hugged, said their goodbyes, then August drove back to San Pedro to get the bonds.

He pulled into Nana's driveway, took the surfboard out, and headed for the wine cellar. He now had the 350 original bonds and the 350 counterfeit ones sitting in front of him.

He popped the three catches on both rails of the surfboard, carefully lifted the fiberglass lid to one of the hidden compartments, put in half of the original bonds, snapped it shut, and then repeated the process on the other side. Before he shut the lid, he wrote out a note. *"I will be out of town on business for no more than a week. I'll call when I get back. You hold my end."*

He put the note on top of the bonds and snapped the lid shut.

He put the other bonds in the Halliburton cases and buried them. He stood, looked at the board, and couldn't detect the hidden seams. He looked at his watch; it was two o'clock.

He loaded the extremely valuable surfboard in the van, and

headed back to Hermosa Beach.

* * *

Later that afternoon, John pulled into the Century Plaza Tower 1 underground parking facility, pulling into a spot marked "deliveries." John and his guy got out, he opened the rear door; they each pulled out a board and casually walked into the lobby, where they got a few strange looks from the business crowd. They could barely squeeze the 10' 6" boards into the elevator, leaning them from corner to corner, leaving almost no room for both of them to stand.

They rode the elevator to the thirty-second floor. The hallways were empty and they entered the Law Offices of Cohen, Preen, & Littcomb. The receptionist gave them an odd look.

"May I help you?"

"I have a delivery for Mr. Cohen."

She got on the intercom. "There's a delivery for you. You better come out here and take a look."

Alan entered the lobby. "Wow, one of my clients said he sent me a present. Bring them into my office."

They followed Alan into his office; John's helper went back to the lobby while John showed Alan how to open the lids.

* * *

After August delivered the board back to John's shop, he took the coastal route back to San Pedro, happy as a clam, now that the weight of peddling the bonds and having possession of them was over. He thought about the last trip to Switzerland, coming up with the idea of selling the bonds back to the government, and meeting Cindy Alden. He realized how much time had flown by since he'd gotten back from Catalina, and that he needed to call her.

As soon as he got back to his house, he pulled out his wallet, got her number, and placed the call.

"Hello."

"Hi, Cindy, it's August Taracina." Silence on the line. "We met in Catalina?"

"Oh, that August. The guy that was going to give me a call, and take me out?"

"Same guy. Hey, I'm sorry, beautiful; I'd have called sooner, but I've been out of the country."

"I was wondering when I might hear from you."

She's pissed. Better come up with something good. "You hungry?" he said, sheepishly.

The phone went silent; August thought, "I fucked this one up good."

"I haven't had dinner, if that's what you're asking."

"Can I take you to dinner?"

"If you let me pick the restaurant," she chuckled.

She gave him her address; August said he'd pick her up at seven.

On the way to her apartment, August stopped by a floral shop and bought a dozen red roses. He knocked, and she opened the door, looking as radiant as she did when he first laid his eyes on her.

She loved the roses and invited him in while she put them in a vase. "So, where do you want to go?" asked August.

"How about The Reef?"

They had a wonderful time, and enjoyed each other's company. It was a work night, so after dinner, August took her home and walked her to the door. She gave him a kiss and thanked him. He said he was going out of town for business and would call her as soon as he got back.

He drove home. As he pulled into his driveway, he spotted two of his men sitting in a Ford truck, keeping an eye on his house. Since Eddie Burger ransacked his home, and Diz and boys roughed him up, August didn't want to risk walking in on someone or have anyone walk in on him. He had to be careful during this bond transaction.

41

No one, but Jim and Dusty, knew about the counterfeit bonds, and no one but August knew what he intended to do with them, and he intended to keep it that way.

Andy had not only set up the deal with Steve Workman, but sat with him while negotiating with the greedy motherfuckin' Swiss bankers, and August wanted him by his side when they finally closed the deal. He'd also be part of the security team needed while traveling with the bonds. He picked up the phone and gave him a call.

"Andy, it's August; the guys accepted my offer. Join me for another trip?"

"Hell, yes. That's great news. Let me know what I can do."

"I'll call you back as soon as I know when and how we're going."

August hung up. He was going to transport 350 counterfeit one-million-dollar bonds to Switzerland. Hiding them in the lining of a suitcase was no longer an option, and neither was flying to Europe on a commercial airliner. He called Tony Amada. "Tony, I need to charter a jet with enough range to fly to Europe. Any ideas?"

"Yeah. Remember that time when Sweet Willy charted that 727 to pick up a load we set up for him in Guadalajara? The charter company's name was strange. Ah . . . Oh yeah, it was called Whatsa McCullough Air, named after the owner."

"Thanks, man, I'll give Willy a call."

He hung up, and then called Willy, who answered on the second ring.

"Hello."

"Hey, it's August."

"What's happening?"

"I need a big jet. You still in contact with Whatsa McCullough Air?"

"Yeah. How big?"

"Big enough to fly to Europe."

"Something to do with those bonds?"

"Yeah, I might have an opportunity to unload them."

Opportunity my ass. He has a fuckin' buyer. "I haven't talked to him for a while. I'll give him a call and set you up with him."

"Thanks, Willy."

"No problem, talk to you later." He hung up the phone, and began to pace back and forth, his Irish temper rising. He had made a few inquiries and had some possible interest. *Fuck! I could make a shitload of money. This could be my way out. I could move back to Ireland fat and happy. This is too large of a score to pass up. I'm sick and tired of hustling these loads for the Colombians, and being a middleman for the mob. But that little prick isn't leaving me any room to get a piece of the action. After all we've been through. Fuck! If I don't get the chance to fence them, then fuck him. I'll take that little greedy fuck out. He won't even know where it came from. If he gets in the way—I'll kill the fucker.*

Willy owned a twin engine Cessna. He called Whatsa McCullough and set up an appointment, headed to the private airport, then flew to Topeka, Kansas, home of Whatsa McCullough Air.

Whatsa McCullough was a colorful World War II pilot who started a charter business in the Midwest. "Whatsa" was a name given to him by the men he flew with during the war, and Sweet Willy never knew his real name. He even named his charter operation, Whatsa McCullough Air. He had a fleet of planes, mostly jets and some prop jobs, of all sizes, including Boeing 737s.

Sweet Willy sat across from Whatsa McCullough, who sat behind his ornate desk. After catching up with their lives since they last talked, Whatsa asked, "So what can I do for you?"

"A business associate of mine needs to charter a jet large enough to fly nonstop to Europe."

"No problem, we have three 737s that have plenty of range."

"Great, but that's not why I came here to talk to you. I want to know when and where this business associate of mine is going, and to be informed early enough so that I can be there to meet him."

"Why?"

"Never mind, but it's worth fifty grand to you for the information."

"Well, partner, all I need to know is your associate's name and we have a deal, as long as he's not hauling drugs, weapons, or anything illegal."

"His name is August Taracina."

"My plane isn't going to get fucked up, is it?"

"No way, but I would recommend that you collect your fees in advance."

Before he took off, Willy called August with Whatsa's private number.

* * *

After receiving Whatsa's number August called and chartered a 737 with a range of 6200 nautical miles, capable of flying to Amsterdam. It cost him $25,000. Celebrities, like Hugh Hefner, and presidents of large companies used the 737 because it had sufficient range to fly to Europe, nonstop.

Tony was certified to fly the jet, and August wanted him to be the co-pilot, making sure the flight went as planned.

He arranged to depart from Topeka on Thursday, fly to Mexico City, refuel, and land in Amsterdam, then drive to Switzerland and meet the bankers on Monday.

As soon as Whatsa McCullough had the flight information, he called Sweet Willy. Then Willy, a.k.a. William Kelly, placed a call to his cousin, Adam Kelly, in Belfast. "Willy, me boy, it's damn good to hear from you."

"Adam, I need a favor and I will make it worth your while."

"Whatever you need."

"Could you round up a few of the boys and meet me in Amsterdam? I plan to take something away from a business associate."

"I presume, not on a peaceful note."

"You presume correctly, and you'll need to acquire some weapons."

"Shouldn't be a problem. We'll fly over on my friend's plane, and bring our weapons. Matter of fact, why don't you fly into Belfast and go with us?"

"Excellent idea. Pick five good men to come with us." He gave him August's itinerary and confirmed that he would pay all the expenses, hung up, then arranged to fly to Ireland.

* * *

August called Diz and arranged to have him along for protection. Andy and Steve flew down to LAX and were picked up by August and Diz. They drove to Torrance Airport where Tony was readying the King Air for the flight to Topeka.

All intended to carry handguns, except for Steve. Andy couldn't bring his gun from San Francisco so August had Diz bring an extra Glock .45 automatic with three extra magazines for him.

The King Air B200 had maximum seating for thirteen; August's interior was custom-made. It seated eight with a lot of legroom, had several tables, and a much nicer galley. Powered by two Pratt and Whitney turboprops, it had a cruising speed of 333mph, and a range of 2,075 miles, making it an easy nonstop flight to Topeka, Kansas.

It was 1,530 miles, as the crow flies, to Topeka. They had a comfortable flight, cruising at 30,000 feet, and they landed at Forbes Field five hours after take-off.

After a perfect landing, Tony taxied the King Air to Whatsa McCullough Air and parked the plane near the 737 that August had chartered. They moved their luggage to the new ride and climbed aboard.

Thirty minutes later, they took off from Topeka and flew to Mexico City's Benito Juarez International Airport, where they refueled and took off again to Amsterdam's Schiphol Airport.

They were a little more than halfway across the Atlantic when Tony got on the P.A. system. "We're going to run into some pretty bad weather in ten minutes, so if you're not buckled up do so, we're in store for a rough ride."

Everyone got to their seats and secured their seatbelts. Ten minutes later, the plane began to shudder from the turbulence. Then, all of a sudden, the plane was knocked to the left, as if a huge hand had slapped its side. Then it dropped, sending bile billowing up into August's throat. The plane shook violently, and went straight up, so fast they could feel the G-forces pushing them down into their seats.

After twenty minutes of hell, the turbulence settled down enough for everyone to let go of their armrests. Tony got back on the PA. "That was a little scary. We're experiencing a problem with the hydraulic system. So far, it doesn't seem too serious but the captain has radioed ahead and if necessary, we're cleared to land at Lisbon Portela Airport for repairs."

The pilot was confident they could reach Amsterdam's Schiphol Airport and radioed ahead, explaining their problem. He was instructed to taxi after landing, to the private plane section, where an airport repair service representative would meet them.

The pilot received instructions to land and set the jet down on the tarmac. He spotted the service truck and followed the service technician's directions to a spot, and cut off the engines.

The passengers stayed onboard, while the pilot and Tony had a discussion with the service tech as they inspected the plane.

In the terminal, four men stood by the window and watched. One of them turned to the others. "It looks like something is wrong with their plane," said Sweet Willy, a.k.a. William Kelly.

"Could that affect their plans?" asked Adam.

"I doubt it. My man told me they were spending the night at the Airport Hilton, if he needed to contact them."

"So what do you want us to do?"

"Tell the boys to be ready to follow them when they leave the airport."

Tony climbed on board and went into the cabin. "What's up?" asked August.

"A hydraulic pump is leaking and has to be replaced. The tech thinks he can get one tomorrow morning and have the plane repaired within a day or two."

"Good, then it won't affect our plans. Let's rent a car and get to the hotel."

"I'll go to the terminal and rent a car," volunteered Andy, who handed his gun to Diz. "Just in case someone stops me."

Fifteen minutes later, Andy pulled up in a Mercedes 500 sedan. The pilot opened the luggage compartment and the guys began to transfer their bags to the trunk. Everything went into the trunk, except the two Halliburton cases held by August.

August turned to the pilot and engineer. "You two coming with us?"

"The engineer is staying with the plane; I'll go with you guys, if that's okay."

"No problem, let's go."

Sweet Willy kept the binoculars on the two Halliburton suitcases, as August slid into the backseat of the Mercedes. *He's out of the country and in possession of the bonds. Not on his turf, making him more vulnerable. I'll take those fuckin' bonds, and he'll never know I was behind it. That is, if he stays alive.*

"Let's get to our car!" ordered William. They briskly walked out of the terminal and waited for the Mercedes to leave. He got on a walkie-talkie.

"Patrick."

"Yes."

"They're in a black Mercedes 500 sedan. You take the lead; a mile later, we'll take over. Don't get too close now. We don't want them to spot us."

"They're pulling out," said Patrick.

William watched the Mercedes drive by, followed by his men. He started his car and pulled out, staying a comfortable distance from Patrick's car.

After a mile, Patrick turned left and William moved behind August's Mercedes. Patrick sped around the block and took position behind William.

Andy was driving and spotted the tail. "August, I think we've picked up a tail."

"Why the fuck would anybody be following us? No one even knows we're here."

August spotted a hotel coming up. "Pull into that hotel."

Andy pulled in front of the lobby entrance; August jumped out and went in. He walked up to the reservation counter, asked for the rates, thanked the clerk and left. He jumped back into the car and shut the door. "Did the tail stop?"

"No, the white car drove by, but a blue sedan stopped across the street."

"Let's go. We'll see if he follows us."

Andy pulled out and the blue sedan took the position behind them.

Less than a mile down the road, the white sedan pulled ahead of the blue car, as it faded back into the traffic.

August was sitting on the passenger side, watching the side view mirror. "Who the fuck are those guys?" He spotted a Sheraton Hotel. "Pull into the Sheraton."

"Andy, pull up to the curb and keep the car running, while I check in," said August, who jumped out and headed toward the lobby.

Both Andy and Diz saw the blue and white sedans pull up, and park in the Sheraton's lot, but no one got out.

"Doesn't look good," said Diz.

"Not acting like cops," said Tony.

"Then who the fuck are they?" asked Andy.

August paid cash for a suite and a room across the hall, and gave the clerk a huge tip. Ten minutes went by, when August walked out and climbed in. "Drive into the underground parking garage."

William watched through his binoculars. "They were supposed to stay at the Hilton. Why have they changed their plans? Adam, go inside and see if they're checking in; try to find out what room they're staying in."

Andy parked the car; they piled out, got their luggage, and took the elevator to the lobby.

While waiting for the elevator, a bellman wheeled his cart up and asked, "Your room number?"

"Sixteen twenty-two," said August.

Adam entered the lobby and took a seat.

Tony leaned toward August. "We have company."

They followed the bellman to suite number 1622 on the top floor. He opened the double doors and unloaded the luggage. August gave him a healthy tip. As soon as the bellman got into the elevator, and the doors closed, they moved all of the luggage to the room across the hall, and piled in.

Steve and the pilot looked apprehensive. "Why are we all in this room?" asked Steve.

"I don't know who the fuck is following us, but we don't think they're cops. Which means, whoever they are, they could be dangerous. So we're going to sit tight and see what their next move is."

The bellman stepped out of the elevator and Adam walked up to him. "Excuse me, but I was on the phone when you took the luggage up for my friends. I don't even know the room number."

"It's suite number 1622."

Adam stepped into the elevator. "Thanks a lot."

He pushed the button for the sixteenth floor, the door opened; he pushed the number 2 and rode the elevator down, then took the stairs to the parking level, and walked back out to his friends. He slipped into the rear passenger seat. "They're in suite 1622."

"Let's give them an hour to settle in; then you and the boys will pay them a visit," said William.

August had a gut-wrenching bad feeling about these strange events. He had someone watching the hallway at all times, by keeping the door cracked open. An hour later on Diz's watch, the elevator sounded, the door opened, and a bunch of guys piled out with silenced guns drawn.

Diz quietly shut the door and whispered, "Here they come."

August watched the action through the peephole. The guys were facing the front door of the suite. One guy aimed at the doorlock and fired, blowing the lock apart. Another guy kicked the door in, while the rest of them charged in.

"The place is empty," yelled one of the intruders.

Another asked, "Are you sure you had the right number?"

"I'm positive."

"Could be a trap. Let's get the hell out of here!" said Adam.

August and his team had their weapons ready, while August watched the intruders rush out of the suite and head down the hall.

August whispered, "Diz, we'll run across the hall and take cover in the suite. Tony and Andy take them from here. Ready."

He opened the door and ran, with Diz on his heels, the backs of the bad guys facing them.

One of the intruders reached the elevator and turned to push the button. He saw Diz running into the suite. "Ambush!" he yelled, pulling his .45 automatic from the small of his back and firing. They were sitting ducks with nowhere to hide.

Everyone on both sides opened up, bullets ricocheting off the walls. Andy shot one of them in the leg and he fell to the floor, while his companions fired, keeping August and his team at bay. The elevator chimed, as Diz came around the corner in a crouched position and fired, hitting one of them in the chest. Diz watched him buckle over, as the elevator door slid open. Everyone fired wildly, as the intruders piled into the elevator, pulling the guy with them that was shot in the leg, but leaving the critically wounded guy on the floor.

Diz and August ran down the hall. The guy was still breathing and holding his wound. Diz grabbed him by his shirt, pulling him close. "Who sent you?"

Blood was running out of the guy's mouth. "Fuck you!"

"Fuck me? Fuck you!" Diz jammed his finger into the bullet hole; the guy screamed in pain. "Tell me who you're working with or I'll rip your fucking heart out!" The guy spat at him, blood and spit running down his face. Diz jammed two fingers in the wound and pulled. The guy's eyes bulged in pain, as he attempted to scream.

They only heard a gurgle, as more blood poured from his mouth, as his body went limp.

Diz frisked the dead intruder, pulled out his wallet, and slid it into his pocket. "We should get the hell out of here."

They turned to go back to the room, to their luggage. Halfway down the hall, Andy and Tony stood, guns in hand, with Steve and the pilot in shock from what they had just witnessed. As August and Diz reached them, the elevator opened and a couple stepped out. Seeing the body lying in a puddle of blood, the woman screamed, while the man pulled her back into the elevator.

"Get the luggage, we'll go down the stairs," said August.

They raced down the stairs to the parking level. They threw their luggage into the trunk and piled in the car. Before Diz could shut the rear door, Andy punched it, peeled out of the parking space and sped into airport traffic, before the authorities could arrive.

Andy pulled into the Hertz Car Rental row. "We should rent another car and return this one. August and Tony jumped out and headed for the Hertz office, while Andy pulled to the side.

August rented a white Fiat van; Tony pulled up behind Andy where they transferred their luggage to the van. He followed Andy to Avis where they returned the Mercedes, leaving any possible evidence behind.

"Who the fuck were those guys?" asked Steve.

"I don't know, man, but whoever they are, they meant business," said August. "Think it could have been one of the bankers who set up the take down?"

"God, I never thought of that. Guess it's possible. Fuck, I did give them our itinerary."

"Well, if they had something to do with this the deal is dead, and so are they if I get my hands on them. One thing's for sure, whoever knew when we were arriving, probably knew we had reservations at the Hilton. Tony, find us another hotel for the night."

Tony drove past the airport and turned into a Howard Johnson's. August got three rooms, two queen beds in each. The pilot and Tony shared a room, Steve and Andy another, and August and Diz took the third. It was late and everyone was exhausted, but Diz insisted on setting up a watch for the night. He took the first three-hour shift, Andy, the second, and Tony took the last.

"Diz, give me that wallet."

August went through the contents, found a few British pounds, no ID, and no credit cards. He did find a piece of paper with a phone number and "246" written on it. There wasn't an area code listed.

He picked up the phone and dialed the number.

"Airport International Hotel, can I help you?"

"Yes, room 246, please."

August waited. On the third ring, someone picked up. "Hello." August didn't answer. "Hello, who is this?"

August hung up, totally stunned and disappointed. He recognized the voice. He looked at Diz. "That was Sweet Willy. I can't believe it. That motherfucker was planning to off us and take the bonds." He sat on the edge of the bed, anger rising off the scale. He looked at the two Halliburton cases. "This is fucked up."

"Let's go fuck him up," said Diz.

"Not now. We know the bankers aren't involved so I want to get this business over with and get out of Europe. You and Chucky can pay that motherfucker a final visit after we get back to L.A."

42

August lay awake most of the night, fitting the recent chain of events of this puzzle together. *We landed in Amsterdam, where there are no customs, or any type of inspection of luggage. We arrived on time, only the airport, and the pilot—oh, and let's not forget Willy's buddy Whatsa McCullough, knew our schedule. I wonder how much Willy paid him for the information.*

Whether it was a queer isolated incident, or a warning of future events, August wasn't going to take any chances. He looked at his watch. It was 6:30. He woke Diz and called the other rooms, waking up the guys.

They left their weapons in a locker, rented two Mercedes 380SE sedans from different agencies, and bought some walkie-talkies with a five to seven mile range. His plan was to follow the other car through the German border, then to the Swiss border, staying back three or four miles. If the first car encountered any problem, they could warn him. He could turn around and attempt to cross the border another way.

They dropped off the pilot at a hotel, instructed him to hang loose until they got back, and to be prepared to take off at a moment's notice. The pilot was thrilled to be left behind this time; the possibility of getting shot had been reduced to zero. August didn't want to tip Sweet Willy that he was onto him.

They were 430 kilometers, or 260 miles from Zurich, and didn't waste any time getting on the highway; Andy and Steve in the lead car and August, Tony, and Diz in the other. They maintained a distance of four miles apart, driving at ninety miles an hour.

They drove through the town of Arnhem; next stop was the German border. The traffic was moderate. August was driving the second car and he kept a lot of vehicles between him and Andy's.

Andy pulled up to the border; they showed the guard their passports and he waved them through. He grabbed the walkie-talkie and called August. "Went through like sliding on slick grease."

"Thanks, I'll call you as soon as we're in Germany."

August was carrying a passport and driver's license under the name, Frank Cutri. He stopped at the border; the guard checked their passports and waved them through. He called Andy, relieved. "We're in Germany."

They drove through Cologne, Bonn, through the Rhineland, passing by Heidelberg, enjoying the scenery through the Black Forest, reaching Freiburg, now only a short distance from the Swiss border.

Cars were backed up at the border crossing, as Andy's Mercedes got close, he could see why. The guards were having the passengers get out of their vehicles, searching the interior and the contents in their trunks. He didn't wait till he crossed the border, he pushed the speak button on the walkie-talkie. "Something's up, they're searching the cars."

August made a U-turn and drove away, not really knowing what he was going to do. He drove back to Freiburg and checked into a small motel. Andy and Steve were told to check into the Zurich Marriott and wait for a call from August if anything went wrong. As usual, fucking Murphy's Law—which has no international boundaries—had kicked in.

August sat in his room, totally frustrated, along with Tony and Diz. Tony was thumbing through a "where and what to do in Freiburg" magazine, and Diz was lying down on one of the beds, half asleep.

"Have any ideas how we can get across the border?" said August.

Tony laughed, "Maybe we could ski cross country?"

August had an epiphany. "No way, but what if we buy some skis, put them on a rack and take a road trip to a ski resort in Switzerland."

"I just happened to be looking at a map here of the local ski resorts," said Tony.

August slid his chair next to Tony and they studied the map. Tony put his finger on the map. "We could drive up to Flumserburg Ski Resort; it's right across the border in St. Gallen. I'll bet you're not going to find a border guard on the way. When do you want to go?"

"I'm exhausted; we need to buy some skis and a roof rack. I'll call Andy and let him know that we're okay, and then we'll go shopping, have dinner, and get some rest. We'll get up at seven, have breakfast, and take off." He looked at the map. "It couldn't be more than an hour drive to Zurich. If everything goes as planned, we'll be having lunch with Andy and Steve."

August called Andy and told him what he planned to do; he'd see him tomorrow. He got another room for himself, then the three of them drove to the nearest sporting goods store. August bought three pairs of used skis, a roof rack, sweaters, and wool knit caps.

They loaded the stuff inside the car, picked up some take-out food and beer, drove back to the motel, stuffed themselves, and hit the sack.

They were up at six and secured the ski rack on the roof—happy they had bought the sweaters and caps—because it was freezing. They drove to a café and had breakfast, then headed to the Flumserburg Ski Resort.

The only sign that they crossed the border into Switzerland was, in fact, a sign welcoming them to the country. August drove past the turnoff to the resort, stopped in the town of St. Gallen, called Andy to tell him they were on their way to Zurich, and to have Steve set up an appointment with the bankers.

Steve called Bank de Priv'e Zurich and spoke to one of the partners, Hans Gruenfelder, who set up an appointment at ten the following morning.

They arrived in Zurich at eleven thirty, pulled into the Marriott Hotel driveway and checked in. Tony and Diz were in one room and

August was in the other. As soon as they settled in, August called Andy's room. "Ready for lunch?"

"Where are you?" asked Andy.

"Down the hall from you, room 2210."

"Steve's right here. We'll see you in a minute."

There was a knock, and August opened the door. Andy gave him a hug. "Good to see you."

"Went through a lot of fuckin' shit to get here." August shook hands with Steve." I'll bet you never thought you'd have to go through all this to make this deal?"

"Not in my wildest dreams."

"Let's go to lunch," said August.

They took the elevator to the lobby; August handed the ticket to the valet. Two minutes later his Mercedes pulled up to the curb.

"What's with the skis?" asked Andy.

"Oh, those. They were our ticket into Switzerland."

"What?"

August laughed. "I'll tell you over lunch."

Tony and Diz joined them and they went to a restaurant down the street. They followed the maitre d' to a private room, ordered drinks and looked at the menu.

"So what's the plan for tomorrow?" asked Andy.

"After we finish lunch, we'll get rid of the skis and the rack. Tomorrow morning, Tony and Diz will stay at the hotel. I'm going to rent a limo to visit the bankers. When we finish with them, the driver will drop us off at the hotel. Tony will call Whatsa McCullough Air, tell them to have our pilot fly to Zurich to pick us up, and have him call our hotel when he arrives. Then we'll get the hell out of Europe.

"As for the rest of the day, I'm going back to the hotel and go to the spa. You're welcome to come if you like. I'm going to sit in the steam bath till I can't take it anymore, then have a one hour massage and lie around the rest of the afternoon.

"Dinner's on me at a restaurant nearby, then I'm going to get some rest."

* * *

The following morning, the three of them were in the lobby waiting for their ride. A black Mercedes limo pulled up to the curb. The driver got out and opened the door for August, who held a case in each hand. He let Andy and Steve climb in first, then he handed Andy the cases, and joined them.

Steve told the driver, in French, where he wanted to go; he headed to the street and pulled into the traffic. Fifteen minutes later, he stopped in front of the Bank de Priv'e Zurich.

An attractive woman met them at the front door, and escorted them to the same conference room they'd shared their previous meeting. The two partners, David Zubriggen and Hans Gruenfelder, were sitting at the conference table and stood to greet them.

They shook hands. "Mr. Lira, so good to see you again. I hope you had a good trip back to Zurich?" said Gruenfelder.

"I don't know if I'd call it good, but it was certainly exciting," said August, a.k.a. Tony Lira.

"Steve told us about you getting caught in a storm and your plane experiencing some problems, having to delay our meeting. I hope it wasn't too much of an inconvenience."

Oh, no problem at all. We could have crashed, almost got whacked, and had to sneak into Switzerland. "No, not really, it could have been worse." *Yeah, like never to be seen or heard from again.*

August set the two cases on the table; everyone shook hands, and the three of them sat on one side and the two bankers on the other. The bankers' eyes zeroed in on the cases as August set them on the table, opened them, and pushed them toward the bankers.

Then the unexpected happened, or maybe August knew it had to happen. One of the bankers stood, reached across the table, and pulled the two open cases toward him. "We'll need to examine these before we release your funds."

"I wouldn't expect anything else."

The bonds were not consecutively numbered. Each positioned a stack in front of himself and began to examine the bonds, one at a time. When they finished, David and Hans turned to each other, then addressed their guests. "Would you excuse us for a moment?"

August shrugged his shoulders. "Take your time."

Ten minutes later, the bankers walked in and took a seat. Hans smiled. "How would you like to be paid?"

August pulled out a piece of paper and slid it across the table. "You can wire the money to this account number at the Cayman National Bank."

"Mr. Workman, we will wire your share to your account at Credit Suisse at the same time."

"That would be fine, thank you."

Zubriggen stood. "I'll be right back."

Hans asked, "Could I get any of you a drink?"

"It's a little early for a cocktail, but I'll have some coffee," said August.

Hans picked up the phone, placed an order, and another woman brought in a tray with coffee and scones. She served each of them and left.

Hans looked at August. "When will you be leaving Zurich?"

"Not to be rude, but as soon as I verify the deposit in my account."

"Sorry to hear that. I was hoping we could take all of you to dinner this evening."

"I wish I could stay here for a week and relax, but I have some pressing business to take care of. But thank you anyway."

David walked into the conference room and took a seat. "Your money has been wired and verified; they have received the funds."

"Mr. Lira, you can go into the adjoining office and call your bank to verify the deposit," said Hans.

August got up, went into the next office, called the Cayman National Bank and asked for his representative, Carl Johnson.

"This is Carl Johnson, can I help you?"

"Carl, it's August Taracina. I need to verify that $35 million has been wired to my account." He gave him the number.

"Good to hear from you, Mr. Taracina, one moment please." A

minute went by. "It is in your account. Anything else I can help you with?"

He smiled. "Not at this time. Thank you, Carl." He hung up and sat there, elated.

Epilogue

Now that August wasn't burdened, carrying the bonds, and Whatsa McCullough's pilot had moved the 737 to Zurich International, August decided to make a change in his itinerary. Before he left the hotel, he made a call to the leaders of the Canadian biker gangs that controlled the distribution of the whites he produced, and set up a meeting in Montréal.

He told Tony to contact their pilot, change the flight plans from Mexico to Canada, drop him off in Montréal, proceed to Topeka and return to Los Angeles in the King Air. August planned to stay in Montréal overnight, and then fly to Vancouver to meet a young associate, Colin Lane, about a new business venture, growing high-grade marijuana.

He had Diz accompany him to Montreal and had Mickey fly up to Vancouver to meet them. August had decided beforehand to pull Mickey and Diz into this new venture, as a way to repay them for their hard work and loyalty.

He felt that this was the wave of the future. By setting up his two friends, he could keep his finger on the pulse of this new operation.

They landed at Vancouver International, and met Mickey at the Vancouver Hotel where he secured three adjoining rooms. August put in a call to Colin and set up a meeting at his hotel room at six. Colin owed August $600,000 for a thousand pounds of high quality pot, which he had sent him several months ago. Colin said he was bringing the cash with him.

At six o'clock sharp, there was a rap on August's door. Diz

opened the door to let Colin in; they shook hands. "Good to see you, Diz."

He waved, "Hey, Mickey."

He walked over and shook hands, and gave August a hug.

"Good to see you. How was your trip?"

Well, Colin I'm now 35 million dollars richer. "Couldn't have been better. Want a drink?"

"Maybe later." He handed August the briefcase full of bundled hundred-dollar bills. "Payment in full."

He set the briefcase on the coffee table. "Thank you."

"I'd like to go over the details first, if that's okay with you."

August gestured with his hand, "Fine, let's sit down."

Colin went into detail about how they were going to grow high-grade marijuana in Canada; it was practically legal. "I found the perfect property to start our operation, but I need to raise more money to pay cash for the land. Then we can get it started."

August pushed the briefcase toward Colin. "I'm bringing Mickey and Diz in as partners and they will be working with you, handling my share. This is our investment in the new venture. Okay with you?"

Not that Colin had any choice, but he really did like the deal. "You kidding? I love it. I've worked with Mickey and Diz; together, we could build a solid business up here."

"Good. I'm going to fly back to L.A. in the morning, and leave Diz and Mickey here to work out the details. I don't know about you guys, but I'm starved. Let's have our first board meeting over dinner."

Colin drove them through Stanley Park, to the very secluded Sequoia Grill on Fergusson Point. They drank and enjoyed the scenery, watching the sunset over the Northern Pacific. They had a fabulous dinner and were back at the hotel by ten.

August left the three business partners in the bar and went to his room. He took a hot shower, threw on a robe, and kicked back on the couch. He was thrilled with his decision to bring in Mickey and Diz. His operation at the harbor was over and he really didn't want to stay in the whites operation much longer. There was too much heat on him. His Columbian and Mexican sources either had been killed or were in jail. The whole business was changing. Cocaine, meth, and crack turned him off, as well as the people that dealt in it. The tide had changed, honor amongst thieves and smugglers was now in the past. *Fuck it, maybe it's time to retire. Hell, I'm 35 million dollars richer, and this new pot deal will provide me with a steady cash flow and a great future.*

He got up, walked over to the bar, poured himself a drink, lit up a Marlboro, then picked up the phone, and called Cindy Alden for a date.

* * *

While August was landing at LAX, Alan Cohen received a call from Agent Nick Cutler. "Agent Cutler, what can I do for you?"

"We have the letters of immunity, and the representative from Lloyds of London will be flying in this evening. We can have the meeting at our office. Let's say at ten tomorrow?"

Alan laughed. "I'm sure you're joking. See you at my office at two o'clock, but if you're not joking, forget the deal."

Cutler chuckled. "We'll be there."

Now that he had a date and time, he needed to inform August. He left his office and dialed August's pager from the phone booth, and waited ten minutes—no one called back. He tried every hour, using payphones on other floors, with no luck.

It was five o'clock and the only payphones the feds could not see him use were on the floors of his building, so he tried once more. This time, August called him back. "Jeezzz, August, how come you haven't called me back?"

"I just got back in town. I left my pager home, and just turned it on fifteen minutes ago."

"Well, you got home just in time. The feds and a rep from Lloyds of London will be at my office at two tomorrow to settle the deal. Why don't you come by at five and pick up the board? Oh, park on the third level next to the loading dock and service elevator; use the passenger elevator to come up to my office, that way no one, like the feds, will see you in the lobby. When we leave, I'll take the other board through the lobby and out to my car, while you use the service elevator to the cargo dock."

"Looks like you thought of everything. See you then."

* * *

After John delivered the boards, Alan leaned the real board on the wall behind his desk. Then he walked over to the bar, pushed a concealed button and a wood panel slid open, revealing a room four-feet wide and four-feet deep.

He used the room to conceal his private documents. There was also a safe in there, where he stored cash, sensitive information from some of his legal cases, and the one bond that August gave him to show the feds. He transferred the bonds to two extra large leather briefcases and put them and the board in the room, then closed the panel.

After talking to the feds, and having trouble contacting August, Alan had a hell of a time getting to sleep. He woke up at four A.M. and lay in bed until six. His wife was sound asleep; he got up, went to the kitchen, and turned on the coffee pot. He cleaned up, put on some shorts and a T-shirt, had some coffee while he read the paper, then went for a brisk walk.

This was the big day. When he got back, his wife was up. He took a quick shower, got dressed, kissed his wife goodbye, and left for the office. It was no surprise that he spotted a tail as soon as he pulled out of his driveway.

When he walked through the lobby, he saw the same two guys standing by the guard kiosk watching him as he walked to the elevator. When he got to his office, he took the two cases from the hidden room, locked them in his office closet, and went to work.

At two o'clock sharp, Nick and Leo, both carrying large Halliburton case's, Agent Thomas from the U.S. Treasury Department assigned to verify the authenticity of the bonds, and William Noland from Lloyds of London, walked into the Law Offices of Cohen, Preen, & Littcomb. The receptionist was expecting them and escorted the four men to Alan Cohen's office.

Alan had his assistant, John Whitcomb, join them to witness the transaction. He was seated by the window next to Alan's desk. Cohen stood and walked around his desk to greet the visitors. "Good afternoon." He shook hands. "Nick, good to see you— Leo—," he began to shake hands with the third agent, while introducing himself, "Alan Cohen."

"Agent Earl Thomas."

Alan turned to the fourth man, shaking his hand.

"William Noland, I represent Lloyds of London."

Alan gestured with his hand, "Please, take a seat."

While the four men sat down, Alan walked around his desk and also sat down. He turned toward his assistant. "John, for the record, FBI Special Agent Cutler and Lloyds of London representative William Noland are here to settle a transaction, negotiated between them, myself, and my clients. Agent Cutler, you have the floor."

He looked past Alan. "Nice board."

"Yeah, one of my clients gave it to me as a token of his appreciation for saving him over fifty grand. I can hardly wait to ride it. In fact, I'm thinking of going to the beach tomorrow morning." Alan gestured for Cutler to continue.

"Not that I'm thrilled with this transaction, but I've been instructed to hand over four letters of immunity for the stolen shipment of stock certificates, municipal bonds, and 350 one-million-dollar bearer bonds, missing from a shipment originating at the Seattle Federal Clearinghouse, consigned to Brinks, and shipped via Western Airlines. It departed from SeaTac and went missing upon arrival at LAX.

"Agent Thomas is from the U.S. Treasury Department and is here to verify the authenticity of the bonds and take possession.

"Upon verification, William Noland, from Lloyds of London, will turn over the 3.5 million dollars in unmarked one-hundred-dollar bills as settlement to you, releasing Brinks and Lloyds of London of any further liability to the U.S. Government. If that sounds reasonable with you, I'd like to get this over with."

"I have to admit, I'm not comfortable with this transaction either. May I see the money and the four letters of immunity?"

Nick handed Alan the letters of immunity, while Leo and Noland set the cases on the desk and opened them up, turning them around toward Cohen. Alan read each letter of immunity, then randomly picked up and inspected the bundles of one-hundred-dollar bills to make sure they weren't marked. Satisfied, he stood and walked to the closet, unlocked the door, picked up the two large briefcases and placed them on his desk.

He realized how vulnerable he was at this moment. He only had a verbal agreement with the feds, for the four letters of immunity and the cash from Lloyds of London. He thought, *I'm glad I had John sit in as a witness. Hell, these guys could take the bonds and the money and simply walk out of my office. What could I do? Sue them?*

Cohen squirmed in his chair, while the treasury department's agent inspected the bonds. Fifteen minutes later, Agent Thomas turned to Cutler. "They're authentic and the serial numbers match."

Alan took the cash out of the large metal case's, concerned that the feds might have put some type of device in with the money and could remotely detonate it, marking or destroying the cash. He began stacking the cash on his desk, then the treasury department agent and Leo transferred the bearer bonds to their now-empty Halliburton cases.

Alan turned to Agent Thomas. "So, what happens to the bonds?"

"Not that it's any of your business, but they'll be destroyed."

"Well then, I guess we're finished here," said Nick, as he reached over and shook Alan's hand, while making direct eye contact. "This transaction never happened."

"What transaction?" asked Cohen.

Nick said, "One other thing. I hope the stocks and muni-bonds were destroyed, as you said, or we'll open a whole new case, and you'll be our prime suspect."

"Look, Agent Cutler, I told you that my clients told me the certificates and municipal bonds were destroyed: carefully burned and the ashes scattered, because they had no value. There's no reason to harass me if one might show up, and like you just said, this transaction never happened."

"You make a valid point. We'll leave it that way."

The four men stood, and left the office, escorted by John Whitcomb, per instructions from Alan.

John walked back into Cohen's office. "They're gone. That was one scary deal."

"Yeah, I'm glad it's over. You got that all on the recorder?"

"Yeah." John walked over and handed Alan the cassette tape.

"Thanks, and thank you for being my witness."

John walked out of the office, leaving Alan leaning back in his chair, smiling, and $583,000 richer.

* * *

The three agents and Lloyds of London's representative drove back to the FBI Los Angeles Field Office. Ten minutes later, they were sitting in Assistant Director James Warner's office with their boss, Agent Paul Higgins.

"Well, how did it go?" asked Warner.

"I gave him the letters of immunity, Mr. Noland gave him the money, and he gave us the bonds, then we left."

Higgins knew that Nick wasn't happy with this deal. He interrupted him, "Well, I guess we can close the file on this one and move on."

"Yeah, I guess we can," grumbled Nick, as he and Leo stood and walked back to their cubicles. Agent Thomas and William Noland remained in Warner's office with the briefcases. "Can we take a look?" asked the director. Thomas opened one of the briefcases. Warner pulled out a few bonds and examined them. "How the hell did they get these?"

Nick began to work on his closing report. A half-hour later, Leo found him staring into space, looking totally frustrated. "Ready to get out of here?"

Nick looked up at his buddy, then down at the open file. He closed it for the last time, shaking his head in disgust. "Yeah, I'm finished, let's get the hell out of here."

* * *

August had some magnetic signs made that said "Flowers by Florence" on them. He put them on the doors of the van and drove to Century City. He pulled into the underground parking garage, drove down three levels, parked next to the loading dock and elevator, and locked the doors. Then he took the passenger elevator to Cohen's floor and walked to his office.

The receptionist told him to go right in; Alan was sitting at his desk, with his surfboard leaning on the wall. "August, good to see you."

Alan stood, walked over to the bar, pushed the hidden button, the false panel slid open, revealing the hidden room and the other board. "I was wondering where you hid the other board."

"The case agent commented on the board leaning on the wall. I told him that I'm taking the morning off and going surfing with my new board. I'm ready to leave, and I'll take this board with me. You, on the other hand, can take yours to the cargo dock and take it home." He handed August a key. "You'll need this to use the service elevator."

The feds will see me leaving the building with my new surfboard sticking out of my wife's Mercedes wagon and will follow me home, and probably watch me surf tomorrow."

"Great plan; I'll get the key back to you."

They walked out of the office, August to the freight elevator and Alan to the other. One of the FBI agents in the lobby radioed the two agents in a Crown Vic, who spotted Alan going to his car, watched him slide the board into the rear of the wagon and leave.

They followed him home.

* * *

August put the board in the van, waited a few minutes before he pulled out, drove around awhile, making sure he wasn't being followed, then went to Nana's house, took out his share of the money, hid it, and put the board under the house and left. On the way home, he stopped at a payphone and called Scott's pager. A few minutes later, Scott called. "You guys surfing tomorrow?" asked August.

"Yeah, I think so. What's happening?"

"Time to settle up; I want to go surfing again."

"Can't wait to tell the guys. See you at three-thirty."

* * *

At 3:25, August pulled the Ford Aerostar van to the curb in front of the beach house. He wore baggy flowered trunks, a blue T-shirt, and leather sandals. He pulled out the board, grabbed his gym bag and headed for the front door. It opened as he reached the steps.

"Looks like you're ready to go," said Randy, who was standing at the entrance. August walked in and set his board and bag down. Scott, Terry, and Jeff were sitting at the table nursing a beer. "Want a beer?" asked Jeff, who pointed to the fridge.

August helped himself and sat down. "Nice board," said Randy.

"I'm glad you like it, because it's your present."

Randy looked a little confused. August put his finger to his lips, and then cupped his ear like he was hearing something. The guys instantly caught on. Their house could be bugged, in fact, August had warned them previously, not to talk about him or the bonds.

Randy played along. "Wow, thanks a lot, my old board has about had it." They kept talking while August popped the snaps on the rail of the board, lifted the lid, exposing the compartment full of bundled one-hundred-dollar bills. The guys stood there, in amazement, while August closed the lid and pointed to the other side, indicating another compartment.

"I didn't drive all this way to bullshit with you guys, let's go ride some waves," said August. August picked up the new board and leaned it against the wall with the three spares, and grabbed the board he used the last time he was there.

The guys just stood there, a bit overwhelmed, knowing that $2,232,000 was hidden in a surf board leaning against their living room wall. August wanted to leave it there, unattended, and go surfing.

They followed August out the door, making sure it was locked, and headed for the beach. As August walked through the sand, toward the water's edge, a wave of relief came over him, knowing that this burdensome journey—bonds and all was finally coming to an end.

He waded through the water until he was deep enough to jump on his board and paddle out through the surf. He joined the guys who were sitting on their boards, talking while waiting for the next set.

They were all anxious to find out what had gone down. August sat up on his board; they all started in unison. He held up his hand and pointed to Scott. "You first."

"Where'd you get that board?"

"A friend altered it for me. I didn't think it was a good idea to walk into your house with a couple of stainless steel cases."

"We have your money hidden in the house," said Scott.

"Good, let's catch some waves."

The westerly winds hadn't come up yet and the waves were in perfect form. The sets were four to five feet high and the five of them were in their element.

The last wave in a set was building in front of August, who turned his board around, took three strokes, stood and dropped into a perfect left. He made a hard turn at the bottom of the wave pushing him up to the crest. He moved toward the nose, dropping him into the curl, and got tubed, he shot out like a cannon ball and kicked out.

As he paddled back, exhilarated from his ride he thought, "I've been working way too hard."

Unfortunately, the westerly winds began to howl, blowing out the waves, causing the guys to give it up for the afternoon. They paddled in, not too soon for the nervous, now rich dudes, and headed for the beach house. August took a quick shower, got dressed, and joined the guys in the living room.

Scott was holding a brown grocery bag and handed it to August, who stuffed it in his gym bag and set it on the table. Scott handed him a beer and motioned for all of them to go out on the deck, just in case the house was bugged. "I wanted to thank you for everything you've done for us. I know you went over the top for us, trying to unload the bonds, doing this with your attorney."

Scott chuckled, "I hid your cash in my attic with a bunch of other boxes. I spotted rat droppings in the house and thought, Ohhh fuck! They ate the money." Everyone laughed.

"I ran out to the garage and got the ladder. As I ran back into the house, my wife looked at me as if I was crazy. I frantically climbed into the attic and shined the flashlight around. All I could see was rat shit and boxes with holes chewed in the sides. I freaked out, and began to throw everything aside, until I got to the box with the cash.

"Then I remembered that I didn't use a cardboard box, but an old steel tool box that my dad gave me. That fuckin' box was so strong a bomb wouldn't damage it. I sat there sweating and laughing, while my wife was yelling, 'You okay?' Anyway, your cash was intact, and we're going to have more than enough money to build our hotel, and retire. Well, I hope everything works out for all of you; I'll look forward to visiting you in Costa Rica." He paused. "You know, I came here with a surfboard; I think I should leave with one."

"Take the one you had today, I never use it anyway," said Terry.

They went back inside the house, hugged, and shook hands. August picked up the bag and Terry's old board and left. He walked to his van, put the surfboard in the rear with his gym bag, got in, turned on the ignition, and drove away.

About a block away, two FBI agents had been staked out since noon. The driver radioed in to the L.A. office. "Yeah, they came home from work, a friend joined them and they went surfing as usual. Their buddy just left. These guys will probably do the same thing they always do. The supervisor will go home to his family and the three bachelors will go to the market, buy some beer, bring home a pizza or sandwiches, smoke some pot, watch TV, and go to bed."

"Yeah, I agree; see you in the morning." The FBI agent turned to his partner as he started the engine. "We're done here."

* * *

Six months later

It was 9:00 A.M. in San Francisco when Andy pulled to the curb in front of a construction site. He got out of his Mercedes and stood there, admiring his new 200-unit apartment complex, paid for by his cut of two million from the bond deal.

Around the same time, Jim and Dusty were entering their new 100,000 square-foot office building, stopping to admire their new sign "J & D Printing and Graphics" paid for from their share of one million dollars each.

Tony bought a Grumman Goose, and started his new venture in Micronesia, called "Inter-Island Transport" from his share.

While Andy, Jim, and Dusty admired their investments, Linda Workman walked out on the deck of their new eighty-foot yacht, now motoring through Prince Edward Sound, with two fresh cocktails. She handed a glass to her husband, Steve, and sat in a lounge chair next to him.

He took a sip of his cocktail. "It's so beautiful here."

"I'm glad we bought this yacht. It's going to be fun cruising Alaska."

"Yeah, and we still have more than half of what we made in our account in Switzerland."

"Good, we'll need the income to cover the crew and the captain, plus the fuel and maintenance, as well as the entertainment."

"Speaking about entertainment, I spoke to August. Cindy and he are flying to Ketchikan, joining us for a week or two on our inaugural cruise to Alaska."

ANGELS GATE

* * *

Three months later

A Lear Jet taxied to the private plane section of a small airport, the door opened, August and his wife, Cindy, climbed down the air stairs to the tarmac. A blue Suburban pulled up and Scott McCarran jumped out dressed in shorts and a Hawaiian-print shirt, and waved. "Welcome to Costa Rica." He hugged August. "Man, it's so good to see you."

"Good to see you too. This is my wife, Cindy."

Scott held out his hand. "Scott McCarran, welcome to paradise."

Cindy was going to shake his hand, but decided to give him a hug. "Nice to meet you."

"Well, let's get moving; everyone is waiting to see you."

Scott turned onto a private road, where a sign mounted on a post read, "Welcome to Hotel Costa Rica."

Scott pulled up under a thatched roof that led into a small lobby. As they got out of the Suburban, Randy, Jeff, and Terry, wearing trunks, and four women in bikinis, one pregnant, another holding an infant, and Scott's two kids, Kati and Josh, ran out to greet them.

Introductions were made. Scott's wife, Karen, and their two kids, Jeff and his Costa Rican wife, Maria, Terry and his wife, Lorrie, who met and married while they lived in the States, and their baby boy, Zach, and Randy and his girlfriend, Carolyn, who he met while she was vacationing in Costa Rica. It was love at first sight. After spending a week together, Carolyn flew back to Miami, took care of her personal business, gave notice to her landlord, quit her job, and flew back to live with the love of her life, and now carried his child.

Scott asked his bellman to take the luggage to the Taracina's room. "Let's get you settled into our best suite," said Scott, as he gestured for August and Cindy to follow him.

"You probably noticed that there's still construction going on. We have fourteen rooms completed, plan to add ten more, and later build eight free-standing two bedroom casitas when we can afford it." Scott handed August the keys to the suite as they walked up to the door.

August opened the door to a tropically decorated suite with a veranda overlooking the white sandy beach, palm trees, and the Pacific. "It's beautiful," said Cindy, as she walked out on the deck.

Scott grabbed August's arm, holding him back. "We never told anyone about the bonds. We did tell the girls that we made a big hit, selling some pot that made enough money to build the hotel."

"They know I was involved?"

"Yeah, sorry, but we . . ."

"Don't worry about it. I'm happy for you. You guys have really fulfilled your dreams."

"What was that, honey?"

"Nothing, I was just telling Scott what a great job they've done."

"It's a beautiful spot. I can see why you all wanted to move here. August, I think we should buy something down here," said Cindy.

"Why buy something when you can stay with us anytime you want?" asked Scott. "I'll let you guys settle in. We'll be waiting in the outdoor bar."

They unpacked; Cindy put on a skimpy bikini, August, a pair of baggy trunks; then they joined their hosts. As they walked up, Karen handed each of them a frosty Mai Tai. "Welcome to our little piece of paradise." She waved her hand across the table covered with plates of colorful fruits, clams, fish, lobster, and shrimp. "Thought you might be hungry after your flight. Please help yourselves." A pretty young woman brought another plateful to the table. "This is Sarrita. She's in charge of our staff and helps Lorrie take care of Zach. If you need anything, she will take care of it."

They sipped on their Mai Tais and enjoyed the appetizers, while talking about Costa Rica, breaking ground on their hotel, and about August and Cindy's wedding. Randy stood and looked toward the surf. "Hey, August, the waves aren't going to get better and it's getting late. Want to ride a few?"

Five minutes later, the guys were paddling out to the point break. The waves were head high and perfect form; they were the only surfers in sight. As the sun fell toward the horizon, the wind began to blow offshore, holding up the face of the waves.

The guys were having a ball, while the wives sat at the bar, watching another beautiful sunset. While they were waiting for another set, August asked the guys, "So tell me how everything went since the last time we surfed together?"

"Everything went as smooth as it could," said Scott. "Thanks for having Tony Armada call and offer to take us surfing in Costa Rica, it made everything so much easier. We used the surfboard to transfer the money down here, deposited it in the bank, and put the immunity letters in a safe deposit box.

"I quit my job first and left for Costa Rica via Miami. A month later, Randy gave notice, and told Western he was going back to college. Then Terry got married and told them he was moving to Canada. Jeff was the last to leave, telling them he was joining the professional surfing tour. Since then, we've been working our asses off and just opened the hotel."

There were a few dark clouds laden with moisture hanging over the horizon. As the sun fell below them, its rays changed to a spectrum of colors from gold to orange, red, and pink, glistening on the calm water. Randy spun his board around.

"We can talk later." He took two strokes and took off down the face of a perfect wave. The others followed; they surfed until dark then paddled to shore.

Randy said he was going to clean up and left with Carolyn. As the rest went to clean up, August and Cindy walked to their suite, took a quick shower, and changed, Cindy into a flower print summer dress, and August into shorts and a T-shirt. They left the suite from the veranda and walked through the sand to the open cantina, where Scott and Karen were nursing a drink, dressed in light colorful attire. Within ten minutes, everyone returned refreshed and ready to party.

Earlier, Jeff loaded the large built-in barbeque with mesquite wood, and while they were surfing, his wife, Maria, put a match to it. By the time everyone returned to the cantina, the flame had subsided and Jeff spread the coals, sending sparks in the sky, like little fireworks making popping sounds. He lowered the grills, getting them preheated, while Randy brought out fresh Wahoo and lobster tails and put them on to grill.

The table was set; they were all seated, enjoying a fantastic dinner. The kids finished and left the table; Lorrie had Sarrita take Zach.

They were having dessert and coffee; August took in the moment. "Well, it seems like it's been a win-win scenario for everyone."

"Couldn't get much better," said Randy. "We still have work to do, need more money to finish the hotel, but we're now officially open and people are making reservations. There's a small resort being built a mile from here and they're building a marina. We plan to run a fishing charter operation out of the marina, and Karen and Maria are opening up 'Costa Rica Tours.' It'll take some time, but that's one thing we have. We're on the ground floor and we'll grow as the tourism does."

At times, August felt a little guilty; he had not shared his fortune equally with the guys. He pulled an envelope out of his back pocket and handed it to Scott. "When we were in the middle of the smuggle, the profits grew faster than I expected.

"I decided not to give you your total share and made an investment on your behalf; let's say for your future. You'll be very happy with what you guys made. The proceeds are in a numbered account in your name in a Cayman Island Bank."

Scott held up the envelope like he was trying to see what was inside, and then he slowly opened it, pulled out a sheet of paper, and unfolded it. As he read it, his jaw dropped, totally speechless, when he saw the balance in the account was well over a million dollars.

He looked at Randy, and handed him the certificate. "We won't have to wait to complete our dream."

Three days went by and it was time to leave paradise. August promised to visit in a few months to see the finished product and to go fishing.

Everyone piled into the two used Suburbans and drove to the airport. The Lear was fueled and ready to go. They said their goodbyes; Cindy and August boarded their jet, and minutes later took off with a roar."

Randy held his hand above his eyes to shield the sun's rays. "God, I love that guy."

A month later

August was sitting in a boardroom with Young Lee and other officers of the Shanghai office of the Far East Trading Company. Young Lee handed the instrument back to August. "Now, we are very interested."

* * *

WERE THE REAL BONDS
REALLY RETURNED TO THE FEDS?

* * *

Two Chinese brothers, both entrepreneurs, started an international shipping company. They used counterfeit bearer bonds, as collateral to borrow money from banks throughout the world, to build their container ships. As the industry flourished, they paid back the loans. Now that shipping company is one of the largest shipping companies in the world!

No one was hurt, the banks made their profit, and the company prospered. How many other individuals or companies have used this method to get ahead? Who knows?

* * *

Counterfeit money is currency that is produced without the legal sanction of the state or government; counterfeit government bonds are public debt instruments produced without legal sanction with the intention of "cashing them in" for authentic currency, or using them as collateral to secure legitimate loans or lines of credit. Counterfeiting is universally regarded as a criminal act and has been known to be attempted in very large amounts (e.g. Two Japanese men were apprehended by Italian authorities in a recent attempt to smuggle approximately $135 billion in U.S. Treasury Bonds across the Switzerland/Italy border in June 2009). WERE THEY REAL OR COUNTERFEIT? NO ONE'S WILLING TO CONFIRM IT!

Angels Gate
By Andrew Rafkin & Louis Pagano
AWARD-WINNING MANUSCRIPT

"I have read and absolutely loved your book *Angels Gate*. It was a real treat! This is a great book and I am sure you will have a lot of success with it. It will also make a super movie, so make sure you keep the screenplay rights! Thank you so much for sharing the book with me—it was a great page-turner from start to finish."

—C. Clark, Editor

OTHER AWARD-WINNING NOVELS WRITTEN BY ANDREW J. RAFKIN

Red Sky Morning

"Andrew, a gifted storyteller relives the summer he turned seventeen in this coming of age fast moving adventure as a member of the crew on a commercial fishing boat. *Red Sky Morning* is a gripping seafaring adventure written for anyone who loves the ocean."
—Midwest Book Review

"From the moment I opened the book *Red Sky Morning,* I was captivated. Each chapter brought forward a new adventure or trial, and my heart raced as I looked forward to what happened next.
This is a wonderful book. You don't have to like fishing or the ocean to appreciate the great quality of this novel. I would recommend *Red Sky Morning* to anyone, young or old. It's easy to read and hard to put down." —Bryan Draper, Aced Magazine

"*Red Sky Morning* is a fascinating peek inside the life of a commercial angler. Andrew Rafkin has the talent for narrating a story and bringing it to life. This gripping tale is a must read for sportsmen." —Debra Gaynor, Review Your Book.com

<u>Creating Madness</u>

"*Creating Madness* is the first of a series of action thrillers firmly grounded in a world changed forever by 9/11. Andrew Rafkin has put his diverse and impressive background to good use, writing with a technically authoritative voice and a well-conceived plot that keeps firing until the end." —Donna Russo Morin, "Word Warrior"

"A strong plot, technical savvy, and a comprehensive understanding of global political positioning combine to make this a cutting edge novel of international intrigue. Compelling, timely, and believable, a great read. Look forward to *Mediterranean Madness*, the next in the series of O.R.C.A. adventures." —Midwest Book Reviews

"*Creating Madness* has a nonstop action-filled plot. Rafkin combines technology with likable characters and a plot ripped from the headlines. Fans of Cussler and Clancy will want to add Andrew J. Rafkin to their must-read authors." —Review Your Book.com

<u>Mediterranean Madness</u>

"Picking up nearly where *Creating Madness* left off, the second book by author Andrew J. Rafkin brings all the characters of his first book back, including those who pose a threat to the world's population, and adds some new characters, which enrich and expand the story. *Mediterranean Madness* is a multi-layered story with a plot like a five-layered cake, rich and deep."
—Donna Russo Morin, author of *The Courtier's Secret*

"Rafkin keeps the reader turning the pages with a balance of suspense, conflict, play on emotions, and romance. *Mediterranean Madness* is must reading for anyone who enjoys a techno-thriller with riveting action, a complex plot, and true to life characters. Rafkin's writing is superb."—Midwest Book Reviews

Mexican Madness

"The characters that make up the O.R.C.A. team are at their best in *Mexican Madness*, the third novel in the O.R.C.A. series. Rafkin's fan base just keeps growing. I anticipate that announcement of the series will soon be flashing on the movie marquees across the country."
—Richard Blake

"This is Andrew Rafkin's third novel in the Madness trilogy. I have had the honor to read and review all three. I hope there will be many more O.R.C.A. adventures in the future. He has the uncanny ability to engage the reader in a complex, heart-stopping, action-packed novel that would make a fantastic first-rate flick." —Readers Favorite

About the Authors

Andrew J. Rafkin, was born in 1946 in San Pedro, California, grew up in a commercial fishing family. Through high school, he worked on sportfishing boats, and at seventeen went commercial fishing with his father, captain of a large Purse Seiner, during summer vacation. Two years later, he worked aboard a ninety-foot fishing boat, which was caught in a hurricane force storm where Andrew almost lost his life. These events later served as inspiration for his first nonfiction true-life adventure, *Red Sky Morning*.

He served in the Navy during the Vietnam War and later graduated from California State University, Dominguez Hills with degrees in economics and marketing. He is a successful entrepreneur and president of Palos Verdes Security Systems, and certified by the Department of Homeland Security.

Andrew has received the EVVY literary award for *Red Sky Morning* and the Readers Favorite Awards for his Madness trilogy *Creating Madness*, *Mediterranean Madness,* and *Mexican Madness*.

He lives with his wife, Lynn, in San Pedro, California, and spends his spare time reading, fishing, hunting, golfing, and making wine.

Visit his website: www.andrewrafkin.com

Louis Pagono, was born 1947, in San Pedro, California. He worked on the docks on his family's commercial fishing boats, and later in his parent's restaurant, Luigi's. Later he joined the Merchant

Marines, and worked on the freighters moving cargo up and down the Pacific Coast.

He always had the love for the ocean and the bounty it brought him, and his wife, Kathy, and their son Joseph. He now resides in Palm Springs, California, and owns Fisherman's Market & Grill, a successful chain of restaurants in Southern California.

His friendship with Andrew Rafkin began in grammar school. Later in life, they resumed their relationship, and were destined to co-author this phenomenal story.